NORMS,
DEVIANCE,
AND SOCIAL CONTROL

NORMS,
DEVIANCE,
AND SOCIAL CONTROL
Conceptual Matters

Jack P. Gibbs

Vanderbilt University
Nashville, Tennessee

ELSEVIER
New York · Oxford

Exclusive Distribution
throughout the World by
Greenwood Press, Westport,
Ct. U.S.A.

Elsevier North Holland, Inc.
52 Vanderbilt Avenue, New York, New York 10017

Sole distributors outside the USA and Canada:
Elsevier Science Publishers B.V.
P.O. Box 211, 1000 AE Amsterdam, The Netherlands

Library of Congress Cataloging in Publication Data

Gibbs, Jack P.
    Norms, deviance, and social control: conceptual matters.

    Bibliography: p.
    Includes index.
    1. Deviant behavior. 2. Social control. I. Title.
HM291.G495   303.3′3   80-24957
ISBN 0-444-01551-5

Copy Editor Leslie Cohen
Desk Editor Louise Calabro Schreiber
Design Edmée Froment
Design Editor Glen Burris
Openers/Mechanicals José Garcia
Production Manager Joanne Jay
Compositor Lexigraphics
Printer Haddon Craftsmen

Manufactured in the United States of America

Dedicated to the memory
of AUSTIN L. PORTERFIELD

Contents

Preface

This book grew out of a conviction that conceptual issues and problems receive inadequate attention in texts and lectures on norms, deviance, and social control. The slighting of those issues and problems is no mystery. Whether written or inflicted on the audience of a lecture, a conceptualization is intrinsically dull. Indeed, unless presented with a skill that is beyond most mortals, the statement or defense of a definition puts readers to sleep in droves; and no subject can empty a lecture hall quicker. To make bad matters worse, no definition is demonstrably right or wrong, true or false. Nonetheless, scientific or scholarly activity without conceptualizations borders on the inconceivable.

If there is anything more boring than a definition, it must be a defense of the concern with conceptualization; so the present defense shall be mercifully brief. While most philosophers of science recognize a distinction between a conceptualization (which cannot be proven false) and a substantive theory (which may be proven false), they also recognize that virtually all landmark theories in the history of science incorporated a *novel* conceptualization, either new concepts or redefinitions of existing terms. There are also philosophers who deny any clear-cut distinction (if any at all) between conceptualization and theory; and the notion of causation makes the distinction all the more tenuous. Consider Stinchcombe's argument (1968:38): "The first requirement for a concept is that it accurately reflect the forces actually operating in the world. That is, the definition of a concept is a hypothesis that a certain sort of thing causes other things of interest to us.'' The argument suggests this principle: Any definition of a term that denotes a class of things or events should be an implicit claim that instances of that class (so defined) have the same causes and effects. Restatement of the principle would be much more acceptable to philosophers (e.g. David Hume, Bertrand Russell) who have questioned the notion of causation: The definition of a class of things or events should ensure a homogeneity of instances, such that at least one distinctive and ostensibly valid empirical generalization about those instances can be formulated.

Neither version of the principle is particularly informative, but they are not alien to the mentality of scientists. To illustrate, suppose someone invents a new class term ''kleb,'' and defines it in such a way that it denotes all widows, volcanic eruptions, zebras, neutrinos, and political assassinations. No one would believe it possible to formulate an empirical generalization about ''klebs'' (their causes, effects, etc.) that is valid, let alone distinctive (i.e. valid for that class only). Should someone astonish us with such a generalization, then we could no longer dismiss the notion of ''klebs'' as a fiction; but that possibility only introduces the ultimate dilemma that arises when engaging in some conceptual enterprise (e.g. defining norms, deviance, or social control). That dilemma briefly is this: Scientists harbor doubts about a definition of a class term until that term and its definition are employed in at least one defensible theory, but theories require class terms and definitions as their point of departure. So if scientists appear to be chasing their tails, it is precisely because they cannot avoid doing otherwise.

What has been said of the importance of conceptualization (and mind you it was mercifully brief) applies to all of the sciences—physical, natural, social, behavioral, hard, soft, etc. However, a rare mentality would be required to deny that the social sciences are especially haunted by conceptual issues and problems. There may be several reasons for the conceptual difficulties. The most obvious possibility is that the vocabulary of the social sciences emerged largely from, and still reflects, the language of the humanities and of the man on the street. Social scientists strive mightily to answer questions about crime, personality, democracy, cities, revolutions; and in so doing they are understandably reluctant to depart from nontechnical definitions of those terms. Yet, as philosophers monotonously inform us, any science that allows outsiders to define the terms of that science is doomed.

Whatever the reason for the conceptual difficulties in the social sciences, the problems are painfully obvious. Social scientists incessantly engage in debates over not only the ''best'' definition of particular terms (e.g. attitude, social class, power) but also the best form of a definition of any term (e.g. operational or instrumental definitions versus verbal definitions). Yet, despite all of the concern, the typical definition formulated by social scientists appears blatantly arbitrary and/or hopelessly vague. Arbitrary definitions are not likely to be accepted; and the consequence of a vague definition is negligible empirical applicability, meaning that independent investigators will disagree in identifying particular events or things as instances of the class that is defined. For example, whatever the definition of "elites," sociologists are likely to discover that they frequently disagree as to who is and who is not an elite in a particular community.

Some scientific terms (e.g. electron) denote purely theoretical notions, not things or events that can be observed or measured in any direct sense. Neither the distinction between a theoretical language and an empirical language nor its importance is questioned; but since so few definitions in the social sciences promise appreciable empirical applicability, the technical vocabulary of those fields appears excessively theoretical. Yet terms are not somehow naturally either "theoretical" or "empirical"; rather, the distinction hinges largely on the way a term is defined, but that consideration scarcely lessens the conceptual problems of the social sciences. Indeed, definitions in the literature of those fields are typically so vague that the theoretical–empirical distinction itself is difficult to maintain, which is to say that the designation of a term as theoretical or empirical is inherently disputable. The same may be said for the distinction between analytic and synthetic statements. Whereas an analytic statement is either true or false by the very meaning of its constituent terms (e.g. bachelors are men who have never married), whether a synthetic statement is true or false is not indicated by the meaning of its constituent terms (e.g. monogamy is the legally prescribed form of marriage in all highly urbanized societies). However, if the constituent terms of a statement are defined vaguely, the designation of that statement as analytic or synthetic is debatable. Yet such designations are absolutely essential for tests of a theory. If a theory comprises both analytic and synthetic statements (as virtually all theories do), tests of the theory are precluded unless the synthetic statements can be identified, because only those statements are subject to falsification by empirical observations.

Far from being exceptions to the foregoing, definitions of norm, deviance, and social control are studies in conceptual issues and problems. Sociologists agree appreciably in their definitions of a norm; but those definitions do not speak to several questions about norms, such as: What proportion of members of a social unit must subscribe to a belief for that belief to be a norm? The immediate consequence of leaving such questions unanswered is that definitions of a norm promise far less than maximum empirical applicability. The indirect consequence is that the traditional definition of deviance also promises far less than maximum empirical applicability, because that traditional definition refers to deviant behavior as behavior contrary to norms. The conventional sociological definition of social control also promises far less than maximum empirical applicability. The reason is that it makes reference to deviant behavior: Social control is any institution, organization, culture complex, or mode of behavior that counteracts deviance. The point is not just that an empirically applicable definition of deviance is lacking; additionally, there are now two contending camps in sociology regarding definitions of deviant behavior, and the outcome of that conceptual issue may decide the fate of the sociology of deviance.

Unfortunately, this book cannot offer a solution to all of the conceptual problems pertaining to norms, deviance, and social control. However, those problems will not merely go away because sociologists are reluctant to recognize them. Hopefully, this book will make it more difficult for sociologists to avoid confronting the problems and continue deluding students.

Four of my colleagues—George Becker, Ivar Berg, Bob Bibb, and Mike Swafford—encouraged me to continue the line of work that culminated in this book. Although they should not be held liable for the product, I am grateful to them for their encouragement. My wife, Sylvia, suffered through "another book" in reasonable good form; and even my children, Laura and Douglas, were patient now and then. Trudy Masic, Carol Meyer, and Maria Taylor performed miracles in converting my terrible handwriting into type. Their secretarial services and much of the time that I devoted to this book stemmed from my affiliation with a good school, Vanderbilt University.

Jack P. Gibbs

Nashville, Tennessee
August, 1980

NORMS,
DEVIANCE,
AND SOCIAL CONTROL

NORMS
AND
DEVIANCE

I

Sociologists use few technical terms more than "norms," and the notion of norms looms large in their attempts to answer a perennial question: How is social order possible? In pursuing the question, sociologists follow in the footsteps of illustrious names in the history of social thought, particularly Plato and Hobbes; and in this century contending schools of sociology are distinguished by divergent answers to the question. Although Durkheim and Parsons are often designated as leading figures in the functionalist school, it is more accurate to characterize their perspective as "normative sociology." That is true because in various ways they attributed social order to the existence of norms. Stating their argument quite briefly, interaction between members of a social unit tends to be orderly because the vast majority of members subscribe to the same evaluations of conduct, meaning that they hold the same beliefs as to what conduct *ought to be*. That explanation of social order has been debated for decades (Ellis, 1971; Klapp, 1973; Scott, 1971; Stoll, 1968; Wrong, 1961), and the resurgence of Marxist sociology in the past two decades signifies a rejection of the "consensual" explanation of social order. Marxist sociologists, and conflict sociologists in general, do not question the idea of social order itself; but they have no use for the assumption of normative consensus, especially insofar as it implies agreements in evaluations of conduct across social class lines. Rather than attribute social order to normative consensus, Marxist sociologists emphasize the use of State agencies by a dominant economic class (e.g., capitalists) to control dissidents through coercion and the threat of punishment.

In their great debate neither consensual sociologists nor conflict sociologists have emphasized that social order itself is largely a normative notion. If social order is described in strictly behavioral terms (i.e. without reference to beliefs about what conduct ought to be), then it is a matter of *statistical* regularities or uniformities. However, consider this question: If 10% of American adults commit shoplifting at least once a year, would social order be greater if that percentage should become 98? Indeed, what if everyone shoplifted on each visit to a store? Such changes would make behavior in one sphere of life *more uniform,* but that would not justify describing either change as an increase in social order. Nonetheless, sociologists commonly allude to social order as though it pertains to *behavioral* regularities and uniformities (i.e. the extent to which human behavior in a particular social unit is predictable), and such practice ignores the normative dimension of social order. That criticism is not meant to side with Durkheim or Parsons, thereby tacitly rejecting the Marxist argument. It is one thing to point out that the very idea of social order somehow entails normative notions but quite another to assert that there is appreciable normative consensus in even one social unit, let alone all units. Yet pointing out that social order has a normative component does little to clarify the idea of social order, and it may well be that the idea is so abstract that questions about it are not really meaningful. Be that as it may, as long as sociologists are preoccupied with the explanation of social order, the notion of norms will remain crucial.

Despite the preoccupation of sociologists with social order, there are many more theories of deviance than theories of social order. It could be argued that there is no real distinction between the two; and the argument could be furthered by pointing to the predominantly normative character of most theories of deviance, even though the theorists may not have used the term "norms." As a case in point, conceptualizations of Durkheim's (1951) famous four types of suicides (egoistic, anomic, altruistic, and fatalistic) would be made incomprehensible by the exclusion of normative notions. Similarly, two central terms in Merton's theory (1957) of anomie and deviant behavior—institutionalized means and culturally approved goals—denote normative notions; and the part of Sutherland's theory of differential association [see Sutherland and Cressey (1974)] pertaining to variation in the crime rate assumes greater normative conflict or dissensus in some populations than in others.

The foregoing should not be construed as a suggestion that the notion of norms is important only for the sociology of deviance. To the contrary, virtually every major sociological theory has a conspicuous normative quality. Whereas the division of labor can be described in behavioral terms, when formulating his theory on the subject, Durkheim was preoccupied with the normative consequences of an increase in the division of labor. The normative character of Weber's most famous theory (1930) is even more obvious, for he postulated that the emergence of one normative system (Protestantism) was necessary for the emergence of another normative system (capitalism). Like many sociologists before and after him, Weber formulated his theory with the idea of refuting Marx (1909), who attributed the emergence of capitalism to changes in the mode of production. Granting the vast differences between Marx's theory and Weber's theory, one similarity should be noted: Both theories are based on a conceptualization of capitalism as a normative system.

Far from being arcane, major sociological theorists rely less on normative notions in explaining human behavior than do lay persons. If asked by a visitor from another galaxy why there is ostensibly no sexual intercourse between brothers and sisters or parents and children, the typical American probably would reply that such sexual intercourse is wrong, sinful, disapproved, or against the law. No sociologist would fail to recognize that the reply constitutes a normative explanation of behavior and that the person who replied is familiar with the notion of a norm, even though he or she may not use the term. Moreover, it is unlikely that sociologists would dismiss the explanation as entirely naive, for they too indulge in normative explanations of human behavior—both in their personal life and in their professional activities. They commonly assume (perhaps with some reluctance to make it explicit) that human behavior is typically normatively determined or "governed." That assumption runs throughout Durkheim's brand of sociology, but the social psychologist Sherif (1936:3) has made the assumption most explicit: ". . . social norms regulate even the activities involved in the satisfaction of the major organic needs, such as hunger and sex."

There are all sorts of problems with normative explanations of human behavior [see Blake and Davis (1964)]—the most immediate, but least recognized, one being that all such explanations assume norms can be identified. The validity of that assumption hinges on the answers to two questions. First, is there appreciable agreement among social scientists in their definitions of a norm? Second, are the definitions such that, in using them, independent observers can agree in identifying the norms of particular social units? Without agreement in definitions of a norm, the reality of norms becomes suspect; and unless independent observers can agree in identifying the norms of particular social units, there must be doubts about the very existence of norms.

As shown in Chapter 1, there is appreciable agreement in definitions of norms, but there is no truly defensible way to answer the second question about those definitions. Only rarely do sociologists engage in research to ascertain the amount of agreement among independent observers in applying a definition, which is especially the case for definitions of norms. The analysis of several definitions of a norm (Chapter 1) identifies five major problems that would arise in the attempt to apply those definitions. Of the five problems, the one alluded to in the Preface serves best for illustrative purposes, and it is briefly described again for that reason. The vast majority of definitions depict a norm as a shared belief in a social unit as to what conduct ought to be. Few definitions suggest that a belief cannot be a norm of a social unit unless it is shared (i.e. subscribed to) by *all* members or even all adult members. While it would be grossly unrealistic to stipulate *absolute* consensus as a criterion of a norm, no definition can be applied unless it stipulates the minimum proportion of members of a social unit who must subscribe to a belief for that belief to be a norm. None of the definitions in the literature stipulates that minimum proportion, and it appears that any such stipulation would be arbitrary.

The point made in Chapter 1 is not just that conventional definitions of a norm leave several problems unresolved. Additionally, sociologists seem only dimly aware of those problems. Furthermore, the problems are such that no acceptable solution seems likely soon.

Whatever the merits of normative explanations of human behavior, the notion of norms is important if only because it is pertinent to the definition of numerous other major sociological concepts—deviance in particular. The conceptual relation between norms and deviance is paradoxical in that the recognition of deviant behavior casts doubt on a normative explanation of any kind of behavior. Thus, if the extraterrestial visitor previously mentioned is intelligent, that creature would voice reservations about a normative explanation of a sexual relation between brothers and sisters, defending those reservations by pointing to instances of sibling incest. That reservation can be generalized as a principle: If deviance is behavior contrary to a norm, then each instance of deviance casts doubt on normative explanations of human behavior. Indeed, if there were no deviance (so defined) and if there were no problems with the notion of norms, then there would be only one major sociological question: For any given social unit, why are the norms of that unit what they are, and why do they change?

The importance of deviance stems directly from its normative character. Insofar as social change is described in terms of normative transformations, all social change commences as deviant behavior; and deviance is the antithesis of social order—the very concern that has preoccupied sociologists from the outset. Consequently, it is not surprising that for several decades sociologists defined deviance as instances of a *type of behavior* that is contrary to a norm. That definition makes deviance interesting and important. However, as shown in Chapter 2, during the past 15 years numerous sociologists have partially or totally abandoned the traditional normative conception of deviance in preference for a "reactive" conception, according to which a *particular* act is deviant if and only if it is reacted to punitively or in some other distinctive way.

Many sociologists are not fully aware of the change in the conceptualization of deviance, much less its implications. Such is the case because advocates of the new conception of deviance have not been explicit as to their rejection of the normative conception or the reasons for the rejection. The most probable reason for the rejection is an awareness of the problems with the notion of norms. Once those problems are recognized, doubts are cast on the definition of deviance as behavior contrary to a norm. In any case, the shift away from the normative conception was made less conspicuous by the inclination of sociologists to speak of the emergence of the "labeling perspective" in the sociology of deviance rather than the emergence of a reactive conception of deviance. As I point out in Chapter 2, the term labeling perspective appears to denote a single, unitary argument; but sociologists use the term in such an uncritical way that it denotes three distinct, logically independent arguments: the reactive conception of deviance, the theory of secondary deviance, and the societal reaction theory. All three arguments are examined in Chapter 2, commencing with a description of the objections to and the merits of the reactive conception of deviance.

The labeling perspective poses issues that have yet to be resolved, and the fate of the sociology of deviance may rest on their resolution. A step toward their resolution is proposed in Chapter 2, but the more important consideration is that parties to the debate will continue to talk "past one another" until they recognize that the labeling perspective comprises three distinct arguments.

The Notion of Norms

1

Despite the divergent terminology employed by the authors, most of the 14 illustrative definitions of a norm (or social norm) quoted below appear consistent with this brief statement: A norm is a belief shared to some extent by members of a social unit as to what conduct *ought to be* in particular situations or circumstances. The most likely exceptions (Johnson, Newcomb, and Sherif, infra) are quoted because they are atypical, meaning that the selection of the illustrative definitions from the literature of sociology and social psychology was not random. If all of the definitions in that literature were quoted, the convergence would be even more striking.

Illustrative Definitions of a Norm

Bierstedt (1963:222): "A norm . . . is a rule or a standard that governs our conduct in the social situations in which we participate. It is a societal expectation. It is a standard to which we are expected to conform whether we actually do so or not."

Birenbaum and Sagarin (1976:11): ". . . norms may be thought of as legitimate socially shared guidelines to the accepted and expected patterns of conduct. Expectation alone would not make action normative. . . ."

Blake and Davis (1964:456): "... any standard or rule that states what human beings should or should not think, say, or do under given circumstances."

DeFleur et al. (1977:620): "NORMS ... Shared convictions about the patterns of behavior that are appropriate or inappropriate for the members of a group; what group members agree they can, should, might, must, cannot, should not, ought not, or must not do in any given situation."

Dohrenwend (1959:470): "A social norm is a rule which, over a period of time, proves binding on the overt behavior of each individual in an aggregate of two or more individuals. It is marked by the following characteristics: (1) Being a rule, it has a content known to at least one member of the social aggregate. (2) Being a binding rule, it regulates the behavior of any given individual in the social aggregate by virtue of (a) his having internalized the rule; (b) external sanctions in support of the rule applied to him by one or more other individuals in the social aggregate; (c) external sanctions in support of the rule applied to him by an authority outside the social aggregate; or any combination of these circumstances."

Homans (1961:46): "A *norm* is a statement made by a number of members of a group, not necessarily by all of them, that the members ought to behave in a certain way in certain circumstances."

Johnson (1960:8): "A norm is an abstract *pattern*, held in the mind, that sets certain limits for behavior. An 'operative' norm is one that is not merely entertained in the mind but is considered worthy of following in actual behavior; thus one feels that one *ought* to conform to it. This feeling means that one 'accepts' the norm."

Larson (1977:249): "Social Norm: An expected pattern of behavior appropriate in a given situation."

Morris (1956:610): "... norms are generally accepted, sanctioned prescriptions for, or prohibitions against, others' behavior, belief, or feeling, i.e. what others *ought* to do, believe, feel—*or else*. . . . Norms must be shared prescriptions. . . . Norms always include sanctions . . . ."

Newcomb (1950:266): "The term 'norm,' unfortunately, has several meanings. We shall use it, however, only in the sense of 'more or less fixed frame of reference,' whether of quantitative or qualitative nature."

Schellenberg (1970:278, 281): "Norms are patterns of expected behavior . . . . Norms represent standards of what is expected. At the same time they represent standards of what is approved. Approval is always, at least to some degree, a necessary part of normative behavior."

Sherif (1936:3): "We shall consider customs, traditions, standards, rules, values, fashions, and all other criteria of conduct which are standardized as a consequence of the contact of individuals, as specific cases of 'social norms.' "

Thibaut and Kelley (1959:239): "A norm exists when there are (1) agreements, or consensus, about the behaviors group members should or should not enact and (2) social processes to produce adherence to these agreements."

Williams (1968:204): "A norm is a rule, standard, or pattern for action (from the Latin *norma,* a carpenter's square or rule). Social norms are rules for conduct. The norms are the standards by reference to which behavior is judged and approved or disapproved. A norm in this sense is not a statistical average of actual behavior but rather a cultural (shared) definition of desirable behavior."

Problems in Defining a Norm

Sociologists can take small comfort in the appreciable agreement that is realized over several decades in their definitions of a norm.[1] That is true because none of the definitions truly confronts any of five crippling problems—crippling in that they seem to preclude a definition that is empirically applicable and yet not arbitrary. As suggested in the Preface, those problems have gone unconfronted because the definitions do not address several questions about norms. It should be recognized, however, that no definition of a term (sociological or otherwise) is truly complete, meaning that it speaks to all possible questions about the things or events denoted by that term. Stating this differently, it is virtually inconceivable that a definition completely expresses the conception of a norm held by the individual who stated the definition. Whereas one's conception of a class of things or events encompasses everything that one believes is true of that class, a definition need stipulate only the features of that class that distinguish it from all other classes.[2] The distinction between a conception and a definition is all the more important because two sociologists may hold identical conceptions of a norm

[1]Definitions of a norm by anthropologists are similar to those in the sociological literature; hence, instances of those definitions are not included among the illustrations. Anthropologists appear even more insensitive to problems with the notion of norm than are sociologists, and the same may be said of scholars in jurisprudence and political scientists. Were it not for the rarity with which economists use the term norm (especially in the evaluative sense), it would be a truly interdisciplinary concept.

[2]The subject is even more complex because one's conception of a class of events or things may encompass a mixture of two kinds of beliefs, those beliefs as to what is *logically* (i.e. necessarily) true about all of those events or things, and those beliefs as to what *may be* true (i.e. empirically contingent and possibly false). Thus, the belief that human beings do not have functional wings can be taken as logically true (if an animal has functional wings, it *cannot be* a human being). By contrast, the belief that no human being is over ten feet tall can be taken as empirically contingent

and yet employ different terms to define norms; hence, contrasts in the terminology of definitions can be misleading. Nonetheless, granted the importance of the distinction between a conception and a definition, the distinction in no way lessens the problems of the definition of a norm.

Most definitions of a norm in the sociological literature reflect the "superorganic" conception, according to which norms transcend the opinions of particular individuals.[3] That conception (Durkheim's legacy) reflects an aversion to reductionism (more specifically, a pronounced reservation about sociologists using psychological notions). The superorganic conception gives rise to definitions of a norm that promise negligible empirical applicability (i.e. little agreement among independent observers in identifying particular norms of particular social units). Examine the Blake and Davis definition of a norm as one such instance (supra). The logical form of the definition (*per genus et differentium*) is conventional in that it describes norms as subclass of a larger class of phenomena, standards or rules.[4] However, the meaning of "standard" or "rule" is obscure, and many social scientists treat those terms as synonymous with norms. In any case, the distinction between norms and *other* standards or rules remains unspecified; and, whatever the distinction may be, the Blake and Davis definition does not suggest how norms are to be identified.

All definitions that reflect a superorganic conception of a norm create the impression that norms are like fireplugs—tangible and obvious. To the contrary, whatever else a norm may be, it is an *abstraction* from human events (necessarily the behavior of particular individuals); hence, norms

---

(*footnote continued*)
(i.e. though perhaps true for all human beings—past, present, and future—it could be false, as one can imagine a startling disconfirmation). A conception may encompass both kinds of beliefs, and those who hold that conception may not be able to readily distinguish the two kinds. Individuals may differ when it comes to identifying beliefs as being either logically true or empirically contingent. In any case, a conception of a class of events or things is more akin to a substantive theory than is a definition; hence, even if it were possible to express a conception fully in a definition, that would not be desirable if the conception encompasses empirically contingent beliefs. Whatever else a definition may be, it should pertain only to those characteristics that are logically true of all instances (events or things) of the class in question.

[3]For one of the few extensive, critical commentaries on the notion of "superorganic," see Bidney (1953), noting that his observations on the superorganic conception of culture apply for the most part to the superorganic conception of norms. It is not particularly informative to say that the superorganic conception of a norm depicts norms as transcending particular individuals, but the conception is vague in the extreme. Consider the idea that a belief or type of behavior is superorganic *if* no living member of the social unit in question originated, created, or invented it. While that idea is a fairly specific criterion of "transcending particular individuals," actually using that criterion could have strange consequences. For example, the criterion suggests the possibility that the use of aircraft became a norm or a component of American culture the very instant that the Wright brothers died. Or, consider water witching. Evidently, no living American invented that belief or behavior, but is water witching now a norm or otherwise a part of American culture? It is precisely that kind of question which the superorganic conception of a norm (or culture) does not answer.

[4]What is said here of Blake and Davis's definition applies on the whole to the vast majority of all definitions in the literature—not just the illustrative definitions.

cannot be identified systematically without an observational procedure. A procedure cannot be stipulated by a definition, but unless a definition *suggests* a procedure, its empirical applicability is dubious at the outset.

Suggestions as to an identificational procedure are found only in definitions set forth by sociologists who eschew the notion of superorganic and have no abiding fear of reductionism. George Homans is a case in point. His definition (supra) suggests what may be the only systematic way to identify the norms of a social unit, to solicit responses from all members (or a representative sample) to "normative questions" such as: Do you approve or disapprove of smoking marijuana?

The suggestion of an indentificational procedure is the major merit of Homans's definition[5]; but when one contemplates extending his definition to an explicit, detailed procedure for identifying norms and actually applying it, five crucial problems with the notion of a norm surface immediately. Homans did not recognize those problems, nor do most sociologists, not even those who use the term norm extensively.[6]

The Consensus Problem

The assumption of normative consensus is a staple in perennial sociological debates (e.g. functionalism versus Marxism), and those debates suggest that norms and consensus are distinct. Yet if norms are *collective evaluations of conduct,* as most definitions suggest, then a norm represents consensus.[7] However, it would be unrealistic to require that all members of a social unit make or endorse a statement for it to be a norm; hence, the question: What minimal proportion must do so? Any amount less than 100% (e.g. 67%) would be arbitrary.[8] Far from being trivial, the problem lies at what may well

[5]The reason is that Homans identifies a norm as a kind (subclass) of *statement,* and the meaning of "statement" is far more clear than the meaning of rule, standard, pattern, blueprint, or guideline. Moreover, it is obvious that some statements do not pertain to the *ought* or *should* (i.e. they are not evaluative).

[6]Even more remarkable, classic works in the way of logical analyses of norms (deontic logic) pay little attention to the problems in question (Anderson and Moore, 1957; von Wright, 1963). And none of the surveys of the use of the term norm by sociologists recognize all of the problems, let alone resolve them (Blake and Davis, 1964; Gibbs, 1965; Morris, 1956; Rommetveit, 1955; Williams, 1968).

[7]The term "collective evaluation of conduct" is used here not in the sense of normative consensus (i.e. absolute agreement in the normative opinions of members of a social unit) but to signify that the normative opinions of all members (or a sample of them deemed representative) have been solicited. Thus, if a certain proportion of all members of a social unit (say 69 %) make or endorse the statement "smoking marijuana is bad," then the statement is a collective evaluation of conduct to that extent (the term denotes a *quantitative* property of a social unit).

[8]In one of the very few instances where sociologists have confronted the consensus problem in defining a norm, Bates and Harvey (1975:67−68) take the position that an evaluation of conduct (or, evidently, any "idea") may be a norm even if held by only one member of the social unit in question and not necessarily a powerful member. They are to be admired for confronting the problem directly. However, it is doubtful if their solution will be acceptable to many sociologists, the immediate objection being that Bates and Harvey's conception does not attribute any necessary collective quality to norms.

be the central notion in conventional conceptions of a norm: the notion that norms have a collective quality.

Arbitrariness is only one aspect of the ''consensus problem''; additionally, the distinction between *aggregate* consensus and *structural* consensus must be confronted. Suppose that the normative question about marijuana is posed to a representative sample of Americans and 85% voice disapproval. Even so, that percentage could vary enormously among families, races, social classes, communities, and/or ethnic divisions; should that be the case, it would be unrealistic to speak of *the* American marijuana norm. Then consider the assumption that much of human behavior is in some sense normatively determined. Not even Durkheim would argue that the opinions of Episcopalians in Vermont determine a Chicano's behavior in Texas, or deny that the distinction between aggregate and structural consensus remains relevant in assessing the norms of communities and of organizations. As for the idea that ''reference groups'' can be taken as the ultimate locus of norms, sociologists will not carry normative relativism that far. It may well be that many individuals govern their behavior in accordance with what they perceive as the evaluations of conduct held by particular esteemed individuals (e.g. a friend, an employer, a movie star), but that relativism would make norms peculiar to particular individuals.

Normative Contingencies

Suppose that one responds to the marijuana question by voicing approval of that type of behavior. If pressed on the matter, the respondent might balk at the prospect of children smoking pot; but the question does not stipulate ''adults,'' and age is only one of several possibly relevant normative contingencies.[9] Everyday experience surely indicates that evaluations of conduct are contingent on characteristics of the actor, characteristics of the object of the act, and/or various situational considerations (e.g. time and/or place).

Most sociological definitions of a norm recognize contingencies, usually by reference to ''situations'' or ''circumstances''; and it is doubtful if any significance can be attached to the omission of such a reference in some of the illustrative definitions. However, a normative question in a survey of public opinion cannot stipulate all possibly relevant contingencies, especially since they are not the same for all respondents or for all types of conduct. Nor is the

[9]This argument is distinct from the notion that a norm marks off ranges of tolerable behavior. That ''continuum'' notion tends to confound four considerations: (1) actual behavior, (2) contingencies, (3) the intensity of evaluations of conduct, and (4) consensus in those evaluations. Hence, far from clarifying, the notion makes it difficult to realize an intelligible and empirically applicable definition of a norm. Similarly, references of social psychologists to ''norm senders'' and ''norm receivers'' only begs the question: Whatever is being sent or received, why is it identified as a norm?

problem solved by recognition that some, if not all, putative norms of particular social units actually incorporate contingencies. Ponder this normative question: Do you approve or disapprove of people drinking alcoholic beverages? In responding to that question, many Americans might express approval—but only for people beyond a certain age (e.g. 18). While sociologists would recognize such a response as indicative of a role (a collective evaluation of conduct that applies only to particular categories of individuals or statuses), it is an illusion to suppose that the notion of a role solves the contingency problem. Whatever the social unit, virtually all evaluations of types of conduct are roles; but contingencies in evaluations of conduct are not limited to status distinctions, let alone one status distinction (age in the case of drinking). Accordingly, whatever the response to the foregoing normative question about drinking, whether approval or disapproval, the respondent might well admit that his or her evaluation of a *particular instance* of drinking would depend on the age and sex of the drinker, the time, the place, the financial condition of the drinker, whether there had been a death or serious illness in the drinker's family, and so on.

Differential Power

Returning to the marijuana question, suppose that one respondent in the survey is a wealthy senator and another is a skid-row bum. The conventional survey practice would assign equal weight to their normative opinions, but that practice is debatable. Granted that power is a fuzzy notion, in this instance one respondent clearly has more power than the other. Insofar as there is a marijuana norm, the senator would surely have more opportunities to alter the norm through legislative action.

Despite reasons for assuming that some normative opinions "count more" than others, conventional opinion survey procedures run contrary to that assumption; but practical problems seemingly preclude an alternative. Even if an empirically applicable definition of power could be formulated, the relative importance of different kinds of power (e.g. political, economic) is not likely to be approximately the same for evaluations of all types of behavior; and there is no prospect of assigning "power weights" to each normative opinion. Accordingly, it is not surprising that none of the illustrative definitions explicitly stipulate that only evaluations of conduct endorsed by the powerful members of a social unit are norms. Other than practical considerations, there is only one conspicuous rationale for ignoring differential power in the identification of norms. No *definition* answers empirical questions such as: Why do norms change? Differential power might be part of the answer; but the answer would be a substantive proposition, not a conceptualization. Nonetheless, ignoring differential power when identifying norms appears grossly unrealistic.

What People Say and What People Do

Although the vast majority of sociological definitions of a norm are "evaluative," there are two distinct alternatives. The first, a *statistical* definition, equates a norm with average or typical behavior. Such a definition is extremely rare,[10] and some of the illustrations (see Williams's definition, *supra*) explicitly reject the statistical notion; but the idea does touch on an issue. In applying an *evaluative* definition of a norm, investigators must solicit normative opinions; and that procedure, as in attitudinal research, admits divergence between what people say conduct ought to be and what people actually do (Deutscher, 1973). By contrast, a statistical definition admits no such divergence, but it makes a "normative" or "cultural" explanation of aggregate behavior tautological. Thus, if brother–sister marriage is contrary to a norm because rare, it is pointless to argue that such marriages are rare because they are contrary to a norm.[11] Moreover, a statistical definition ignores those subjective states (disgust, shame, indignation, guilt, etc.) that give a sense of immediate reality to norms as evaluations of conduct.[12] That consideration is all the more relevant in contemplating this argument: Even if in some American communities the majority of husbands do commit adultery at least once, their attempts to conceal the act are more indicative of a norm than is the frequency of the act.

The problems that haunt an evaluative definition are not avoided by a statistical definition. Consider this question: With what frequency must a type of act occur before it is a norm? As in contemplating the "consensus problem," any answer would be unrealistic or arbitrary. Then think about the typical American's infrequent attendance at funerals, even though the normative quality of attendance is suggested by its public character.[13] Of course, going to funerals is rare because it is a highly contingent kind of

---

[10]Nonetheless, Rommetveit's survey (1955) concluded that a statistical conception of a norm is one of three ways that social and behavioral scientists use the term. The other two are (1) to designate a particular shared "frame of reference" and (2) to designate the existence of social obligation or pressure.

[11]Yet an individual's perception of regularities in the behavior of others may have an impact of his or her behavior, a significant possibility in connection with the interests of social psychologists in conformity (Aronson, 1976; Newcomb, 1950; Schellenberg, 1970; Sherif, 1936; Thibaut and Kelley, 1959).

[12]No one would deny some connection between norms and such experiences as shame, guilt, and indignation. Accordingly, since the notion of norm bears on the experience of virtually all adult human beings, it may appear strange that the notion is a study in problems. Those problems stem largely from a firm convention. to think of norms as collective rather than as personal or idiosyncratic.

[13]The illustration is also relevant in anticipation of the argument that the average frequency with which individuals engage in a type of act is relevant but not the proportion of them who have engaged at least once. That argument ignores the low average frequency for all manner of *public* types of acts (e.g. marriage, attending funerals, graduation ceremonies).

behavior, but it is not clear how normative contingencies can be recognized by a statistical definition of a norm. Moreover, since acts contrary to widely shared evaluations of conduct (e.g. in some communities possibly smoking marijuana) are commonly concealed, the reported frequency of those acts (e.g. smoking marijuana) is dubious.

Still another alternative to an evaluative definition is also "behavioral," but it focuses attention on *actual reactions* to acts. Here is a brief version of such a reactive definition: A type of act is a norm of a social unit if instances are not reacted to punitively. The definition does not rest on the assumption that people "do what they say"; indeed, it may be that only punitive reactions are indicative of what people truly take as important. Additionally, assuming that the powerful members of a social unit control sanctions, the reactive definition of norms takes differential power into account indirectly. So it is not surprising that some of the illustrative definitions (see Dohrenwend and Morris, supra) allude to reactions to acts—sanctions in particular. The contrast suggests that definitions of a norm are more divergent than casual inspection of them indicates. More importantly, as sociologists truly attempt to realize empirically applicable definitions of a norm, those definitions will become increasingly divergent.

A reactive definition of a norm may appear to come to grips with the problem of normative contingencies, for potential reactors to particular acts presumably take contingencies into account. However, when reactions are impunitive, it is not known whether the act itself precluded a punitive reaction or whether it was the circumstance (e.g. the social identity of the actor). When the reaction is punitive, it is not known whether the act itself elicited the reaction or whether it was the circumstance. In brief, contingencies are not revealed by the proportion of instances of a type of act that result in punishment.

Still another reservation stems from recognition that a reactive definition of a norm does not *explain* punitive reactions and the argument that norms *determine* reactions to acts. The reservation is disputable because definitions cannot answer empirical questions. In any case, since acts contrary to widely shared evaluations of conduct are commonly concealed, it is difficult to estimate the *proportion* of such acts that result in punishment. One can speak of "acts that would be punished if known to others"; but that terminology introduces conjecture, especially since it ignores the social identity of potential reactors. In other words, the idea ignores this question: Who would have reacted punitively had they known of the act?

Even if all preceding objections were irrelevant, a reactive definition cannot be applied without a criterion as to the necessary frequency of punitive reactions. No sociological definition of a norm that stresses the reactive quality (usually by reference to sanctions) stipulates such a criterion. No one is likely to argue that all reactions to all instances of a type of act must be impunitive for that type of act to be a norm, but a defensible alternative is wanting.

Normative Properties Excluded

The evaluative, statistical, and reactive definitions of a norm are all uni-dimensional (i.e. they emphasize only one quality of norms). However, reconsider the ultimate argument for the concern with norms: Much of human behavior is in some sense and in some way normatively determined. The argument forces recognition that in numerous situations individuals orient their behavior in terms of *expectations* rather than evaluations of conduct; and several of the illustrative definitions of a norm refer to expectations (see Bierstedt, Birenbaum and Sagarin, Larson and Schellenberg, supra). Yet those references are troublesome. Specifically, it may be that some authors of definitions uncritically equate "evaluations of conduct" and "expectations of conduct," which is clearly suggested by such qualifying phrases as "appro-priate" [see Larson's definition (supra)]. Yet the distinction is undeniable. Many parents may expect that their children will eventually smoke cigarettes, but persist in the belief that they ought not do so. In a sense the effort of the parents to prevent what they dread is a response to expectations of conduct, not just evaluations of conduct.[14] Viewed in that light, a great deal can be said for those definitions of a norm that recognize both expectations and evalua-tions of conduct; but most definitions simply do not speak directly to the question, and the omission has an unfortunate implication. It may well be that the appreciable agreement among the illustrative definitions (largely in their emphasis on evaluations of conduct) is misleading. If sociologists are to arrive at an empirically applicable definition of a norm, they must direct themselves to several questions (in this case, the relevance of expectations of conduct), but as they confront such questions they will come to disagree. Stated otherwise, as definitions of a norm become empirically applicable, they will become more divergent.

Divergent definitions are especially likely if more sociologists come to take Scheff's argument (1967) seriously. He points out that individuals commonly orient their behavior around their perceptions of *others'* evaluations of conduct.[15] Nor can sociologists deny that *perceived* evaluations of conduct are more social than *personal* evaluations. Finally, since Scheff's argument

[14]Consider this illustration: American parents seldom engage in attempts to prevent marriage between their children (surely far less than they engage in attempts to prevent them from smoking), but they ostensibly disapprove of incestuous marriage much more than they disapprove of smoking.

[15]The difference bears on attempts to characterize people as being "inner-directed" or "other-directed" (Reisman et al., 1953), and it may be the best way to force recognition that the distinction is *quantitative*.

readily extends to expectations of conduct, one can rightly speak of a distinction between personal expectations and perceived expectations.

A unidimensional conception of a norm is not consistent with three conventionally recognized types of norms: mores, customs, and laws [see Davis (1949) and Sherif's definition (supra)]. Unlike mores, commonly recognized instances of customs (e.g. eating breakfast) have no particular affective connotations (i.e. no real bearing on morality or ethics). Yet Americans have expectations as to such behavior, even to the point of being surprised, for example, on encountering an adult who eats only one meal a day. So customs are norms only insofar as the notion of a norm encompasses *both* expectations and evaluations of conduct.[16] Then consider the conventional idea that a law is a type of norm.[17] While a criminal statute ostensibly expresses an evaluation of conduct, the evaluation may not be shared by even a majority of those subject to the law. Moreover, if all unenforced criminal statutes are not laws, the reactive definition of a norm (which emphasizes actual punitive reactions) identifies the relevant normative property.

To summarize, an inclusive definition of a norm would recognize at least five major normative properties: personal evaluations, perceived evaluations, personal expectations, perceived expectations, and distinctive reactions to acts. Yet there is no assurance whatever that even a majority of sociologists would accept such a definition and, in any case, it would be extremely difficult to frame an intelligible definition of a norm that recognizes all five properties. Even if such a definition could be formulated, it would have to be recognized that each constituent normative property is quantitative. Consequently, as long as sociologists continue to think of a norm as being either

[16]Appearances to the contrary, the definitions of Birenbaum and Sagarin, and Schellenberg (supra) would preclude recognition of eating breakfast as a norm even though those definitions recognize *both* evaluations and expectations of conduct. While most Americans probably expect others to eat breakfast somewhat regularly, there does not appear to be any particular evaluation of that conduct (i.e. disapproval of adults who do not eat breakfast). The point is that numerous putative customs can be recognized as norms only if the definition of a norm recognizes (inter alia) evaluations of conduct *and/or* expectations of conduct.

[17]Selznick claims (1961:94) that definitions of law ''are not really so various as is sometimes suggested. . . .'' To the contrary, one would be hard pressed to find any term in the social sciences or jurisprudence that is defined in such diverse ways as ''law.'' Moreover, debates over conceptualization of law have raged for centuries, and contending schools of jurisprudence are distinguished first and foremost by preferences as to definitions of law. Should this argument be doubted, examine a sample of definitions of law (Gibbs, 1972), and then read Bodenheimer (1974), Ehrlich (1936), Fuller (1969), Hart (1961), Hoebel (1954), Kantorowicz (1958), Kelsen (1967), Llewellyn (1951), Malinowski (1959), and Stone (1961). An analysis of the problems and issues in defining law (or *a* law) is outside the scope of this book; however, it should be noted that those problems and issues commence with an unquestioned convention in the social sciences and jurisprudence—a law is a type of norm. If norms are defined as a collective evaluation of conduct that is endorsed by at least a majority of the members of a social unit, then an ''unpopular law'' (or anything akin to that notion) is a contradiction in terms, regardless of how systematically or effectively that law is enforced. Advocates of ''natural law theory'' (Fuller, 1969; Selznick, 1961) seemingly attribute a consensual basis to laws, while advocates of ''analytical jurisprudence'' (Kelsen, 1967) clearly oppose that attribution.

present or absent, the five properties cannot enter into a definition of a norm without the stipulation of a *minimal* amount of each. Any such stipulation is bound to be arbitrary or unrealistic.

Proposal of a Radical Solution

Given the litany of seemingly insurmountable problems, the only solution is to abandon that notion of norms when formulating theories or conducting research and replace it with the notion of "normative properties," meaning any *characteristic* of a type of behavior in a particular social unit having to do with collective evaluations of that behavior, collective expectations of that behavior, and/or reactions to instances of that behavior. That definition is not precise, but it permits whatever distinctions (e.g. personal versus perceived) and specific measurable variables (e.g. perceived evaluative consensus) a theorist may choose to introduce.[18] By contrast, conventional definitions (most of the fourteen previously examined) depict a norm as qualitative and unidimensional.

The proposal is radical, but it would not require that sociologists destroy their lecture notes. They can continue to teach as though norms are as real as fireplugs, provided they separate their pedagogy from their theorizing and research.[19] Nonetheless, sociologists who cling to a superorganic conception of norms will dismiss the foregoing problems as mistaken because they stem from the belief that norms have something to do with the behavior of individuals; but their argument does not even suggest a procedure for identifying norms. Such a procedure would not be required if sociologists

[18]The same is true of normative contingencies. Systematic research on normative properties requires answers to normative questions (including those pertaining to expectations of conduct) from members of a social unit, but the questions would recognize only contingencies that are relevant *for the research at hand*. Relevance is likely to depend on the theory that guides the research; hence, any theory pertaining to normative phenomena should stipulate not only the contingencies that the normative questions should recognize but also how differential power is to be treated in soliciting and/or assessing answers. Needless to say, the proposed strategy departs from the superorganic conception of norms, according to which norms exist independently of particular theoretical or research interests.

[19]A radical alteration of research and theory on deviance would be required if the traditional definition of deviance (briefly, deviant behavior is behavior contrary to a norm) is employed. According to the normative conception of deviance, a type of act in a particular social unit is either deviant or not; but the proposed strategy would treat virtually any type of act in any social unit as deviant to *some degree*. Moreover, deviance would not be treated as unidimensional; rather, at least five logically independent values would be required to express the deviant character of a type of act, with each value corresponding to one of the five major normative properties (supra). Yet the strategy is less radical than it appears. Few sociologists or social psychologists would deny that deviance is somehow a matter of degree; but that recognition is seldom even suggested in conceptualizations of deviance, and for all practical purposes it is completely ignored in research and theory. It has been ignored largely because of the inordinate focus in the history of the sociology of deviance on "serious crimes" (e.g. murder, robbery, rape). That focus prompted sociologists to overlook problems with the notion of norms and deviance, because the identification of those types of acts as deviant is scarcely disputable; but the focus is very narrow, and the conceptual problems remain.

used the term to denote a purely theoretical notion (i.e. norms do not exist in the real world), but they clearly do not use the term in that manner.

Whatever the fate of the proposed solution, it would be idle for sociologists to presume that any existing definition of a norm can be extended in such a way as to avoid the problems. All of the definitions are incomplete, in that they do not speak to several questions about norms; but it is pointless to demand a definition that completely expresses a conception of a norm. For that matter, the problems are such that not even a truly complete definition would solve them. Even if it were possible to realize absolute correspondence between a definition and a conception of a norm, that definition would not solve the consensus problem (to mention only one). Indeed, there is the distinct possibility that as sociologists more nearly realize complete definitions of a norm those definitions will diverge (e.g. one definition will treat expectations as a feature or a possible feature of a norm, while another will explicitly deny their relevance). If the problems are to be resolved, conceptual innovations (atypical definitions) are essential; but the atypical illustrative definitions—those formulated by Johnson, Newcomb, and Sherif—do not resolve any of the problems. They are simply different; and no significance can be attached to the fact that Newcomb and Sherif are social psychologists, because the definitions of Thibaut and Kelley and Schellenberg (also social psychologists) are very much like those of sociologists.

More General Issues

As previously suggested, problems with the notion of a norm emerge when one aspires to realize an empirically applicable definition of a norm, but such a definition would serve no real purpose unless the ultimate goal is to employ it in stating *testable* theories. Despite the ''lip service'' that sociologists pay to the desirability of testable theories, a substantial number of them are committed to a hoary tradition: assessing theories without regard to tests (i.e. rejecting a theory regardless of tests unless it is consistent with one's preconceptions of social reality). Those sociologists will dismiss the foregoing analysis as the identification of only ''technical'' problems. Such a dismissal would be an illusion, for the problems in question bear directly on the arguments that distinguish contending schools of sociology.

The major figures in ''humanistic sociology''—phenomenological sociology, ethnomethodology, and symbolic interactionism—do not use the term norm extensively; and some of the more candid figures (especially those with an analytical bent) voice reservations about the notion itself [see Kitsuse (1975)]. The principle reason is one of the problems previously discussed—contingencies in evaluations of conduct. Consequently, when confronted with a systematic attempt to identify the norms of particular social units (whether in descriptive research or in tests of a theory), humanists are likely to regard the attempt as naive. If the attempt was made by posing normative questions to members of the social units (the only obvious systematic way to identify norms if they are understood as collective evaluations of conduct), humanists will be especially sensitive to the point that normative questions inevitably fail to recognize some possibly relevant contingencies in evaluations of conduct. Thus, if informed that, say, 60% of a representative sample of adult Americans have voiced "disapproval of abortion," a humanist sociologist is likely to dismiss that finding as bordering on the meaningless (perhaps rightly so).

The claim is not that humanists are fully conscious of all problems with the notion of norms, or that their doubts about the notion are limited to the contingency problem. Even dim awareness of any of the problems is sufficient reason to harbor doubts about the notion itself. It is no less significant that sociologists who make extensive use of the term norm appear insensitive to the problems; hence, they cannot understand why humanists do not also treat norms as an absolutely central notion. Humanists themselves contribute to misunderstandings of their perspective by occasional and largely uncritical use of the term norm. Their perspective would be better understood by their opponents if humanists categorically rejected the notion of norms and made the reasons for it explicit. In any case, the seemingly permanent divisions of sociology into contending schools is no mystery; those divisions grow out of and are sustained by problems with the putative central notions in sociology, and the notion of norms is an outstanding case.

Marxist or Conflict Sociology

It is grossly misleading to describe Marxist or conflict sociologists as different from their colleagues (functionalist, in particular) because they reject the assumption of normative consensus; and it would be misleading even if other differences are duly noted. Although they seldom make the point explicit, Marxist and conflict sociologists are bound to harbor doubts about the very notion of a norm, not just normative consensus.

Those doubts stem principally from two problems with the notion of norms: the distinction between aggregate and structural consensus, and differential power. Thus, confronted with the finding that 60% of a representative sample of Americans voiced "disapproval of abortion," a Marxist or conflict sociologist is bound to wonder about the normative opinions on abortion of racial−ethnic minorities, working women, and employers. They would be especially concerned with the normative opinions of wealthy employers, for their theoretical perspective has led them to the conviction (perhaps rightly so) that the normative opinions of members of the dominant economic class are the ones that *really count*.

The reservations of Marxist or conflict sociologists have not led them to reject explicitly the notion of norms or to redefine it so as to confront the consensus problem and the problem of differential power. Like their colleagues, Marxist or conflict sociologists continue to use the term norm without due recognition of the problems. That practice perpetuates the belief that schools of sociology are divided on purely ideological grounds; but they are divided also by implicit reservations about the central notions in sociology, and those reservations are not purely ideological. They stem from problems with those notions that sociologists *in general* rarely confront. Again, the notion of norms is an oustanding case.

The Notion of Deviance

2

Because most of the 19 illustrative definitions quoted below are fairly recent and representative in that sense, they do not reveal the great shift in conceptions of deviance that took place during the 1960s. Hence, only Merton's definition (infra) is truly consistent with the conception of deviance held by virtually all sociologists until about 1965. That traditional conception reduces to this brief definition: Deviant behavior is an instance of a type of behavior that is contrary to the norms of at least one particular social unit.

With the exception of the definitions by Feldman and Kaplan, all of those formulated after 1966 exclude the term norms and/or stress *reactions* to behavior as a criterion of deviance. That stress reflects at least a partial acceptance of the reactive conception of deviance, according to which a particular act is not deviant unless someone reacts to it in a distinctive way (e.g. punitively).[1] That conception was first suggested in definitions of deviance by Becker, Erikson, and Kitsuse in the early 1960s (infra). However, it may well be that not even a majority of sociologists now categorically accept the reactive conception of deviance.[2] Most of them appear to be struggling to find middle ground

---

[1]Some of the illustrative definitions seemingly represent attempts to avoid problems with the notion of a norm and not so much an acceptance of the reactive conception of deviance. For example, Thio's definition makes deviance a matter of degree, which implies rejection of the notion that a norm is either present or absent.

[2]It appears that divergent conceptions of deviance have yet to become an issue in anthro-

between Becker et al., and advocates of the older, purely normative conception of deviance.[3] One conspicuous manifestation of that struggle is the proliferation of arcane locutions in recent definitions of deviance [see Davis, Denisoff and McCaghy, Steffensmeier and Terry, and Thio (infra)].

Before examining the illustrative definitions, it should be recognized that sociologists commonly speak of the labeling perspective but not of the reactive conception of deviance. The two terms clearly do not have the same meaning. For reasons indicated subsequently, the term labeling perspective can be construed as denoting any one or all of three distinct and logically independent arguments, *including* the reactive conception of deviance. Hence, sociologists are not fully aware of the distinctive character of reactive conception or its implications, because the conception is like a tree in a dense forest. That is not to say that the other components of the labeling perspective are unimportant. The fate of the sociology of deviance hinges largely on the issues raised by components of the labeling perspective, and toward the end of this chapter a proposal is made with a view to circumvent some of those issues.

Illustrative Definitions of Deviance

Akers (1977:11) "We consider here only behavior which deviates in a disapproved direction. More specifically, attention is directed primarily to instances of disapproved behavior considered serious enough to warrant major societal efforts to control them, using strong negative sanctions or treatment-corrective techniques."

Becker (1963:9): "The deviant is one to whom that label has successfully been applied; deviant behavior is behavior that people so label."

Bell (1971:11): "Basically the ultimate measurement of whether or not an act is deviant depends on how others who are socially significant in power and influence define the act. . . . One could commit any act, but it is not deviant in its social consequences if no elements of society react to it."

Birenbaum and Sagarin (1976:37): "If one wishes to make this definition

---

(footnote continued)

pology (Edgerton, 1976), which is to say that the vast majority of anthropologists continue to accept the older, normative conception of deviance.

[3]One alternative in the way of middle ground is not a partial acceptance of the reactive conception of deviance (as in the case of Schur's definition) but, rather, simply avoiding references to norms in defining deviance (e.g. the definition by Steffensmeier and Terry). Such definitions are especially vague and difficult to understand, but they are now very common. Consider, as another example, Matza's statement (1969:10): ". . . to deviate is to *stray*, as from a path or standard."

[Schur (1971:24)] more precise, one might expand it to *human beings* as well as human behavior, so as to include those whose deviance comes from what they are and not from what they do. Lepers, for example, may elicit the types of reaction that Schur spells out for conduct. We would also add, to cover the fact that some socially condemned behavior, because of secrecy, never comes to elicit those interpersonal and collective reactions, that the behavior would elicit them *if it came to be known*. It is difficult to locate a single word that covers all the persons and behavior that are usually encompassed by this theme, but we believe that the concept of *disvalued* persons and behavior is as close to it as any.''

Black (1976:9): "Deviant behavior is conduct that is subject to social control.''

Clinard and Meier (1979:14): "... deviance constitutes only those deviations from norms which are in a disapproved direction and of sufficient degree to exceed the tolerance limits of a social group such that the deviation elicits, or is likely to elicit if detected, a negative sanction.''

Cullen and Cullen (1978:8): "... acts and actors violating the norms of society will be termed 'rule-breaking behavior' and 'rule breakers,' while the terms 'deviant behavior' and 'deviant' will be reserved for acts and actors labeled as deviant by a social audience.''

Davis (1975:227): Deviance: "Any form of opposition to established rules, standards, or practices of elites; deviance may be a political label, a popular stereotype, or a form of sanctioned behavior. In conflict theory, deviance is political opposition to coercive control.''

Denisoff and McCaghy (1973:26): "Deviance is the name of the conflict game in which individuals or loosely organized small groups with little power are strongly feared by a well-organized, sizable minority or majority who have a large amount of power.''

Erikson (1962:308): "Deviance is not a property *inherent in* certain forms of behavior; it is a property *conferred upon* these forms by the audiences which directly or indirectly witness them.''

Feldman (1978:5): "Deviance is ... the violation of a norm that somebody believes is important.''

Kaplan (1975:4): "Deviant behavior ... is the failure of a person to conform to the specified normative expectations of one or more of the *specified* groups in which the individual holds membership.''

Kitsuse (1962:253): "Forms of behavior per se do not differentiate deviants from non-deviants; it is the responses of the conventional and conforming members of the society who identify and interpret behavior as deviant which sociologically transform persons into deviants."

Lofland (1969:23): "... deviance is here defined with reference to public definitions embodied in civil rulings and detection and apprehension procedures—not with reference to any human bodies that actually get detected and apprehended. Definition hinges upon the *possibility* of detection and apprehension, not upon *actual* detection and apprehension. The domain of deviance is all that behavior that *could* become an object of defensible apprehension, processing and punishment were the activity known to civil authorities and should they choose to act."

Merton (1966:805): "... deviant behavior refers to conduct that departs significantly from the norms set for people in their social statuses."

Schur (1971:24): "Human behavior is deviant *to the extent that* it comes to be viewed as involving a *personally discreditable* departure from a group's normative expectations, *and* it *elicits* interpersonal or collective reactions that serve to 'isolate,' 'treat,' 'correct,' or 'punish' *individuals* engaged in such behavior."

Scott (1972:11−12): "... there are few natives who actually use the term 'social deviant' as such; most of them, when they confer this property on others, use labels such as 'nut,' 'queer,' 'weirdo,' 'rascal,' 'pervert,' or 'loony.' I employ the generic term 'deviance' to refer to that property that is conferred upon persons whenever labels such as these are used."

Steffensmeier and Terry (1975:4): "Deviance consists of differentially valued phenomena."

Thio (1978:23): "... we may define deviant behavior in terms of public consensus. We may define it as *any behavior considered deviant by public consensus that may range from the maximum to the minimum.*"

Further Observations on the Reactive Conception of Deviance

Granted that the statements of Becker, Erikson, and Kitsuse do not amount to explicit rejections of the older, normative conception of deviance, it does not distort to interpret them as suggesting the following version of a reactive definition: A particular act is deviant if and only if it is reacted to distinctively or "so labeled" by at least one member of the social unit in question.[4]

---

[4]Actually, an even more extreme interpretation of the new conception of deviance could be justified. It appears that allusions to *actual* acts as "objectively real" are alien to that conception; hence, the present version of a reactive definition should perhaps refer to "allegations of acts." However, in recognition that Becker et al. do speak of acts and behavior (not just allegations), the present interpretation is less extreme than it could be.

Whatever the merits of such a reactive definition (there are several), it cannot be reconciled with a normative conception of deviance.

Have Becker and the others truly advocated a reactive conception of deviance? Some of their other statements do raise doubts. For example, Becker (1963) refers to secret deviance, which suggests that "unreacted to" behavior may be deviant. Ambiguity is also introduced by the references of Becker, Erikson, and Kitsuse in stating their arguments to (1) creation of deviance, (2) audience, and (3) behavior. The "creation" argument suggests that deviance has nothing to do with behavior; but, alternatively, it may only make this banal point: no norms, no deviance (Merton, 1971:827). "Audience" may designate either (1) potential reactors to a *particular* act, or (2) all members of a social unit who express some normative opinions about *types* of acts. Finally, "behavior" denotes either a particular act or a type of act, and the distinction is crucial. When members of a social unit evaluate conduct in the abstract or the concrete, they are reacting to behavior. However, norms pertain to types of acts; and, according to the traditional conception of deviance, a particular act is deviant if and only if it is *an instance of a type* contrary to a norm.[5] Yet Becker et al. do not emphasize types of acts, let alone norms; hence, their arguments seem to reduce to this: Whether a particular act is deviant depends not on its typification (e.g. rape, suicide) and reference to a norm but, rather, on *actual* reactions to that act. Of course, even a reactive conception suggests that deviant acts are instances of a class, but it is a class defined only by reference to reactions.

Objections to a Reactive Conception of Deviance

Whatever their intention, Becker et al. have not resolved problems with a normative conception of deviance; and, eventually, sociologists may come to regard those problems as insoluble and intolerable.[6] If so, the reactive conception is the major alternative; but it too is permeated with many problems.

[5]While Becker, Erikson, and Kitsuse commonly ignore the distinction between a particular act and a type of act, in all fairness to them it should be recognized that the same is true of sociologists in general. It may well be that the English language makes it cumbersome to maintain the distinction.

[6]The present argument is that the normative conception of deviance came to be rejected because of problems with the notion of a norm, even though advocates of the new (reactive) conception have not made their rejection of the older conception explicit, nor fully revealed the reasons for the rejection. Note, however, that one difficulty with the normative conception of deviance is not emphasized here; the conception makes the identification of instances of deviance difficult if only because acts contrary to a widely shared evaluation of conduct tend to be concealed. That difficulty *may have* encouraged rejection of the normative conception, but it can be avoided only by denying that deviance has any connection with collective evaluations of conduct (perceived collective evaluations in particular).

What kinds of reaction identify acts as deviant? Critics allege that reactivists (advocates of the reactive conception of deviance) do not provide an empirically applicable stipulation of the relevant kinds of reactions.[7] Such a stipulation is not realized by speaking of "distinctive reactions" or "labeled as deviant," and the failure of reactivists to emphasize punitive reactions is puzzling. Given their preoccupation with officials, both the kind of reaction *and* the social identity of the reactor may be relevant. If so, whose reactions identify acts as deviant? Should the reactivists reply "formal agents of social control," that would generate issues. For example, how could sociologists identify surveys of self-reported acts or reports of criminal victimization as studies of deviance?

Defenders of the labeling perspective (Kitsuse, 1975:276) admit that the relevant kinds of reactions remain vaguely identified, but they appear indifferent to the problem. Many defenders (Schur, 1971:14) have argued this: Since what is deviant for some members of a social unit may not be so for others, a precise definition would be unrealistic. The argument is consistent with a premise of phenomenology, symbolic interactionism, and ethnomethodology—that the "meaning" of an act is inherently problematical. That premise is introduced not to refute, but rather to suggest that the reactivists' real quarrel is with positivism. If this is so, the issue may never be resolved. Nonetheless, sociologists would profit by recognizing that some things are beyond constructive debate.

The epistemology of the reactivists gives rise to a paradox. Kitsuse (1975:276) argues that regardless of their knowledge about the norms of a particular social unit, sociologists are justified in designating a particular act in that unit as deviant *only if* they consider reactions to that act by the unit's members. The paradox lies in this question: If the meaning of an act is so problematical that a sociologist cannot justifiably classify the act as deviant by reference to norms, why is the meaning of a reaction to the act not equally problematical?

The larger question at hand—What reactions identify acts as deviant?—is a major reason why definitions of deviance have come to be markedly divergent.[8] In the case of the illustrative definitions, Cullen and Cullen follow Becker et al. in speaking of reactions and labeling only in general terms; but Schur stipulates particular kinds of reactions. Then observe that Bell, Davis,

---

[7] For references to an extensive number of critiques of the labeling perspective, see Cullen and Cullen (1978). Unfortunately, these authors do not emphasize the point that the reactive conception of deviance is only one of three components of the labeling perspective, and the same is true of all critiques of the labeling perspective.

[8] It is significant that (as suggested in Chapter 1) definitions of a norm have not become divergent. Accordingly, divergence in definitions of deviance reflects the abandonment of the normative conception of deviance and the fact that some sociologists have abandoned that conception more than others.

and Denisoff and McCaghy focus on the identity of the reactors, while Lofland seemingly attempts to identify both relevant kinds of reaction and reactor, and Clinard and Meier do not identify the reactors. Such divergence probably reflects more than purely idiosyncratic choices of terms, and there is no prospect for a reduction of that divergence.[9] Even attempts to emphasize reactions in defining deviance generate paradoxes. Thus, whereas Black (supra) defines deviant behavior by reference to social control, as pointed out in Part II, it is conventional in sociology to define social control by reference to deviant behavior.

Is the notion of norms actually avoided? The most compelling argument for the reactive conception is that it circumvents horrendous problems with the notion of a norm. It does so, however, only if it entails no implicit reference to norms, and that is most doubtful. Carefully examine Scott's definition (supra). A *complete* list of such deviant labels (e.g. "queer") is inconceivable; and not even a complete list would answer this question: How do we know that the labels denote deviance? The labels denote *types* of individuals or behavior that are ostensibly disapproved by numerous members of some English-speaking social units, and that answer reintroduces the normative conception of deviance.

Reactivists would be hard pressed to argue that labels alone are decisive. If a police officer should refer to a woman as "a hooker," a label has been applied, but how would we know that it is a *deviant* label? The problem is compounded because labels alone are not necessarily indicative of disapproval. (In certain U.S. social circles calling someone a "head" is laudatory and not a condemnation of smoking pot.) Hence, attempts to punish someone may be more indicative of deviance than purely verbal labels, but that possibility makes the relevant kind of reaction especially disputable, and it is becoming more so. Cullen and Cullen (1978:12) assert that "labeling and not treatment . . . is the kind of reaction that identifies deviant acts and actors," and they further suggest that the harshness of a reaction is irrelevant. Yet how could saying "bad boy" be relevant but inflicting corporal punishment irrelevant? Far from cleansing "deviant labels" of normative connotations, Cullen and Cullen (1978:30) actually use the term norm: "Deviant labels are definitions that announce (correctly or incorrectly) that a behavior or person has violated the norm of a given group." Even if sociologists are to allow what the

---

[9]That is particularly true in contemplating the relevance of the social identity of reactors to acts. Along with the emergence of the radical, critical, Marxist, or conflict school of criminology [see Inciardi (1979)], there is now much greater emphasis on interpreting reactions to deviance (crime in particular) as manifestations of differential power. That emphasis may reflect recognition that definitions of norms ignore differences in the power of members of a social unit (Chapter 1); but that was not the foremost concern of Becker et al., and they have been castigated for being liberal rather than radical [see commentaries in Goode (1975), Gouldner (1968), and Thio (1978)]. In any case, the identity of relevant reactors entails a major issue.

members of the social unit take as a false announcement, is the norm's existence also irrelevant? Regardless of the answer, it is by no means clear what qualifies as an announcement or who must make it.

Although few sociologists may categorically accept the reactive conception of deviance, they are increasingly inclined to avoid the terms norm and normative in defining deviance. Of the 19 illustrative definitions only five (those formulated by Clinard and Meier, Feldman, Kaplan, Merton, and Schur) include those terms. Not all of the other definitions are purely reactive, but one must surely wonder how the use of such terms as "disapproved" (Akers), "disvalued" (Birenbaum and Sagarin), and "differentially valued phenomena" (Steffensmeier and Terry) really avoids any of the problems with the notion of norms.

Are particular types of acts deviant? The reactive conception even raises doubts about sociologists identifying particular acts as instances of types. The point is illustrated by Douglas (1967:196): ". . . since there exist great disagreements between interested parties in the categorizations of real-world cases, 'suicides' can generally be said to exist and not exist at the same time . . . ." Douglas's argument would surely apply all the more when it comes to members of a social unit designating particular acts as "deviant."[10] For that matter, since the members must use symbols to signify types of acts (e.g. rape, suicide), how can sociologists know that those symbols have the same meaning for the members who use them? The upshot is that the reactive conception casts doubts on the very idea of identifying particular acts as instances of types (e.g. rape, suicide).

Some readers may regard the conceptual issue as pedantic, if not moronic. After all, one can formulate theories about rape, theft, suicide, etc., without using the terms deviance, deviant behavior, or deviant. Yet a synthesis of such special theories (i.e. a general theory of deviance) would require a delimitation of the class of all such behaviors, and employing some term other than deviance to designate that class solves no problems.[11] Nor can reactivists

[10]It is grossly misleading to speak of people as using the label "deviant." The point is not just that lay persons (including police officers) rarely, if ever, use the term; additionally, there is evidence that their conceptions of deviants and deviant behavior are quite divergent (Simmons, 1965). What one makes out of that divergence is another matter, however. Surely no scholar in jurisprudence would be struck dumb on discovering that laymen do not even know the meaning of "barratry"; yet it would not follow that the type of crime denoted by that term is a fiction. As for the dictum that "meaning is problematical," it is all too true, which is to say that the meaning of the dictum itself is disputable. In particular, advocates of the dictum persistently ignore several distinctions as to the meaning of meaning, and the distinction between cognitive meaning and affective meaning is crucial in the study of deviance. Briefly illustrating, if two individuals disagree in characterizing a particular act as deviant (or "criminal" or simply "wrong"), it does not follow that they disagree as to the cognitive typification of that act (e.g. whether it was rape rather than suicide).

[11]The danger is that the audience (whether lay persons or scientists) will become so confused

be reconciled to a theory that treats types of acts as objectively real.[12] For that matter, sociologists do not recognize that the reactive conception stems from a nominalistic epistemology; thus, just as deviance is any act so labeled, a planet is any object so labeled.

But suppose the reactivists grant that types of acts are real. Can some types in a particular social unit be justifiably designated as deviant by reference to reactions? If it is assumed that the relevant kind of reaction is punitive, the immediate question is: What proportion of instances of some type of act must be reacted to punitively before that *type* is deviant? As in contemplating a reactive definition of a norm (Chapter 1), any stipulation of a particular proportion would be arbitrary or unrealistic. So it is not surprising that reactivists refrain from advocating a reactive definition of a norm; yet, without something akin to such a definition, they cannot designate *types of act* as deviant.

The ambiguity in question (types of act vs particular acts) is perpetuated by several of the illustrative definitions that stress reactions. Like Becker et al., several of the authors speak of behavior, conduct, or acts; but it is not clear whether the authors are making reference to particular instances or to types. As for the importance of the distinction: If a woman is forced into a sexual act by a gunman but neither she nor anyone else does anything about it (i.e. no subsequent distinctive reaction, no punishment, no labeling), would the incident have been deviant? One can answer affirmatively and argue that the gunman's behavior was an instance of a type of behavior (forcible rape) that is deviant. But why is the type of behavior deviant? Surely not all instances of that type are reacted to distinctively, labeled, or punished, and none of the illustrative definitions stipulates what the minimum proportion must be. Just as surely, a rare mentality would be required to argue that the reaction to an act necessarily identifies that act as to type (e.g. rape, kissing,

---

(footnote continued)

and irritated by the debate that they will dismiss the notion of deviance as a fiction or as something created by pedantic academicians. In that connection it should be recognized that in all human societies each adult truly believes that some kinds of behavior (including, perhaps, *intolerance*) are wrong, and it is probably the case that any such belief about a particular kind of conduct is always shared to some extent (i.e. it is not purely personal or idiosyncratic).

[12]Needless to say, advocates of the reactive conception of deviance (along with phenomenologists, ethnomethodologists, symbolic interactionists, and nominalists in general) may recoil at the idea of a type of act being real; and to some extent their misgivings are understandable, which is to say that the words "real" and "reality" may well be two pitfalls of the English language. However, there is a criterion of the reality of types of act that deserves mention—a type of act is real to the extent that members of the social unit in question agree in identifying instances of it. No one would argue that absolute, invariant consistency in agreement is the standard of "reality," but the criterion does bear on what is surely a central question: How problematical is meaning? If it is as problematical as advocates of the reactive conception of deviance suggest, one must wonder how social order is possible. In any event, the advocates rarely engage in *systematic* research with a view to substantiating their argument, such as having a representative sample of adult residents examine all cases of death in a community over some period and characterize each case as being either a suicide or not a suicide.

sedition, praising). Thus, even accepting the startling idea that no person has committed murder if they have gone unpunished, that idea becomes truly astonishing if extended to the generalization that all punishments are indicative of murder. To be sure, the meaning of ''murder'' is disputable, but that problem is not resolved by the introduction of an absurdity.

What are the prospects for a reactive theory of deviance? Critics of the reactive conception allege that it puts the cart before the horse, meaning that reactions to acts are distinctive (e.g. punitive) because the acts are deviant and not vice versa. Imagine a police officer saying to a suspect: ''You have committed a crime because I have arrested you.'' Then imagine a judge in a bench trial (no jury) saying to the felony defendant: ''You have committed a crime because I find you guilty.'' The point is that the reactive conception does not explain the relation between acts and reactions. True, such criticisms demand what no definition offers—answers to empirical questions; however, definitions can preclude empirical questions, and that consideration generates more doubts about the reactive conception.

Whereas a normative definition admits the possibility of any kind of reaction (or none at all) to a deviant act, a reactive definition does not. Thus, if all deviant acts are reacted to punitively (i.e. by definition, no deviant act goes unpunished), then it is illogical to ask: Why do some deviant acts go unpunished? So a reactive definition is alien to a theory about variation in the character of reactions to deviance. That is the case because such a theory might purport to explain why the proportion of deviant acts that go unpunished is much greater in some social units than in others. True, a reactive definition would not preclude the question of why some reactions to deviance are *more* punitive than others. But reactivists do not emphasize such questions, nor do they show concern with what was once the major question in the sociology of deviance: Why does the rate of deviance vary? A reactive definition of deviance would not preclude an answer; but reactivists apparently harbor doubts about that question, and their suggestions as to alternatives are fuzzy. But note the consistency: If deviance is ''problematical,'' then both the definition of it and questions about it are best left vague.

In Defense of the Reactive Conception

Previous objections notwithstanding, the reactive conception of deviance has several merits. Despite the voluminous literature on the labeling perspective, those merits have not been clearly articulated. Even those sociologists who partially or totally accept the reactive conception rarely comment on the merits of that conception.

What sociologists actually do. The reactive conception is consistent with the reliance on official records in most studies of crime, juvenile delinquency, suicide, and mental illness. That reliance is hardly surprising. Sociologists study numerous types of deviance (e.g. rape) without observing particular instances (cases) directly, and limited resources alone precludes extensive use of data gathered in surveys of self-reported deviance or victimization surveys.

Even incorrigible normativists use *reactive data*, but they assume that official rates of deviance (e.g. the armed robbery rate as reported by the police) are closely correlated with "true" rates. A defensible assessment of that assumption is precluded because the true rate is unknowable, especially given doubts about self-report and victimization surveys [see Booth et al. (1977)]. Nonetheless, because of the emphasis in the labeling perspective on the problematical meaning of acts, the contingent character of legal reactions to acts, and the self-serving nature of social control agencies, sociologists are now thoroughly skeptical about the reliability of official rates of deviance. However, they are largely oblivious to the point that a reactive definition of deviance can be such that official data are the only relevant data, meaning that the true crime rate *is* what the police report.

Who is a deviant? Extending a normative conception of deviant behavior to a definition of *a deviant* is very difficult; hence, it is not surprising that virtually all of the normative definitions of deviance pertain to deviant acts or deviant behavior, not *deviants*. If a deviant is anyone who has acted contrary to a norm, then "adult nondeviant" is virtually a null class (i.e. there are no instances). The problem is not avoided by speaking only of particular types of deviants. If theft is deviant behavior, when does a person become a thief and cease being one? Consider then the problems in defining a conventionally recognized category of deviants—mentally ill persons. Even if psychiatric terms (e.g. paranoia) and diagnostic criteria were empirically applicable, they are not necessarily congruent with the norms of any particular community or society (i.e. "nonpsychiatric" stereotypes of the mentally ill), and no *specific* act or condition is by definition (psychiatric or otherwise) common to all mentally ill individuals. Imagine, for example, a definition of a mentally ill individual as "anyone who weeps unpredictably." The empirical applicability of the definition is likely to be negligible without an answer to this question: How often must an individual weep unpredictably to be classified as mentally ill? Any answer—once, twice, eight times—would be as ludicrous as the definition itself.

By contrast, the reactive conception of deviance readily extends to a definition of a mentally ill individual: anyone so labeled. There is a pressing need to clarify "so labeled," including the social identity of relevant labelers; and clarification will be difficult, especially with a view to cross-cultural application. Nonetheless, reactivists face less formidable logical problems in defining mentally ill individuals (or any other type of deviant) than do normativists.

Avoiding problems with the notion of norms. To silence their critics, reactivists should speak endlessly about problems with the notion of a norm. Only recently have they moved in that direction [see Kitsuse (1975)], and even now they do not stress the possibilities offered by the reactive conception for avoiding problems.

Rather than grapple with the "consensus problem" in defining a norm, reactivists could make this argument: If potential reactors do not react distinctively, they do not truly disapprove of the act in question. Similarly, far from denying normative contingencies, the argument could be that potential reactors take them into account; and reactions can be interpreted as reflecting differential power.

All advantages of a reactive conception will remain unexploited until reactivists identify the relevant kinds of reaction and address this question: What are the reactive criteria for designating *types* of act and *types* of individual as deviant? Nonetheless, the problems are no more crippling than those which haunt the normative conception of deviance.

Preoccupation with the Issue

The conceptual issue is conspicuous in current sociological literature, where sociologists debate it monotonously and busily concoct new definitions of deviance—even attempting to distinguish it from "rule-breaking" [see Cullen and Cullen (supra)]. To illustrate, some of the illustrative "reactive" definitions incorporate a counterfactual notion similar to this: An act is deviant if it is reacted to punitively or *would have been* reacted to punitively had its commission been known to members of the social unit [see Birenbaum and Sagarin (supra)]. Such notions represent a modification of the reactive conception so as to recognize secret deviance.[13] Other definitions reflect attempts to find middle ground by simply combining the reactive conception and the normative conception. The following statement is illustrative: An act is deviant if contrary to a norm of a social unit *and* reacted to punitively [see Schur (supra)].

None of the foregoing "definitional strategies" will resolve the issue, and

[13]The very idea of secret deviance has more implications than are readily apparent. In particular, why would anyone attempt to conceal an act? Should the reactivists reply that those who conceal an act know of previous instances where that type of act was punished, the reply would suggest that types of act are real after all, at least for those who engage in them. When someone conceals the act of smoking marijuana, it is difficult to convince them that the concealment is unnecessary because a police officer is likely to perceive the act as playing a trombone. To be sure, the criticism calls for what no definition offers—answers to empirical questions, such as why individuals conceal acts—but the criticism takes on special significance because advocates of the reactive conception never tire of explaining that they are concerned first and foremost with the way that people perceive the world. Phenomenologists, ethnomethodologists, and symbolic interactionists in general also make that point, but it is noteworthy that many of them [e.g. Blumer (1969) and Lemert (1972)] do not take the extreme position that is exemplified by the reactive conception of deviance. That could be the principal reason why Becker et al. have not been truly explicit in making their arguments.

more problems are created than avoided. Counterfactual notions invite conjecture, especially when the social identity of potential reactors is ignored, as it is in the case of Birenbaum and Sagarin's definition. Specifically, the definition does not handle this question: Who would have reacted? The question becomes all the more significant on recognition that it reintroduces the consensus problem in dealing with the notion of norms (Chapter 1). As for a "compound" definition (such as Schur's), it will satisfy few sociologists, because it avoids objections to neither the normative nor the reactive conception of deviance.

All controversial conceptual questions in the sociology of deviance now reflect the major issue raised by the reactive conception.[14] In particular, sociologists increasingly define *deviants* to include individuals distinguished by certain physical characteristics (e.g. skin color, body dimensions, deformities) or origin (e.g. ancestral nationality). The rationale is that such individuals are "disvalued" [see Birenbaum and Sagarin (supra)]: hence, contrary to the traditional normative conception, being deviant has nothing to do with behavior. Even reactivists may reject the rationale, for it is removed from *actual* reactions to *particular* individuals. Nonetheless, in suggesting that the quality of acts has nothing to do with deviance, reactivists tacitly lend support to the idea that entire categories of individuals may be deviant regardless of their behavior.

Criminologists are not comfortably removed from the debate, for the reactive conception applies to crime and juvenile delinquency no less than to extralegal deviance. Think about this version of a reactive definition of crime: An act is criminal if and only if so labeled by a legal official.[15] If one doubts that such a definition has a following, examine Turk's statement (1969:25): "criminality is not a . . . behavioral phenomenon. . . . Criminality is determined by what the authorities *do*, rather than what they *claim* (or even believe) they are doing in regard to coercing individuals." And some criminologists are busily trying to find middle ground in the debate.[16] Take

[14]The one possible exception is the conceptual treatment of overconformity—that is, whether or not the term designates a type of deviance. That question is not an issue in debates over the normative and reactive conceptions of deviance, perhaps because it is a troublesome question for both camps. Insofar as overconformity is to be recognized as deviant, advocates of the normative conception must consider this difficult question: How often must an individual conform to a norm or to what extent must an individual exceed conformity before such behavior is deviant? Advocates of the reactive conception could stipulate that the bestowal of a reward on someone is the criterion of overconformity (hence, deviance); but that does not avoid any of the objections to the conception, and the notion of a reward may well be more difficult to clarify than is the notion of a punishment.

[15]Lest one reject this definition as totally absurd, note its consistency with this version of a legal precept: One's innocence of a crime is presumed until found guilty in a court of law. Moreover, the reactive conception of deviance has a counterpart in a particular school of jurisprudence. According to "legal realism," law is found in the behavior of legal officials, the rulings of judges in particular (Gibbs, 1972).

[16]A failure to find common middle ground is conspicuous among "conflict" criminologists [for a review of this school of criminology, see Gibbons and Jones (1975), Inciardi (1979), Reid

Sanders's definition (1976:8): "Juvenile delinquency is the characterization of an act as a violation of delinquency laws." Why not say that juvenile delinquency is an act by a juvenile that is contrary to a delinquency law? Ostensibly because such terminology is purely normative, whereas the use of the word "characterization" attributes a reactive quality to juvenile delinquency. Yet a question is left unanswered: What constitutes such a characterization and who must do it?

The Labeling Perspective

If interest in the labeling perspective is waning, the decline probably reflects only the usual dimunition of novelty. In any case, the issues remain and the perspective's ultimate impact depends on their resolution, but none of the issues will be resolved if a particular misunderstanding is perpetuated.

Three Distinct Arguments

Most debates over the labeling perspective center on whether it is really a theory. That issue (Cullen and Cullen, 1978; Goode, 1975; Spector, 1976) is sterile because it erroneously suggests that the "labeling perspective" is a single argument. To the contrary, sociologists use the term in such a way that it denotes any or all of three distinct and logically independent arguments.

The reactive conception of deviance. Reconsider the notion that an act is deviant if and only if it is so labeled. While there is a connection between that notion and the labeling perspective, it should be recognized that some of the major figures in the labeling perspective [e.g. Lemert (1972)] do not advocate a reactive definition of deviance.

The rejoinder commences with previous quotations of Becker et al., *also* major figures in the labeling perspective. If those quotations do not suggest a reactive conception of deviance, then we might as well abandon the English language. True, the quotations may not constitute explicit reactive definitions, perhaps because Becker et al. were unprepared to be explicit. In any event, Kitsuse's position is now more explicit (1975:276): "The new conception of deviance requires that members of the society perceive, define, and treat acts and persons as deviant *before* the sociologist can claim them as subject matter for study." Had Kitsuse made that statement earlier along with Becker and Erikson, a major misunderstanding of the labeling perspective might have

---

(*footnote continued*)

(1979), and Sykes (1974)]. Whereas Turk (1969) accepts the reactive conception of deviance, Taylor et al. (1973) reject it. The conceptual issue poses a dilemma for this newest school of criminology. It would be paradoxical for those members who profess a Marxist orientation to argue that capitalism is conducive to criminal behavior [see Goode's commentary (1975:470)] but at the same time deny that criminality has something to do with behavior.

been avoided. The statement is not quoted to refute it, because not even a suggested definition is true or false. Nor is it argued that the labeling perspective reduces to the reactive conception of deviance; rather, the conception is a *component* of that perspective.

The theory of secondary deviance. Here is a summary statement of the theory of secondary deviance: If a deviant act is reacted to punitively, the actor will engage in further deviant acts as a consequence. That statement is grossly oversimplified; nonetheless, it is an empirical proposition and not a definition. So the theory of secondary deviance and the reactive conception of deviance are logically distinct; and even though some advocates of the conception (Kitsuse in particular) and some advocates of the theory (Lemert in particular) are major figures in the labeling perspective, they are not making the same argument. So why do sociologists speak of the labeling perspective as though it is unitary? One possibility is that the major figures champion the deviant as underdog and/or share a "romantic" view of deviance [see commentaries by Gouldner (1968) and Thio (1978)]. The antipositivistic stance of the major figures is no less relevant. However, whereas the antipositivism of reactivists is reflected in their seeming indifference to specifying the relevant kinds of reaction, that of Lemert and his followers lies in their avoidance of explicit, falsifiable propositions—propositions worded so that it is logically possible to demonstrate that they are false.

The theory of secondary deviance is far from being unintelligible. To the contrary, the general assertion appears fairly clear: Primary deviance is converted into secondary deviance by reactions to it. Nor is the theory implausible. Thus, it does not tax credulity to suppose that the harsh social degradation of women for an alleged moral lapse (e.g. premarital sexual relations) would add to the ranks of prostitutes, make that status irrevocable, and contribute to the infanticide rate (Lemert, 1972:65). Similarly, if convicted felons are deprived of employment opportunities, it is not difficult to imagine that such deprivation generates recidivism. Even primary deviance is a fairly clear notion, for in numerous ways Lemert (1972) describes it as behavior contrary to a norm and *prior to reactions*.

Nonetheless, the theory is a study in problems, most of which stem from two questions left unanswered by Lemert. First, does the theory apply to all types of primary deviance *and* all kinds of reaction? Second, given a relevant type of primary deviance and a relevant kind of reaction, do *all* instances of the primary deviance become secondary deviance? The theory's plausibility would be diminished by an affirmative answer to either question; yet a simple "some" answer would make it unfalsifiable. The general point is that the theory does not comprise explicit and testable propositions. Furthermore, not even explicit propositions would make the theory testable without clarification of secondary deviance. Numerous sociologists seemingly equate the notion with *more* deviance. Yet that interpretation cannot be construed as "more of what was originally primary''; and it is an oversimplification, though one encouraged by Lemert's assertion (1972:ix) that social control leads to deviance.

The notion of secondary deviance is scarcely clarified by Lemert's explicit definitions (1972:48, 63). ''Secondary deviation is deviant behavior, or social roles based upon it, which becomes means of defense, attack, or adaptation to the overt and covert problems created by the societal reaction to primary deviation. . . . Secondary deviation refers to a special class of socially defined responses which people make to problems created by the societal reaction to their deviance.'' One interpretation is that secondary deviance does not necessarily take the form of more deviance, and there are even doubts as to whether more deviance is necessarily secondary deviance. Hence, there can be no consensus as to the kinds of evidence that would corroborate or falsify the theory.

Societal reaction to deviance. Consider this proposition: In any jurisdictional unit (e.g. city, state) for any given year, the proportion of lower-class individuals arrested is greater than the proportion of other individuals arrested. The proposition does not imply that arrest is a criterion of criminality; so it is distinct from the reactive conception of deviance. Nor does the proposition assert anything about the criminality (however defined) of anyone *subsequent* to their arrest; so it does not bear on the theory of secondary deviance.

While the proposition does not bear on either the reactive conception of deviance or the theory of secondary deviance, it does bear on ''societal reaction theory.'' That theory can be explicated briefly only by pointing to its central assertion—the character of the reaction to a real *or* alleged deviant act by an individual is primarily contingent on (1) the social identity of the individual; (2) the social identity of the reactors; (3) the operating rules of the reactors' organization; and/or (4) circumstances before, during, or after the act. The assertion is not a definition of deviance, let alone a reactive definition; and tests of it would neither support nor refute the theory of secondary deviance. Some sociologists might insist that the assertion is peculiar to ''societal reaction theory'' or ''the societal reaction perspective''; but most sociologists do not distinguish either term from labeling perspective. Gove has commented (1975:3): ''In 1938, Tannenbaum published a statement that was to become a landmark of what is now known as either the societal reaction or the labelling perspective.'' That identification is entirely consistent with conventional terminology.

Advocates of societal reaction theory evidently do not agree among themselves as to the crucial contingency (e.g. social class, race, sex) in reactions to deviance [see Rushing and Esco (1977)]. However, such disagreements are not fatal for the theory. It would be premature to demand agreement at this point, and the most relevant contingency may not be the same for all alleged acts or conditions (e.g. robbery, homosexuality) or for all reactors (e.g. police, psychiatrists). Nonetheless, even if all advocates of the theory should identify one crucial contingency (e.g. the "power" or "status resources" of objects of reactions), a major issue would survive that agreement. That issue stems from other components of the labeling perspective.

Assume overwhelming evidence in support of the illustrative proposition, meaning that in all jurisdictional units the arrest rate is much greater for the lower class. That evidence would only give rise to the reason for such a difference. If the alleged reason is class differentials in the "true incidence" of criminality, it is a tacit acceptance of the normative conception of criminality, according to which an act is a crime if it is a violation of a criminal law. So one interpretation of the evidence would be that the true incidence of crime is greater in the lower class. Yet that interpretation would be rejected by sociologists who advocate societal reaction theory or the reactive conception of deviance (recall that the two are logically independent). Advocates of societal reaction theory would argue that lower-class individuals who commit crimes are more likely to be arrested, while advocates of the reactive conception of deviance will not entertain the idea of the true incidence of crime (i.e. the arrest rate is *the* crime rate). So, while the illustrative proposition about arrest may appear removed from the debate over contending conceptions of deviance (in this case of crime), when it comes to interpreting evidence that supports the proposition, the issue is bound to surface. That is the case for all similar propositions about deviance—crime or otherwise. Consider the long line of research on differential rates of mental hospitalization by occupation (Rushing and Ortega, 1979) and then contemplate another illustrative proposition: In any community for any given year, the rate of involuntary admissions to mental hospitals is greater for the lower class. Given positive tests of that proposition, some sociologists would view the findings as support of the argument that deviance is more a function of social identity than behavior. However, a normativist or a psychiatrist who subscribes to the "disease model" of mental illness (Gove, 1975; and Krohn and Akers, 1977) could advance the hardly incredible argument that mental disorders tend to be more severe in the lower class and that severe mental disorders are the most likely to result in an involuntary institutionalization. While the argument is disputable, the point is that interpretations of tests of "societal reaction" propositions are inherently controversial.

Clarification of Issues

In debating the labeling perspective, sociologists commonly "talk past" one another because they interpret the term in different ways (perhaps unwittingly). Thus, in his rejoinder to critiques of the labeling perspective, Kitsuse

(1975) defended the reactive conception of deviance; but the critiques themselves (Gove, 1975) focused on either the theory of secondary deviance or societal reaction theory, without due recognition of the distinction.

Since there is no defensible basis for limiting the labeling perspective to any one of its three components—reactive conception of deviance, the theory of secondary deviance, or the societal reaction theory—the only alternative to more sterile debates is to abandon the term "labeling perspective." Abandoning the term will not resolve any of the issues, but it would clarify the issues by separating them.

Toward a Resolution

While the concern with the labeling perspective has furthered interest in the sociology of deviance, the drift toward conceptual anarchy cannot be indefinitely constructive. Sociologists will appreciate that argument only when they recognize that their research is being assessed largely in the context of a conceptual issue. The point is that sociologists who conduct research on deviance are involved in the great debate whether they know it or like it.

The issue has increased doubts about the reliability of official data to the point that even numerous normativists advise against their use. As for reactivists, they hardly can endorse surveys of self-reported deviance or victimization surveys, and they tolerate official data only if the reactive quality is made paramount. For example, Douglas (1967:223–227) has dismissed positive tests of a theory of suicide by arguing that (1) the independent variable, status integration, is correlated inversely with urbanization (not a variable in the theory); and (2) urbanization is correlated directly with the official suicide rate because in a highly urbanized population there is less reluctance to label deaths as suicide.[17] Nothing would be gained by pointing out that the 1960 *official* U.S. suicide rate differed little from the 1910 official rate, despite an enormous increase in urbanization over the 50 years. Nothing would be gained because Douglas interprets the official suicide rate as a function of the predisposition of officials to label deaths as suicide; hence, he rejects the assumption that the official suicide rate is largely a function of the true suicide rate, which in turn is a function of some "etiological" variable (e.g. unemployment, status integration). Similarly, critics are predisposed to reject works that rest on the reactive conception of deviance, as when Turk is severely criticized (Gibbs and Erikson, 1975:39)

---

[17]In other words, Douglas argues that the *only* connection between status integration and the official suicide rate is that in populations with a low degree of status integration officials are less reluctant to label deaths as suicide than are officials in populations with a high degree of status integration. Hence, so the argument implies, there is no association between level of status integration and the "true" suicide rate. Yet the true rate is unknowable, and some of Douglas's statements (1967:196) cast doubt on even the idea of the true incidence of suicide.

for ignoring the actual behavior of men and women in a purported explanation of differential arrest rates (for robbery in particular). All such partisan assessments are harbingers of the ultimate danger—that the sociology of deviance will degenerate into a debating club, where research findings only fuel disputes.

Proposal of a Strategy

The initial step in circumventing the issue is to take explanation of variation in the *official* rate of each type of deviance (e.g. armed robbery) as the goal of theory. Thus, such a theory would purport to explain why the armed robbery rate as reported by the police is greater for California than for Mississippi. The second step is to assume that the official rate is a function of two variables: (1) the true rate of the type of behavior in question and (2) the disposition of officials to report instances of such behavior. Hence, theories should treat both the true rate and the dispositions as intervening but purely theoretical variables and identify two corresponding sets of independent and mensurable variables: (1) those postulated as antecedent correlates of the true rate (e.g. possibly unemployment) and (2) those postulated as antecedent correlates of dispositions (e.g. possibly the number of police officers per capita). In more conventional terms, the theory would be predicated on the assumption that there are things that cause behavior and things that cause officials to report that certain behaviors have taken place.

The *form* of such a theory is suggested by the following graphic representation, where T is the true rate of some type of behavior (e.g. suicide) for each of several social units (e.g. cities): D is the disposition of officials to report that instances of such behavior have occurred; E is the set of "etiological" variables that are postulated antecedent correlates of T; S is the set of sociocultural variables that are postulated antecedent correlates of D; R is the *official* rate of the type of behavior in question; ⟶ signifies a postulated direct relation, one not subject to observation or measurement; - - - -→ signifies a testable assertion of a time-lag statistical association between change in variables; and ▷ or ⊏ signifies a multiplicative *or* additive combination of variables.

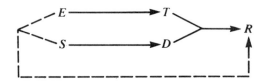

Each theory in the prescribed form would pertain to a particular type of behavior (e.g. robbery), and the designation of that type must correspond to a label employed by officials in reporting incidence.[18] Such a restriction is hardly a cause for objections, since the pursuit of a *general* theory of deviance has been singularly unproductive. However, if critics reject purely theoretical variables (T and D), the proposed strategy has no utility.

Neither normativists nor reactivists will adopt the proposed strategy without reservations. Normativists may balk at taking variation in the official rates as the explanandum, for it suggests acceptance of the reactive conception of deviance. Be that as it may, practical problems (e.g. limited resources) alone preclude extensive use of *unofficial* rates; and since official rates are "societal products," they are hardly less real than unofficial rates.

The reservations of reactivists will be more complex. Should they argue that the strategy equates the true rate of behavior with the true rate of deviance and reject the latter notion, it would be a misinterpretation. One can speak of the true rate of, say, smoking marijuana without implying that any instance of that *type of behavior* is deviant; and the term "disposition" refers to pressures on or opportunities for officials to *report* instances of behavior rather than to the "probability that an instance of a type of behavior will be reported as such by officials." Otherwise, the strategy would suggest that officials report only actual instances of behavior; instead, it admits the possibility that officials report instances of behavior that even by their own perceptions are fictions.[19] True, if reactivists are nominalists, they will object to the idea of particular acts being instances of types; but even that objection is relevant only when sociologists typify particular acts, and the strategy actually treats the true rate of some type of behavior as purely theoretical. Finally, if official data are used in the numerical expression of E and S (e.g. possibly the unemployment rate, number of police per capita), reactivists cannot object that the data reflect a social reality "constructed" only by sociologists.

The most crippling objection to the proposed strategy would be directed toward its purpose, the explanation of variance in official rates of deviance. Given their antipositivistic stance, reactivists may reject "variance explained" as a criterion for assessing theories; if so, the issue dividing normativists and reactivists may never be resolved.

---

[18]The problem is that the official label must be a "deviant label"; otherwise, the theory scarcely pertains to deviance. Since an illustrative list of deviant labels will not suffice, the alternative is to define deviant labels as designations of types of behavior which are disapproved by officials who authorize reports of instances of such behavior. That definition is limited to the use of official data, and it is a partial retreat to the normative conception of deviance; but the consensus problem is minimized because no one is likely to deny, for example, that police chiefs both authorize reports of alleged robberies and voice disapproval of robbery.

[19]Lest the idea be rejected as preposterous, advocates of societal reaction theory can point to all sorts of reasons why officials report instances of behavior that never took place (e.g. the police may charge an "agitator" with reckless driving in order to prompt the agitator to leave town). Normativists would do well not to deny the reality of such incidents but, rather, to question the frequency of such incidents. The answer is crucial when assessing the reliability of official rates of deviance. Paradoxically, there is no place in the reactive conception of deviance for "deliberate mislabeling"—as if to say that in the case of crime there is no such thing as a "bum rap."

The prescribed strategy would not end the controversy completely, nor should it be ended, because controversies can be constructive. Even if the E and S variables jointly explain all variance in R, ascertaining the relative importance of E and S could be a constructive quest. However, a comparison of the two statistical associations, E-→R and S-→R, would not be decisive because the identification of a variable as E or S is inherently disputable. To illustrate, suppose that R is the official suicide rate and the unemployment rate has been designated as an E variable.[20] Even if some conventional measure of statistical association, M, between the unemployment rate and the official suicide rate is truly substantial, it would not demonstrate that the unemployment rate is associated with the official suicide rate (R) primarily through the true rate (T). Reactivists could argue that officials are more predisposed to label a death as suicide if the deceased was unemployed (Douglas, 1967:222). Given such arguments, the justification for identifying a variable as E or S requires evidence beyond M_{er} and M_{sr} (i.e. the $E-R$ and $S-R$ statistical associations). That evidence must come in the form of unofficial rates (U) of the type of behavior in question, with the data gathered in surveys where members of the social unit (excluding officials) are asked questions about their own behavior or that of others.[21] If parties to the debate are willing to assume that the U values are closely correlated with the T values, then evidence can be brought to bear upon the presumptive identification of variables as E and S, which is necessary to assess the relative importance of "etiological" and "reactive" phenomena.

Given a U value and an R value for a social unit, a "disposition" index (d) is the ratio of R to U (i.e. $d = R/U$). That index would be postulated as an epistemic correlate of D, meaning that it presumably reflects the inclination of officials to report more (or less) instances of the type of behavior in question than indicated by unofficial data. Accordingly, given the assumption that E is associated with R primarily through T, identifying a variable as E is justified only to the extent that $M_{eu}>M_{ed}$ and $M_{eu}>M_{er}$. Similarly, since any alleged S variable is assumed to be associated with R primarily through D, then its identification is justified only to the extent that $M_{sd}>M_{su}$ and $M_{sd}>M_{sr}$.

If tests of a particular theory indicate that neither identification (E variable

[20]This simple illustration notwithstanding, a theorist may identify several E and S variables, but the variables (or measures) in each set must be somehow combined. Moreover, the prescribed form does not preclude premises in the theory and deductions of the relations in the diagram. Those premises may encompass whatever notions a theorist cares to introduce, but the notions are likely to be more abstract than the present illustrations of E and S variables (the unemployment rate, police officers per capita).

[21]For example: During the past year have you taken some item from a store without the consent or knowledge of the owner, manager, or any employee of the store? If so, how many times did you do it during the past year? The alternative form of the question would be: During the past year, have you committed shoplifting? If so, how many times did you shoplift during the past year? Given evidence that the answers do not depend appreciably on the form of the question, several problems in interpretation would be avoided.

and S variable) is justified, then the relative importance of the variables becomes a moot point, especially if M_{er}, M_{eu}, and M_{sd} are negligible. However, if test findings justify both identifications, then the relative importance of E and S hinges on the magnitudes of M_{er} and M_{sr}. A no less relevant comparison would be between M_{ur} and M_{dr}. To the extent that $M_{dr} > M_{ur}$, then the official rates are "reactive phenomena"; and to the extent that $M_{ur} > M_{dr}$ the rates are "behavioral phenomena."[22] While esprit de corps may prompt normativists and reactivists to take such comparisons seriously, the more important consideration is the extent to which the multiple association, $M_{r.es}$, exceeds each bivariate association, M_{er} and M_{sr}. If $M_{r.es}$ is substantially greater, then the long-standing controversy will have borne fruit after all; and the protagonist can jointly pursue more constructive work, identifying additional E and S variables with a view to explaining more variance in R.

---

[22]The relative importance of the E and S variables cannot be revealed by one comparison (i.e. one test of a theory), and it could well be that their relative importance depends on the type of behavior.

CONCEPTUALIZATION OF SOCIAL CONTROL

The immediate reason for a lack of progress in the study of social control is a long history of defective conceptualizations. That argument is distinct from but related to the criticism that the preoccupation in conceptualizations of social control with social order ignores conflict and reflects a conservative ideology. The more immediate point is that the preoccupation leads to a conception of social control that is little more precise than this: Social control is anything that contributes to social order. Such a conception of social control is intolerably vague and denotes an all too broad class of phenomena for purposes of research and theory. No less important, the conception makes this question illogical: Does social control contribute to social order? Of course, the notion of social order is so vague that, whatever the definition of social control, inquiry about it may well be unproductive. In any case, if by definition social control contributes to social order, then questions about the *empirical* relation between the two are precluded.

Social scientists have been unsuccessful in their endeavors to supplant vague conceptions of social control with a precise definition that does not reflect a preoccupation with social order, and the review of definitions that follow in Chapter 3 identifies various pitfalls. Some definitions of social control are so broad that they seemingly equate social control with the influence that any individual has on the behavior of others. Such definitions do not even restrict social control to the *intentional* manipulation of behavior, and for that reason it would encompass virtually the entire subject matter of the social sciences. A more specific objection is that such a definition does not suggest what is "social" about social control. To be sure, the idea of influence entails at least two individuals, which excludes internalistic control (i.e. self-control); but that entailment scarcely distinguishes social control from externalistic control in general (i.e. the control of humans by other humans one way or another). Yet most illustrations of social control in the literature clearly suggest that social control is somehow normative and distinct from everyday interaction. Thus, in robbing a liquor store the typical gunman is clearly engaged in externalistic control, but it is difficult to see how coercion in and of itself is normative. Then consider a customer who asks a store clerk for change. The act is clearly externalistic control, and it could be construed as normative in one sense or another; but surely it would not be regarded as anything other than everyday or "normal" interaction.

There are various ways to avoid a broad definition of social control (one that equates it with influence or externalistic control in general) but there are several pitfalls. If a definition limits social control to the activities of legal officials, then the phenomenon is both distinct from everyday interaction and normative in one sense or another. However, anyone who has given serious thought to the subject will quickly dismiss such a definition as unrealistically narrow. A less conspicuous problem is that such a definition makes those with political power the arbiters of social control, and that alone gives rise to the allegation that a concern with social control reflects a conservative ideology. Appearances to the contrary, that allegation extends to the most common contemporary conception of social control, the *prophylactic conception,* which equates it with the "counteraction of deviance." That conception is by no means narrow, but it entails all of the seemingly insoluble problems in defining deviance. Those problems have been described in Chapter 2, and it will suffice to say again that most of the problems stem from enormous difficulties with the notion of a norm and the idea that deviance is behavior contrary to a norm. The major difficulty is the specification of "sufficient consensus," and to ignore that difficulty is to assume absolute normative consensus, or to use another expression, monolithic norms. That assumption ignores normative conflict, especially along class, ethnic, or racial lines. The immediate implication is that a dominant class or caste may determine what is deviant and, hence, what is social control. Thus, if the normative opinions of dissidents are ignored, then terrorists in that social unit are deviants rather than agents of social control.

To equate social control with the counteraction of deviance is to answer three of the conceptual questions that are pursued in Chapter 3. What is subject to social control? Deviant behavior. What is the end or consequence of social control? Reduction of deviance. Who is subject to social control? Deviants. The pursuit of such questions serves to identify problems in formulating a definition of social control, but none of the various answers yield a defensible definition. Therefore, an unconventional definition of social control is proposed in Chapter 4 and defended in Chapter 5.

Since the proposed definition is lengthy and a brief version would be a gross distortion, it is not stated at this point. However, even now note that the definition truly departs from the "institutional" conception of social control, which equates social control with religion, socialization, and law. Any list of institutions is bound to be complete. No less important, to say that religion, socialization, law, etc., are social control does not answer this question: Why are they social control? The point is not just that terms denoting institutions (e.g. religion) are difficult to define; additionally, by any reasonable definition they denote classes of events so broad that it taxes credulity to suggest that all of the events are social control. To illustrate, making the sign of a cross is a facet of Catholic religion, but it hardly follows that all instances of that act are social control. Indeed, one must wonder why certain religious practices do not *require* social control rather than constitute social control. Yet the definition of social control set forth in Chapter 4 does not preclude recognition that certain features of religion, socialization, law, etc., may have something to do with social control. For that matter, the definition serves to describe the sense in which some institutions or organizations have more import for social control than others.

Whatever the descriptive utility of the new definition of social control, the ultimate goal is the use of that definition in a theory. That use is all the more desirable because no definition is right or wrong, true or false. Rather, definitions are useful to varying degrees; and the ultimate use lies in the statement of theories, in this case theories about social control. Accordingly, if only to suggest how the definition can be used, a theory of social control will be set forth in Chapter 6.

Definitions of Social Control and Major Conceptual Questions

3

As suggested in the introduction to Part I, concern with social order is perhaps the central theme in the heritage of the social sciences, sociology in particular. One may lament this theme and argue that it ignores change and conflict; nonetheless, it gave rise to the use of the concept social control to designate features of social life that supposedly contribute to social order, meaning features that ostensibly create and maintain uniformities in human behavior, especially conformity to supposed norms. The concept was first used extensively in a sociological treatise by E.A. Ross (1901), who employed it loosely to denote (inter alia) public opinion, law, belief systems, education, persuasion, and religion. The only common denominator among those phenomena is that they purportedly contribute to social order, and that very loose meaning of social control is still with us.

Illustrative Definitions of Social Control

As suggested by Hollingshead about 40 years ago (1941), the contrast among definitions of social control is largely one of how broadly the phenomenon is construed. However, Hollingshead did not systematically describe the sense in which a definition of social control (or control in general) can be broad or narrow, and even casual inspection of the following quotations will indicate that the distinction is not obvious.[1] Casual reading is all the more advisable since the quotations are given only to set the scene for a consideration of problems in defining social control.

Adams (1975: 21): "The teacher stands in a position that allows him specific controls over certain papers and marks on papers. These marks on papers are physical facts of the environment that are of particular interest to the student because he believes that his grades are of importance for his successful future, for his prestige among his fellows, for avoiding tongue-lashings at home, for staying in school, etc. The marks on the paper are part of the student's future environment, and the teacher controls them. By virtue of this, the teacher has power over the student. . . . control over the environment is a physical matter. An actor either has it or does not. . . . But, once he [the teacher] has it, there immediately comes into being a particular quality in the relationship between the teacher and the student. The teacher now has power over the student."

Bernard (1939: 11−12): "Control itself is a process by which stimuli are brought to bear effectively upon some person or group of persons, thus producing responses that function in adjustment. These responses may be desired or anticipated on the part of the person or persons exercising control or by persons responding to the controls. or they may be unanticipated. The essential fact which renders them controlled responses is that they function in some sort of adjustment situation, which may or may not be the conscious objective of the controllers or of the controlled."

Berndt (1962: 11): "Social control . . . covers all the processes and procedures which regulate behavior, in that they exert pressure on persons and groups to conform to the norms."

Cohen (1966: 39): "Whether people in society think of them in this way or not, we have been using the expression 'social control' to refer to social processes and structures tending to prevent or reduce deviance. The expression is also used to refer to anything that people do that is *socially defined* as 'doing something about deviance,' whatever that 'something' is: prevention, deterrence, reform, vengeance, justice, reparation, com-

---

[1]Although the quotations are thought to be representative definitions of social control, at least one of them (Adams's statement) may not have been intended as a definition of control or of social control. In any case, the distinction between a conception and a definition made in Chapter 1 applies in this chapter. Accordingly, while critical comments are made about the ambiguity or incompleteness of the illustrative definitions of social control, it is recognized that no definition is likely to be free of ambiguity or truly complete.

pensation, the moral enhancement of the victim (e.g. by 'turning the other cheek')."

Dowd (1936: 6, 11): "I use the term *control* . . . as *contra*, against, or contrary to, any momentum, as 'guidance,' 'direction,' 'as to control an engine by a lever.' . . . When I use the term *paternal* or *social control* . . . I mean control only in its telic sense, and I consider the folkways as exercising control only as an instrument. . . . The sole source, or controlling agency, in any society consists of one or more individuals who, on account of some kind of prestige, are able to bring people together for some common purpose, and to induce or compel them to conform to the group interest."

Hollingshead (1941: 220): ". . . the essence of social control lies not so much in the mechanisms society has developed to manipulate behavior in a crisis or in the subtle influences so important in the formation of personality, as it does in a society's organization. . . . social control inheres in the more or less common obligatory usages and values which define the relations of one person to another, to things, to ideas, to groups, to classes, and to the society in general. In short, the essence of social control is to be sought in the organization of a people."

Landis (1956: 7): "Social control . . . is . . . concerned primarily with an understanding of (1) how society makes its members susceptive to its regulative system, and (2) how it makes them conform to it. The basic problem is not one only of how social order is maintained, but of how society itself is maintained and perpetuated. The emphasis is on the way in which the individual is made to fit into the social scheme, rather than on the way the group, through the development of public opinion, establishes the abstract system of control . . . these two approaches are in many respects similar. It is a matter of placing the emphasis. The emphasis is here placed upon how social influences operate on the individual to control him rather than upon an analysis of society's regulative scheme as such."

Lumley (1925: 13): "Social control has usually meant that kind of life pattern which a government, through its officers, imposes upon the citizen. But . . . social control means vastly more than that. We might speak of it as the practice of putting forth directive stimuli or wish-patterns, their accurate transmission to, and adoption by, others, whether voluntarily or involuntarily. In short, it is effective will-transference."

Parsons (1951: 297, 321): "The theory of social control is the obverse of the theory of the genesis of deviant behavior tendencies. It is the analysis of those processes in the social system which tend to counteract the deviant tendencies, and of the conditions under which such processes will operate. . . . Every social system has, in addition to the obvious rewards for conformative and punishments for deviant behavior, a complex system of *unplanned and largely unconscious mechanisms* which serve to counteract deviant tendencies.'' (Italics added.)

Sites (1973: 1): ''. . . the concept of power, the basis of control, is central to all existing social theory. . . . it is around the concept of control (power is action) that this synthesis is attempted.''

Wilson, A. (1977:6): "Social control is used here as the generic term for response to nonconformity and, as such, comprises both perception of and reaction to rule breaking.''

Wood (1974: 53): "It is appropriate to define *social control* for purposes of our discussion as the use of power with the intention of influencing the behavior of others.''

Major Conceptual Questions

Whether a definition of social control is broad or narrow depends on its implied answer to six questions. First, is the exercise of social control necessarily intentional? Second, what is subject to social control? Third, who is subject to social control? Fourth, who exercises social control? Fifth, by what means is social control exercised? And, sixth, what are the goals or consequences of social control?

Preliminary Considerations

Bernard's definition (supra) of control reduces to this: the influence that the behavior of one individual has on the behavior of some other individual. Described in terms of the foregoing six questions, the definition is extremely broad, implying that virtually any kind of behavior is subject to control, whether intended or not; anyone can exercise control to any end by any means; and anyone could be subject to control. As such, it may be significant that Bernard's definition actually pertains to *control;* hence, it does not distinguish social control from other kinds of control over human behavior, and it may be very broad for that reason alone. The point is that a definition of social control should distinguish it from control in general.

Now consider an extremely narrow definition, one so much so that it resembles none of the illustrative definitions: Social control is the legal incarceration of political criminals to prevent terrorism. The definition is very narrow, as it suggests that social control is necessarily intentional, and that (1) only political crimes are subject to social control; (2) only legal officials exercise social control; (3) only political criminals are subject to social control; (4) incarceration is the only means of social control; and (5) the only goal of social control is the prevention of terrorism.

The meaning of "control" inevitably becomes somewhat vague when the notion is extended beyond the physical manipulation of objects; but such extension is necessary in the social and behavioral sciences, for no one would limit social control to pushing, pulling, restraining, or immobilizing human bodies. Yet, granted the necessity of extending the meaning of control beyond the purely physical, it is pointless to conceptualize social control through the use of terms that are no less difficult to define—power in particular. Few terms in the social sciences are vaguer than power, and its definition has been debated for generations (Clegg, 1975; Nagel, 1975; Parenti, 1978). To illustrate the semantical swamp, whereas Sites and Wood describe control in terms of power, Adams describes power in terms of control. Sites further complicates matters by his cryptic reference to control as "power in action." The expression only gives rise to a question: How can power be defined independently of action? Similarly, in the case of Wood's definition, how could power be used without "influencing the behavior of others"?

First Question: Is Social Control Necessarily Intentional?

The notion of intention is implicit even in the control of inanimate objects (e.g. diverting a stream for irrigation). Nonetheless, while some writers appear to argue that social control is necessarily intentional (see the definitions by Wood and Dowd, supra), others (e.g. Bernard and Parsons) explicitly deny the relevance of intention, and the remainder either do not address the question or allude to it ambiguously. Nothing can be said for speaking ambiguously to the question. The issue will remain if ignored, and the failure to answer the question hardly clarifies a definition. Nor is a definition clarified by the common practice of using the term "influence" in defining social control. Since the meaning of that term does not exclude unintended consequences of human behavior, using the term in a definition of social control may be only an implicit denial of the relevance of intention. The objection to that denial is not just that "unintentional control" appears contradictory; additionally, if social control is defined as "the influence of any individual's behavior on the behavior of others," then the study of social control would have to be based on the dubious presumption that all consequences of any particular act can be identified. It may be that virtually all of human behavior has some influence (direct or indirect) on the behavior of others. If so, social control is not a distinct type of behavior. Indeed, it would be difficult to identify any kind of behavior that is clearly not social control, which is to say that for all practical purposes social control cannot be distinguished from the subject matter of all of the social sciences.

In light of the foregoing, the most strategic initial way to limit the meaning of social control is to define it tentatively as *an attempt on the part of one or more individuals to manipulate someone else's behavior.*[2] The immediate consideration in contemplating this tentative definition is a question: What if the attempted manipulation is unsuccessful? The appropriate answer might seem to be that social control has not taken place, but it is difficult to imagine a rationale for denying that the study of social control should encompass both successful and unsuccessful *attempts*. Indeed, the distinction could be crucial in regard to this question: In any given instance, why is social control attempted one way rather than another? One answer is that some commonly recognized specific means of social control (e.g. inflicting physical pain) are perceived as more successful than others, at least in particular contexts. So there is a real justification for defining social control in terms of attempts, as only that strategy permits the distinction between successful and unsuccessful social control.

The notion of attempt takes on special significance in light of the many definitions that equate social control with "the counteraction of deviance," notably those formulated by Berndt, Cohen, and Parsons. Those definitions either exclude reference to intention or deny its relevance; as such, social control becomes any kind of activity that counteracts deviance, whether intended or not. The objection is not just that such a definition is difficult to apply, meaning that one must demonstrate that a particular act or kind of activity does counteract deviance before identifying it as social control. Nor is the objection only that the definition makes social control a potentially very broad and heterogeneous class of phenomena (e.g. if it is shown that the custom of wearing wedding rings promotes marital fidelity and infidelity is deviant, then the custom is social control). It is no less important that if such a definition is accepted, it is illogical to ask if social control counteracts deviance.

Whatever form an attempt at social control may take, the attempt must be manifested in *overt behavior*. It may appear obvious that an attempt at social control requires overt behavior; but that point is obscured in most definitions, and only Adams's conceptualization truly emphasizes "control behavior." His idea seems to be that the behavior of one individual, X, can have no influence on the behavior of another individual, Y, unless X's behavior somehow alters Y's environment. It is difficult to think of any way that X could control Y's behavior, especially since the notion of altering another's environment is not limited to purely physical means (e.g. incarceration, pushing, hitting, etc.). One's symbolic environment can be altered by any kind of communication or message (e.g. a plea, a command, a gesture); hence, Adams's conceptualization makes "control" a very broad class of phenomenon.

[2]This tentative definition is expanded in Chapter 4.

Granted the many merits of Adams's conceptualization, it does have some shortcomings beyond delimiting a very broad class of phenomenon. For one thing, the definition is ambiguous as regards intention, and it should be obvious that we often alter the environment of others without intending to do so.[3] Even when one individual intentionally alters the environment of another individual with a view to manipulating the behavior of the other individual, it is only an attempt at control and one that may fail. To illustrate, if X alters Y's environment with a view to seducing Y, but Y slaps X, in what sense has X controlled Y's behavior? Indeed, altering someone's environment does not necessarily alter their behavior, let alone in the way intended. One reason is that in such a situation there are two environments, that perceived by the would-be "controlee," Y, and that perceived by the would-be "controller," X. Even though X may perceive his/her act of winking as altering Y's environment, Y may not perceive it (i.e. X's wink is not noticed by Y). For that matter, even if Y does perceive the alteration of his/her environment in the same way that X perceives it, Y will not necessarily alter his/her behavior, let alone in the way anticipated by X. The general point is that Adams's exclusion of any reference to perception or intention from his definition creates as many problems as it may resolve.

The major issue. The foregoing tentative definition attributes an intentional quality to social control by reference to an *attempt* at the manipulation of behavior. That attribution creates a problem in the application of the definition, for no one will ever see, touch, hear, or smell an "intention." The "thing" denoted by that term is inherently unobservable, and hence intention must be inferred from overt behavior. However, although there is no method or procedure that insures valid inferences, it does not follow that any definition which incorporates the notion of intentionality is false or cannot be applied. No definition in itself is true or false. Moreover, granted that some definitions may be more useful than others (especially when formulating theories), there is a more *immediate* question as to the merits of a definition: To what extent is the definition empirically applicable?[4] Stated another way: To what extent can independent observers agree in applying the definition to identify particular events or things? In that connection, it is ludicrous to argue

[3]Recall (footnote 1) that Adams's statement should not be taken as an explicit definition of control, but it surely suggests a conception of control. That conception is very broad because it ignores intention, and Adams does not indicate how social control is distinguished from externalistic control in general. None of Adams's other statements (1975) suggests that "intention" enters into the distinction, whatever it may be.

[4]It is recognized that some scientific terms are "theoretical" in that they denote postulated entities, properties, or relations that are not subject to observation or measurement in any direct sense. So, extreme operationalism notwithstanding, it is pointless to demand empirically applicable definitions of all terms. However, social scientists do not use the term social control as though it is theoretical; rather, they use it as though it denotes observable events.

that the empirical applicability of a definition is necessarily negligible if it incorporates the notion of intentionality. As remarked by Justice Holmes, even a dog can distinguish between being tripped over and being kicked. Holmes grossly underestimated the problem of making inferences as to intention; but intentionality is emphasized in conventional definitions of all manner of types of behavior in numerous cultures, and evidently considerable empirical applicability is realized in the use of those definitions. As an example, Anglo-American law is a study in such definitions (Marshall, 1968), one being the legal definition of first-degree murder. However, the claim is not that the empirical applicability of the tentative definition of social control is assured; rather, the extent of its empirical applicability can be determined only by attempts to use it.

Even if the tentative definition should prove to be empirically applicable to the maximum degree, many social and behavioral scientists would have reservations about it, and the reason transcends the conceptualization of social control. A much more general issue is introduced. Extreme behaviorists or empiricists are prone to argue that only terms that denote overt behavior can be used effectively in the social and behavioral sciences. Their rejection of terms that denote covert behavior (commonly designated as cognitive, affective, or predispositional terms) stems primarily not just from a concern with empirical applicability. Additionally, they regard the use of such terms in explanations of overt behavior as superfluous, if not appeals to the fictitious.

Sociologists have a special reason for doubts about terms that denote covert behavior. Their doubts reflect not just a concern with empirical applicability (far from it) but also an abiding fear that the use of such terms is an ill-advised step toward the reduction of sociology to psychology. The fear of reductionism ignores the point that the meaning of the vast majority of terms in the sociological vocabulary cannot be fully explicated without at least implicit reference to covert behavior (Lachenmeyer, 1971). That is the case not only for terms that sociologists commonly treat as primitives (i.e. leave undefined), such as interaction, driving, reaching for, commanding, voting, and shopping. It is also the case for most, if not all, of the major sociological concepts, such as revolution, authority, formal organization, and sanction.

There are at least two reasons why sociologists are not prone to recognize that their terminology is inundated with implicit references to covert behavior. First, in using primitive terms (e.g. robbing a bank) as though they denote only overt behavior, the covert facets of that behavior (e.g. intention, perception) are simply taken as understood in the cultural contexts with which sociologists are familiar and within which they do most of their research. And, second, sociologists have grown accustomed to vague definitions of their major concept (e.g. class conflict); hence, it is only when they attempt to realize empirically applicable definitions that the inclusion of reference to covert behavior is forced upon them. Nonetheless, since many of the major sociological concepts (e.g. value, sentiment, norm, attitude) are scarcely anything less than denotations of covert phenomena (albeit at the collective level), it is strange that sociologists rarely recognize intention or perception in their definitions (Lachenmeyer, 1971:73). However, an attempt to cleanse the sociological vocabulary of covert terms would be a study in futility, just as such attempts have been in psychology (initially by J. B. Watson; more recently by B. F. Skinner); and the attempt would be contrary to the fact that the more advanced sciences are a warehouse of terms that denote unobservable phenomena (no one has observed an electron or gravity).

As for the objection that the use of covert terms in definitions would reduce sociology to psychological explanations, a definition does not explain anything. To illustrate, if suicide is defined as an act by an individual that was intended to end his or her life and did have that consequence, the definition explains nothing whatever about suicide. Thus, to say that Ernest Hemingway shot himself with the intention of ending his life hardly explains (even if true) why he did it, why he had that intention, or why he chose that method (not to mention where and when). The example should not be construed as suggesting that covert terms are appropriate when defining terms that pertain to the behavior of individuals (such as Hemingway's death) but inappropriate when the terms pertain to aggregates, such as rates of behavior. As a case in point, the most vocal of all opponents of psychological explanation of sociological phenomena, Emile Durkheim (1951), defined suicide in covert terms—his definition clearly implies that suicide is intentional. The fact that he concerned himself with explaining variation in the suicide rate in no way changes the character of that definition. Durkheim's implicit recognition of intention is not surprising. When sociologists use the terms of any natural language, eschewing such notions as intention in defining those terms is a dubious practice.

Whatever the rationale for excluding covert terms from definitions of sociological concepts, their exclusion ignores what may well be the most conspicuous feature of human behavior—its purposive quality. That quality cannot be observed (as, say, the *movement* of the hand to the head), but it is so much a part of everyday experience that a denial of it would be an absurdity. Perhaps no less relevant for sociology, in everyday life we commonly attribute intention to the acts of others. To be sure, what one makes of the purposive quality of human behavior is another matter. To characterize a particular act as goal-oriented hardly constitutes an explanation of it, especially when some other kind of act could conceivably realize the goal in question. For that matter, a truly satisfactory explanation of the purposive quality of human behavior has yet to be formulated, but that explanation will not be realized by attempting to banish covert terms from the social and behavioral sciences. It matters little that the explanation of the purposive quality of human behavior is perhaps the task of psychologists rather than sociologists, for it is difficult to see how a sociological terminology can be defended if predicated on a denial of the purposive quality of human behavior.

Arguments against the attribution of an intentional quality to social control are not limited to a denial or belittlement of the purposive quality of human behavior. One can freely grant that purposive quality but argue that the unintended consequences of human behavior are more important than the intended consequences. For obvious reasons, many sociologists seem sympathetic to that argument, and it is clearly consistent with the tradition of "debunking" in the history of sociological theory. Yet the argument suggests a curious conclusion—that only the most important sociological phenomena should be conceptualized. In particular, even if social order is largely crescive, it would not follow that conscious and deliberate attempts to manipulate human behavior (as when legislators pursue a deterrent penal policy) are completely irrelevant, meaning that they play no role in social order. For that matter, the argument admits no relativity, meaning it asserts that regardless of the type of society (nonliterate or post-industrial) only the unintended consequences of human behavior play an important role in the maintenance of social order or the promotion of social change. As such, the argument is contrary to the principle of socio-cultural relativism and to Ward's theory (1903) that depicts societies as evolving from genesis to telesis (i.e. from a crescive social order to one that is planned or deliberately maintained).

Reconsideration of the Tentative Definition

None of the foregoing considerations touch directly on the major shortcomings of the tentative definition of social control. Even though the recognition of intention reduces the scope of social control, the definition nonetheless delimits a very broad class of behavior. That class would include, among other things, instances of the following: asking for some item in a store, incarcerating a felon, proposing marriage, performing a lobotomy, asking a friend for a loan, waving a gun at a bank clerk and demanding money, hailing a taxi, requesting directions from a stranger, ringing a door bell, and shooting a president. The list could be extended indefinitely, and the extension would surely suggest that social control (so defined) encompasses virtually all of human interaction.

The shortcoming of the tentative definition is not that it delimits a very broad class of behavior. Rather, the class of behavior is broad because, inter alia, the definition ignores a persistent theme in the literature on social control, though one that is seldom made explicit. The examples of social control in the literature typically suggest that social control is not ubiquitous—not a conspicuous feature of normal or everyday human interaction. As such, most sociologists would likely agree that asking for an item in a store and inviting a friend to lunch are not instances of social control, though they would be according to the tentative definition.[5] Yet, in defining social control, little would be gained by making reference to everyday or normal interaction. That reference would make the definition impossibly vague, for the notion of normal or everyday interaction is ambiguous without an answer to this question: For whom and in what circumstances? It is difficult to imagine a succinct answer; nonetheless, the idea that social control is somehow distinct from normal or everyday interaction (however defined) should not be ignored. For that reason alone the tentative definition is unsatisfactory.

Just as the tentative definition ignores distinctions between kinds of human interaction, it also excludes normative considerations, and that exclusion is contrary to all manner of observations about and definitions of social control. As a case in point, according to the tentative definition "pointing a gun at a clerk in a store and demanding money" would be social control; but that act would be regarded by virtually any sociologist as deviant or criminal.

Second Question: What Is Subject to Social Control?

None of the definitions heretofore considered speak directly to the second major conceptual question, perhaps because one possible answer is obvious—people are controlled. Obvious or not, that answer is misleading. For all practical purposes, human behavior rather than physical bodies is subject to social control, meaning that rarely does control take the form of mechanical (purely physical) manipulation.

The foregoing may seem trivial, but it is not with regard to narrowing the definition of social control. One way is to limit the kinds of behavior that are recognized as subject to social control; but several of the illustrative definitions do not suggest such a limitation—nor does the tentative definition. That feature of the definitions is hardly strange, as it is difficult to think of any kind of overt behavior that is literally beyond manipulation; but observe that the control of human behavior in general cannot be equated with social control. That is the case because social control is a subclass of externalistic behavior control, the manipulation of the behavior of others.

---

[5]Though seldom recognized, sociologists regard the notion of "controlling others" as so distasteful that they are reluctant to recognize that they frequently control others. Thus, when inviting a friend to dinner, no one is likely to think of that invitation as an attempt to control behavior; but it is difficult to deny that it is. Whereas control is merely distasteful, political considerations make social control dangerous. Both connotations—distasteful and dangerous—may make conceptualization more difficult and controversial than anyone has recognized. It is difficult because critics will recoil from a definition of social control that would include their own behavior, and it is controversial because of the inclination to demand a conceptualization that stresses the dangerous character of social control.

An attempt to identify kinds of behavior that are subject to social control could be guided by the perennial concern with social order. If social order is a matter of the consistency between behavior and collective evaluations of conduct and not just statistical uniformities in behavior, then it may appear that in all social units one vast category of behavior is not subject to control. Some evaluations of conduct are "permissive," meaning that the individual making the evaluation is *indifferent* about the kind of behavior in question; he or she simply regards the behavior as a matter of personal choice and one free of moral or ethical connotations.[6] To illustrate, in some American social units (a particular family or perhaps an entire community) the following appear to be permissive behaviors for adults in certain situations: drinking coffee, attending movies, watching television, and foregoing an early morning meal. As such, there is a basis for presuming that attempts to promote or repress those behaviors (i.e. control them) are negligible.

The argument becomes more understandable and conventional when its major implication is made explicit—efforts at social control are directed toward deviant behavior. Specifically, when individuals evaluate a kind of behavior *proscriptively*, they are likely to engage in activities with a view to prevent that behavior; and when individuals evaluate a kind of behavior *prescriptively*, they are likely to engage in activities with a view to promote that behavior.

The prophylactic conception of social control. While no one is likely to argue that only deviant behavior can be controlled, it is now virtually a tradition for social scientists, sociologists in particular, to think of social control as directed primarily at deviant behavior [e.g. Hawkes (1975)], and that tradition is clearly reflected in most of the illustrative definitions formulated after 1950. Such definitions reflect the "prophylactic" conception of social control, according to which social control is any practice, institution, social process, mechanism, etc., that *counteracts* deviant behavior.[7] Parsons was the key figure in promoting the prophylactic conception, but an anthropologist, Berndt, has set forth the most succinct definition (supra).

Although the rationale for the prophylactic conception is commonly left unstated, the conception is consistent with two previously discussed themes in observations on social control: (1) It is not part of normal or everyday interaction and (2) it has a normative quality. Nonetheless, that kind of

[6]Examples of "normative questions" in Chapter 1 notwithstanding, when conducting a survey of normative opinions each question should be worded so as to make it possible for a respondent to give an "indifferent" evaluation of the type of conduct.

[7]In spite of Wood's definition (supra), the title of his book, *Deviant Behavior and Control Strategies*, signifies an acceptance of the prophylactic conception of social control. So in the list of illustrative definitions, of the seven cited authors who wrote after 1950, only two of them, Sites and Adams (an anthropologist), did not explicitly or implicitly accept the prophylactic conception of social control. No less significant, none of the definitions formulated prior to 1950 suggest acceptance of the prophylactic conception.

definition has failed to provide firm ground for research on social control, because no one has defined deviant behavior in a manner that promises substantial empirical applicability and is acceptable to even an effective majority of sociologists.[8] The reasons for that situation have been described in Chapter 2, but a brief commentary on related objections to and problems with the prophylactic conception of social control is in order.

First off, nothing would be gained by describing social control as directed at any behavior *other than* permissive behavior. That terminology avoids reference to deviance, but by any definition there are few, if any, kinds of behavior that are absolutely permissive for all members of any social unit (adults and children, men and women, Mormons and Catholics) regardless of the situation. The problem is a corollary of a point made in Chapter 1—that evaluations of conduct (especially of *actual* behavior, as opposed to evaluations of types of acts in the abstract) are so contingent that it is doubtful if all of the relevant contingencies can be identified in soliciting answers to normative questions from members of a social unit. Then it should again be recognized that even if all possibly relevant contingencies could be stipulated in normative questions, that would not solve the "consensus problem."

Now consider what appears to be clearly permissive behavior in some social divisions of the United States, such as going to movies or drinking coffee. What about the unceasing efforts of advertisers to promote such behaviors? It could be argued that advertisers, be they small-town merchants or Madison Avenue types, might admit (albeit regretfully) that no potential consumer is under some moral or ethical duty to buy a particular commodity; and the typical consumer rarely, if ever, contemplates a purchase in those terms. So it may be that the activities of advertisers would not qualify as social control in light of definitions set forth by Berndt, Cohen, and Parsons. However, that conclusion is debatable precisely because of problems in defining and identifying instances of deviant behavior (or permissive behavior). Moreover, the activities of advertisers would qualify as social control in light of several of the definitions [see Lumley and Adams (supra)], and perhaps rightly so. Since hundreds of thousands of Americans are employed in the advertising industry and since advertising may well have an enormous impact on the economy and the lifestyle of consumers, it would be dubious to argue that advertising is not social control because it has no practical importance.

The allusion to advertising suggests a fundamental, though somewhat

[8]Perhaps the problem has been virtually ignored in commentaries on the conceptualization of social control (Pitts, 1968; Roucek, 1978) because the vast majority of critics since 1950 have accepted the prophylactic conception of social control. For that matter, commencing with Cohen (1966), virtually all books on social control bear a title in which "deviance" or "deviant behavior" is a constituent term; and even writers who identify with Marxist sociology either accept the prophylactic conception or simply leave social control undefined. Perhaps even more significant, authors of introductory sociology texts long ago subscribed to the conception [see Bredemeier and Stephenson (1962)].

vague, objection to the prophylactic conception of social control. It excludes various highly organized activities in which large numbers of individuals consciously and deliberately attempt to manipulate the behavior of large numbers of individuals.[9] As an example beyond the advertising industry: On what grounds could one argue that the activities of Hitler and other Nazis to manipulate the behavior of millions of Germans were not social control?[10] Yet, if those activities were described as the "counteraction of deviance," it would lead to sterile arguments not only as to whose norms are relevant but also as to what the norms of Germany really were during the 1920s and 1930s. Similarly, unless one can demonstrate that slavery was deviant in the United States prior to the Civil War, then the highly organized efforts of abolitionists [see Dillon (1974)] to alter the behavior of millions of individuals was not social control.

The general point can be appreciated only by contemplating what is commonly referred to as repression or oppression, terrorism, governmental regulation, welfare measures, strikes, blacklisting, boycotting, propaganda, and protests.[11] Although such phenomena are highly organized or in-stitutionalized and clearly involve attempts to control behavior on a vast scale, it would be questionable to characterize them as social control in light of the prophylactic conception. The reason should be obvious—all such phenomena reflect normative conflict, and in that condition the identification of behavior as deviant is especially debatable. The same is true of phenomena or categories of individuals that appear particularly subject to highly organized attempts at control, such as collective violence, dissent, slaves, inmates, rebellions, racial–ethnic minorities, heresy, terrorism, race relations, in-surgencies, students, the poor, children, debtors, strikes, and military subordinates.[12] There are even doubts as to how the prophylactic conception

---

[9]Parsons (1951) has created another problem in his distinction between social control and socialization. He describes social control as compensating for ineffective socialization, meaning social control counteracts deviance that was not counteracted by socialization. Since both counteract deviance, the distinction rests on the presumption that we know (for any given individual) when socialization commences and ends. The presumption is dubious in the extreme; hence, as Martindale (1978) has suggested, Parsons's distinction between socialization and social control is a conceptual quagmire.

[10]For examples, see Allen (1965), Bullock (1962), Grunberger (1971), Waite (1977), and Wighton (1962).

[11]For examples, see Blauner (1972), Caute (1978), Harring (1977), Janowitz (1976), Kanfer (1973), Kirchheimer (1961), Lowenthal and Guterman (1970), Skolnick (1969), Thomas (1973), Wakeman and Grant (1975), Wilson et al. (1977), Wilson, J. (1977), Wise (1976), and Wolfe (1978).

[12]For examples, see Adamek and Lewis (1973), Blauner (1972), Coleman (1969), Denisoff (1974), Finn (1971), Gamson (1968), Genovese (1974), Goffman (1961a), Golden (1958), Hall (1971), Janowitz (1968), Kamen (1967), Kisch (1970), Krüger and Silvert (1975), Laquer (1977), Lea (1963), Lee (1954), Leites and Wolf (1970), Lens (1969), Lipset (1976), Mandell (1975), Marshall (1972), Piven and Cloward (1971), Platt (1969), Pollinger and Pollinger (1972), Radine (1977), Rock (1973), Russell (1974), Schreiber (1978), Shorter and Tilly (1974),

applies to numerous early works that were identified as social control studies, notably studies of race relations, business, unemployment, taxation, stock exchange, industry, and consumer credit costs.[13] Finally, granted that deviance is the antithesis of social order, the prophylactic conception of social control is somehow alien to the classic arguments about social order, such as certain works of Plato (Gouldner, 1965), Hobbes (1953), Machiavelli (1952), Malinowski (1959), Michels (1915), Moore (1966), Mosca (1939), and Sorel (1915).

In attempting to avoid the objections just made, advocates of the prophylactic conception of social control may argue that they do not assume monolithic norms or even approximations of normative consensus. Rather, the argument could be that those who engage in social control do so to promote conformity to *their norms*. That view admits the possibility of normative dissensus and even conflicting norms, but it solves less problems than first appearances indicate. Granted that each social division of a society has its own norms, is absolute normative consensus a criterion of a norm in each division? If so, norms may be largely if not entirely peculiar to very small divisions of a society (e.g. families). Moreover, if social control takes place only *within* divisions of a society, then it plays no role in the attempts of one division to dominate, exploit, or impose its norms on another division. In particular, the attempts of the Ku Klux Klan to control the behavior of blacks is counteraction of deviance—hence social control—only if one ignores the norms of blacks or makes the astonishing assertion that Klansmen and blacks share the same norms. Even if the "consensus problem" in defining and identifying norms would be lessened by abandoning the idea of societal norms (i.e. treating norms as though they are peculiar to small social units), the idea that social control takes place only within divisions of a society (e.g. families, companies) runs contrary to three persistent identifications in the literature of criminology and jurisprudence. First, law is a type of norm (Raz, 1970; Davis, 1949); second, crime is a kind of subclass of deviance (Gibbons and Jones, 1975); and, third, law is a means of social control (Black, 1976; Litwak, 1956; Parsons, 1962; Pound 1968; Stone, 1961). There is further agreement that law transcends divisions of a society (Kelsen, 1967; Weber, 1954); for that reason alone it is dubious to define social control as though it takes place only *within* societal divisions.

The reference to law reintroduces a previous illustration: someone pointing a gun at a store clerk and demanding money. Again, most sociologists would

---

(footnote continued)
Skolnick (1968), Stampp (1967), Sykes (1958), Tilly et al. (1975), Wilkinson (1977), and Wilson, J. (1977).

[13]See Brown (1940), Clark (1939), Finney (1926), Hayes (1936), Heer (1937), Merrill (1938), Modlin and McIsaac (1938), and Phelps (1951).

characterize the act as deviant, but suppose the gunman is acting under orders, as a member of a well organized gang of terrorists and as part of a strategy to bring about a political crisis. What basis is there for denying that the act is social control? The difficulty posed cannot be avoided by limiting social control to the actions of "authorities," as authority is a normative notion. Fewer problems would be posed by defining social control as the promotion of conformity to criminal laws, or by equating it with the actions of legal officials. That is the case because few scholars in jurisprudence would argue that the notion of criminal law or legal official presumes normative consensus, but such a definition of social control would be subject to at least two major objections. First, it would represent a very narrow view of social control, one limited to the legal sphere. And, second, the definition would make the will of legislators or other political superordinates the criterion of social control, thereby confirming what Friedland (1973: 513) said about the attitude of sociologists toward the study of social control: "Social control became a kind of no-no for most of us when the issue of *who controlled* came to the fore. As long as social control was discussed in terms of the development of self-control mechanisms, things were fine; once deviance became an issue, the study of social control became somewhat deviant for many sociologists."

Another strategy for advocates of the prophylactic conception of social control is to abandon any pretense of defining deviant behavior in conventional normative terms and to adopt the *reactive* conception of deviance. Specifically, any attempt to control behavior (i.e. to promote or to prevent it) can be taken as indicative of the would-be controller's evaluation of that behavior (i.e. whether he or she regards the behavior as deviant). That strategy would avoid the unrealistic assumption of monolithic societal norms, or, for that matter, normative consensus in any social unit. Nonetheless, the strategy would give rise to all manner of problems and objections.

As for the problems, inferring evaluations of conduct from attempted behavior control is especially dubious when the would-be controllers *may have acted* only as agents for other parties. Thus, while legislators and police officers attempt to manipulate behavior, according to orthodox Marxist theory, they do so as agents of capitalists. However, since that assertion is debatable, there are real doubts as to whose evaluations of conduct are reflected in the control activities of legal officials. In any case, there is the distinct possibility that some individuals (e.g. police officers, teachers) may admit to a lack of conviction in the very norms that their control activities supposedly support, rationalizing their activities as "only obeying orders." Such obedience may be construed as normative; but, even so, it casts doubt on the idea that those who engage in social control do so with a view to promoting conformity to *their* norms. Indeed, the distinction between those who enforce norms and those who formulate them reintroduces a point made in Chapter 1—that it appears grossly unrealistic to conceptualize or identify norms without recognizing differential power, which is to say without recognizing that the normative opinions of some individuals *count more* than those of other individuals.

Even if the foregoing problems were somehow resolved, there would be several objections to the proposed strategy, the most obvious being the strategy's circularity. Whereas the initial goal was to define social control by reference to deviant behavior, the strategy would have the effect of defining deviant behavior by reference to social control, as in Black's definition (Chapter 2). Moreover, in some societies virtually all kinds of behavior are subject to attempts at control, meaning that a purely "control" conception of deviance negates the very idea of permissive behavior. As previously suggested, going to movies, drinking coffee, and purchasing a car appear permissive for adults in some small American social units (again, especially particular families and perhaps entire communities), but many Americans make a living by promoting those behaviors. Of course, one can argue that advertisers do not really view the failure of particular individuals to attend movies, drink coffee, or to purchase a car as "deviant"; but that argument is a tacit admission that inferences of evaluations of conduct cannot be justifiably drawn from attempts to control behavior.

Some of the foregoing suggested possibilities for circumventing objections to the prophylactic conception imply that social control is intentional; but the most remarkable feature of the conception is the failure of its advocates to attribute an intentional quality to social control, and some of the definitions (Parsons, supra) explicitly deny the relevance of intention. One consequence is that the conception delimits a class of behavior that is too narrow (e.g. it ostensibly excludes advertising, activities of terrorists, and manipulations of millions of individuals to political ends) but is at the same time extremely heterogeneous. As for narrowness, there is the exclusion of the control activities of the Nazis and the abolitionists. As for heterogeneity, according to the prophylactic conception legal executions *would be* social control, regardless of the intention of those who prescribe or administer criminal sanctions, if they promote general deterrence; but wearing wedding rings also *would be* social control (regardless of anyone's intention or perception) if it is shown that the custom does promote conformity to some assumed norm (e.g. marital fidelity). Considerable significance is attached to the *conditional* identification of legal sanctions and customs as social control: They are social control only if it is shown that they promote conformity to some assumed norm. Yet it is extremely difficult to demonstrate that a given behavior, practice, or institution promotes conformity to an assumed norm. Then consider the implication of a demonstration that some behavior (e.g. an increase in fines for speeding) does *not* promote conformity to any assumed norm, even though those who engage in it anticipate that consequence (i.e. they intend to prevent deviance). Since the prophylactic conception denies the relevance of intention, the behavior would not be social control: Hence, the distinction between successful and unsuccessful attempts at social control is precluded by the prophylactic conception. Perhaps most important of all, observe again that the conception makes it illogical to ask whether social control counteracts deviance.

The absence of a defensible basis for answering the second major conceptual question (What is subject to social control?) by reference to deviant behavior has two unfortunate implications. First, there is no obvious alternative in the literature, let alone one that attributes a normative quality to social control; and, second, the prophylactic conception offers the only *conspicuous* possibility for distinguishing social control from normal or everyday interaction.[14] So it is not surprising that those who have voiced reservations about the prophylactic conception admit to doubts about a defensible alternative [e.g. Gibbs (1977)]. Moreover, there are articles and books on social control in which the authors or editors scarcely concern themselves with the conceptualization problem.[15] Such omissions probably

[14]Stating the matter another way, the prophylactic conception of deviance is more defensible than the present criticisms of it suggest, especially if (1) deviance is limited to those types of acts in each social unit that are disapproved by all members; (2) the intention of preventing such an act is attributed to agents of social control (Zald, 1978); (3) the possibility of unsuccessful social control is admitted—that social control does not *necessarily* prevent or reduce deviance. Given those qualifications, no one would be likely to question the identification of *some* aspects of law enforcement, extralegal disciplinary measures, and other kinds of attempts to prevent "deviance" as social control, nor to question the identification of occupants of various statuses (e.g. police officers, teachers, parents, jurors) as agents of social control (Akers and Hawkins, 1975; Akers and Sagarin, 1974; Banton, 1964; Bittner, 1970; Conrad, 1965; Lemert, 1945; Marshall, 1972; Mercurio, 1972; Robertson and Taylor, 1973; Ziegenhagen, 1977). However, when legislators criminalize acts without victims, embark on moral crusades, or further the interests of the wealthy, then the characterization of their activities as "social control" becomes controversial; and the same is true when police officers, prosecutors, and judges are grossly selective in the enforcement of laws [see, especially, Baumgartner (1978), Bean (1974), Becker (1955), Chambliss and Mankoff (1976), Currie (1968), Duster (1970), Erikson (1966), Hagan (1977), Harring (1977), Humphreys (1972), Kirchheimer (1961), Kogon (n.d.), Lea (1963), May (1931), Monahan (1977), Packer (1968), Quinney (1970, 1974), Scheff (1966), Schur (1965), and Skolnick (1966, 1968)]. To be sure, the activities of legal officials are attempts at "control" but whether these constitute social control in light of the prophylactic conceptions is another matter. One major reason for possible doubt is evidence of normative dissensus with regard to the types of act that officials are ostensibly attempting to prevent, and another reason may be evidence that they do not seek to "counteract" such acts as an end in itself (a point ignored in the prophylactic conception of social control). When it comes to commonly recognized extralegal agents of social control (e.g. psychiatrists, employers, private detectives, and religious leaders), doubts are accentuated by the distinct possibility that they are not promoting the evaluative standards or interests of all members of the social unit (Frank, 1961; Goffman, 1961a; London, 1964; Pope, 1942; Scheff, 1966; Spitzer and Scull, 1977; Steadman, 1972; Szasz, 1965).

[15]For examples, see Bean (1974), Bianchi et al. (1975), Bordua (1967), Breed (1955), Broadhead and Rist (1976), Cook-Gumperz (1973), Hughes (1976), Julian (1968), Robertson and Taylor (1973), Rock and McIntosh (1974), Scott and Scott (1971), Spiller (1960), Stewart and Cantor (1974), Vallier (1970), and Weinberg (1974). Most of the authors just cited are sociologists, but the practice of eschewing a concern with conceptual problems is also very common in the anthropological literature on social control (Brown, 1952; Gulliver, 1963; Howard and Howard, 1964; LeVine, 1959; Lieban, 1962; Nadel, 1953; Reay, 1953). Given the widespread indifference in social control studies to conceptual problems, Zald's concern (1978) with those problems is especially noteworthy.

do not represent mere oversights; instead, it may well be that the authors had misgivings about the prophylactic conception but could not formulate an alternative. It is indeed a testimonial to the horrendous problems in defining social control when authors worry over conceptual matters at great length but stop short of endorsing the prophylactic conception or formulating an explicit alternative [e.g. Watkins (1975)].

Third Question: Who Is Subject to Social Control?

None of the illustrative definitions speak directly to the third question, perhaps because the answer appears obvious—any individual. To be sure, in some social units there are individuals (e.g. an absolute dictator) whose behavior appears uncontrolled by anyone. Yet it is difficult to imagine an individual whose behavior is literally beyond control, or an individual that no one attempts to control in any situation (even the more despotic Roman emperors had to contend with a conniving parent or a shrewish wife).

Subordinate statuses. Granted that everyone's behavior is controllable, it does not follow that everyone's behavior is subject to *social* control. (Note again that it is a subclass of externalistic control.) Stating the argument so as to make it even more defensible, certain socially recognized categories of individuals appear *especially* subject to control. In Anglo-American countries the "status terms" employee, army private, child, and inmate are possible illustrative designations of such categories.

A response to the third major conceptual question in "status terms" deserves serious consideration if only because it emphasizes the normative quality of social control (individuals in some particular statuses are supposedly subject to the authority of individuals in certain other complementary statuses, such as child and parent). No less important, the answer excludes from social control various kinds of normal or everyday interaction, notably that between "status equals," such as friends or strangers. Unfortunately, however, the answer would be a study in problems.

The immediate problem is that in some instances one cannot readily ascertain when a given individual is acting in one particular status capacity and not another, or whether individuals in certain statuses (e.g. client) are supposedly subject to the control of individuals in other statuses (e.g. lawyer). Even if there were no such instances, the sheer number of possible subordinate statuses in Anglo-American countries is astonishing. Moreover, the terms denoting those statuses are peculiar to English-speaking countries, and a definition of social control (in this case, one couched in status terms) should not be limited to a particular culture. An ethnocentric enumeration of particular statuses could be avoided by simple reference to "individuals in subordinate statuses" as an answer to the third question. But even if that designation were perfectly clear (thereby promising empirical applicability), such individuals are commonly controlled through acceptance of the authority exercised over them by individuals in complementary superordinate status, and it is difficult to imagine anyone arguing that social control rests only on authority. Indeed, it could be argued that social control is most conspicuous when authority is defied; and, in any case, there is no obvious rationale for excluding coercion as a means of social control.[16] Then there is the commonly accepted idea that law is a means of social control, but law and its enforcement (especially criminal law) cannot be readily described in status terms. More specifically, whether an individual becomes subject to "legal control" appears to be more contingent on acts by that individual than on his or her statuses.

Pareto's theory. With a view to designating a category of individuals who are especially subject to social control (regardless of the society, culture, or context), there are two alternatives to "individuals in subordinate statuses." Those alternatives are all the more important because both are components in major theories about human societies.

The central sociological distinction in Pareto's theory (1963) is that between elites and nonelites, and the distinction is especially strategic for present purposes because Pareto clearly depicts the nonelites as being controlled by the elites. Unfortunately, Pareto's distinction is a study in vagueness, and no clarification of that distinction would justify answering the third major conceptual question by reference to nonelites. The immediate reason is Pareto's recognition of two divisions of the elites, the governing elites and the nongoverning elites. Evidently, the governing elites and the nongoverning elites (or a faction of them) *may* differ as to their economic interests (e.g. a land owning aristocracy versus a mercantile class) and/or ideological orientation (especially as regards political beliefs). Yet Pareto's observations suggest that the only universal differences (i.e. true by defini-tion) is that the governing elites (or a division of them) are in the dominant position as regards political power. The governing elites seek to maintain the status quo—their power position in particular—and to that end they may be concerned primarily with thwarting the nongoverning elites. The latter, in turn, seek to seize power, and to that end their ultimate concern is overthrowing or destroying the governing elites.

---

[16]Ponder Janowitzs's statement (1975:84): "The opposite of social control can be thought of as coercive control; that is, the social organization of a society which rests predominantly and essentially on force—the threat and the use of force." Social control is a controversial subject and inherently dangerous (see footnote 5), but it is an illusion to define it in such a way as to deny those qualities (i.e. to define it as though it were benign, democratic, and imbued with a liberal spirit). Janowitz's statement is all the more puzzling because he refrains from an explicit definition of social control.

The foregoing interpretation of Pareto is disputable, of course, and the same may be said for all interpretations of his theory, which is a testimonial to the vagueness and inconsistencies that pervade it. In particular, some interpreters do not recognize and emphasize the possibility that at least some factions of the nongoverning elites differ from the governing elites in terms of social class, economic interest, residues,[17] or some other significant feature—whether biological, psychological, or sociological. Yet casual observations suggest that contending, if not warring, factions among the elites are common. To illustrate briefly, if the elites are concerned only with controlling the nonelites, what is one to make of the American Civil War, the War of the Roses, or the Puritan revolution? As for the Puritan revolution, it will not suffice to identify Cromwell and his military−political associates (who acted not as isolated individuals but as an organized body) as nonelites, as that would make the distinction between elites and nonelites subjective to the point of being meaningless. Nor will it do to make the point that Cromwell and his associates were leaders of nonelites because to identify an individual as a leader is to recognize that individual's elitism. For that matter, even if the nonelites are led by "dissatisfied" nongoverning elites from the same social class as the governing elites, those leaders do not act as isolated individuals, which is to say that they are a distinct faction, though perhaps not the only one among the nongoverning elites.

The foregoing is not a denial of one of Pareto's main arguments—that the elites strive to control the nonelites. But the governing elites and one or more factions of the nongoverning elites may do so largely with a view to controlling their contenders among the elites (i.e. to remain in power or seize power). Thus, demogogues in ancient Rome (hardly less than elites) specialized in inciting the "mob" (nonelites) to attack officials or leaders of opposing factions, whether governing or nongoverning elites (Heaton, 1939). Recent events in American history are no less illustrative. During the administration of Richard M. Nixon, it was discovered that his subordinates had compiled a list of American citizens as targets for special surveillance and harassment. Commentators duly noted the abundance of Democrats on the "enemies list," but even more conspicuous was the absence of laborers. Of course, had laborers appeared on the list, it would have been a cause for astonishment. Rather, the list comprised influential people, including celebrities, many of whom could be identified as nongoverning elites. The list suggests that the immediate concern of the governing elites (in this case, Nixon and his associates) is the control of the nongoverning elites.

---

[17]This is one of many of Pareto's exotic terms, and it virtually defies definition. Its closest equivalent term in psychology is "drives"; but it is perhaps better to think of residues as the real forces that prompt human beings to certain lines of action, as opposed to the rationalizations they offer for such actions.

What the enemies list does not reveal is the preoccupation of factions among the nongoverning elites with controlling the governing elites. After all, anarchists, rebels, and revolutionaries have no special antipathy toward laborers. When they compile a "target list" it is scarcely less selective than one compiled by the governing elites.

A focus on attempts to control the nonelites would mark an end to the preoccupation of sociologists with studying the social control of seemingly apolitical kinds of deviants (e.g. the homosexual, the petty thief, the drug addict). Perhaps even more important, the focus would amount to a rejection of the assumption of normative consensus. Indeed, the focus would force recognition of three or more sets of *contending* collective evaluations of conduct (i.e. normative dissensus)—one subscribed to by the governing elites; another by at least one faction of the nongoverning elites; and yet another by the nonelites. Even so, reference to nonelites as an answer to the third question (Who is subject to social control?) will not bear examination. Even if the elites do strive to control the nonelites, one division or faction of the elites may be no less concerned with controlling the other divisions or factions. However, once that point is granted, there is no basis for argument that only the nonelites are subject to social control; or, depending on the society and historical period, that even the nonelites are especially subject to social control.

Marxist theory. Rather than speak of elites and nonelites, Marxists see the fundamental conflict in all but communist societies as that between a *propertied* class (those who own the predominant mode of *productive* property, be they nobility or capitalists) and a propertyless class (slaves, serfs, or industrial proletariats).[18] Since the propertied class is unable to exploit those members of the unpropertied class who will not accept the prevailing economic relations, tolerate conditions of work (e.g. wages, salaries), or respect property rights, members of the propertied class are depicted as concerned primarily with maintaining control over the propertyless class.

There are several grounds for objecting to an answer to the third question by reference to a propertyless class, and the reasons transcend the point that such a class is extremely heterogeneous, as it includes, for example, laborers and archbishops. Unless one is prepared to assume that all legislators are members

---

[18]It is misleading to cite one of Marx's publications [e.g. Marx (1909)] as though it offers a theory of social control, let alone a theory of deviance or crime [see Hirst's commentary (1972)]. Nor is it realistic to think of such a theory as is scattered throughout hundreds of Marx's articles, books, letters, and newspaper pieces, awaiting someone to put it together. One may be inspired by Marx to formulate a theory of social control and incorporate some of his assumptions and terms in that theory, but it is inconceivable that even a majority of the constituent statements will be quotations from Marx or even approximations. Much to his credit, Spitzer (1975b) has attempted to state such a theory. Spitzer initially characterized it as a "Marxian theory of deviance," but in replying to a critic (*Social Problems*, 24:364–366) he speaks more accurately of a "Marxian theory of social control."

of the propertyless class, Marxist theory itself negates the idea that only the members of that class are subject to social control, or even especially subject to social control. That is the case because in capitalist societies legislators are supposedly controlled by capitalists. Indeed, in the early stages of capitalism the capitalists scarcely could fail to be concerned with the control of still another propertied class—the landed aristocracy, who contend with the capitalists for political power. "Activist" Marxists accept the argument that the propertied class is greatly concerned with controlling the propertyless class; but unlike the "mechanist" Marxists, the activists assume that revolutionaries are necessary to promote change from one economic order to another—capitalism to socialism. So revolutionaries, including terrorists, seek to control the propertied class, just as members of that class are concerned with eliminating revolutionaries and silencing dissenters; and neither concern necessarily has to do directly with the control of the propertyless class.

Objections to both theories. Although Pareto's theory and Marx's theory do not suggest the same answer to the third major conceptual question about social control, there are at least two objections that apply to both theories. First, control in the context of all manner of superordinate−subordinate status relations (e.g. parent−child, husband−wife, teacher−pupil) is not peculiar to any particular class, stratum, or faction. Hence, it is unrealistic to argue that only one particular class, stratum, or faction is subject to social control.

The second objection is more complicated. While adoption of the orientation of either Pareto or Marx would shift the traditional focus of social control studies from apolitical deviance or criminality (e.g. drug addiction, homosexuality) to the control of some economic−political divisions over other divisions of society,[19] it is difficult to imagine the argument that deviants or criminals (however defined) are not really subject to control. Yet there is scarcely any basis for classifying criminals or deviants (political or apolitical) as a subclass of any particular social class, stratum, or faction (e.g. nonelites, propertyless class). Accordingly, if any one particular class or stratum is taken as subject to social control, then deviants or criminals who are not members of that class or stratum are tacitly identified as not subject to social control.

---

[19] It is precisely the control of one division of a society over another (e.g. nobility−serfs, masters−slaves, employers−employees) that raises what may well be *the* issue as regards the prophylactic conception of social control. Such control is not social control unless the behavior of those who are controlled is deviant, but whose evaluations of conduct are to be taken as the norm? Of course, if the assumption of normative consensus were not disputable (e.g. both serfs and the nobility disapprove of serfs hunting on land owned by the nobility), the question would not pose a problem for the prophylactic conception of social control. To be sure, the conception does yield an explicit answer to the third question (Who is subject to social control?): deviants. But that answer is subject to all sorts of objections and gives rise to all kinds of problems if only because (as suggested in Chapter 2) it is even more difficult to realize a defensible definition of "deviant" than of "deviant behavior."

Fourth Question: Who Exercises Social Control?

Of all the definitions heretofore discussed, including the tentative definition, only Dowd's seems to limit the exercise of social control to a particular category of individuals—those who have "some prestige." That limitation is extremely dubious, for in the history of human societies some despised and feared autocrats have exercised virtually absolute control over their subjects. Indeed, Caligula, Louis XIV, and Ivan the Terrible might well have regarded Dowd's definition as amusing.

The fact that the other definitions do not address the fourth question probably reflects recognition that in any society virtually everyone exercises some control over others. Yet, with a view to defining social control, it is no less important (or obvious) that in any society some categories of individuals appear to exercise more control than others. Some of the more obvious categories in Anglo-American countries are designated by the status terms of parent, employer, warden, general, admiral, governor, president, and police officer. However, such status terminology gives rise to the same problems in answering the fourth question as it does in responding to the third.

Pareto's theory is more defensible in connection with the fourth question (Who exercises social control?) than with the third question (Who is subject to social control?). In the context of Pareto's theory the fourth question can be answered by reference to one particular category of individuals—the elites (governing or otherwise). However, the meaning of elites may be far too vague for the study of social control,[20] and various superordinate–subordinate relations (e.g. parent–child) transcend the elite–nonelite distinction.

The response to the fourth question suggested by Marx's theory—members of the propertied class—is subject to the same objection made in the case of Pareto's theory; it would ignore superordinate–subordinate status relations that transcend particular classes or strata. Additionally, if only the propertied class exercises social control, revolutionaries cannot be taken as agents of social control, whereas in the context of Pareto's theory revolutionaries can be identified as a faction among the nongoverning elites.

Other theories. Any theory about social order can be characterized as "positive" or "negative." In the latter case, coercive or punitive reactions to certain kinds of behavior are emphasized as the basis of order; and those reactions are especially likely to be not only deliberate but also socially organized (i.e. administered largely by persons in particular statuses). So a "negative" theory of social order virtually justifies focusing social control studies upon the control activities of persons in particular statuses. Those statuses are identified only in the more extreme versions of the Marxist theory of social order, in which legal officials are described as essential for the

---

[20]From Mills (1959) to Domhoff (1978) there is no problem more conspicuous or intractable than realizing an empirically applicable definition of "elites."

repression of revolutionaries or dissidents—those who seek to alter economic relations. Yet it is productive property owners (the bourgeoisie in capitalist societies) rather than legal officials who supposedly benefit from the exploitative economic relations; and, according to Marxist theory, legal officials are only *agents of that propertied class*. So it is not clear whether a Marxist study of social control would focus upon legal officials alone, a propertied class, or both.

Unlike either Marx's theory or Pareto's theory, a positive theory of social order seemingly postulates not only substantial normative consensus but also that conformity to norms is rewarding. As illustrative instances, Malinowski's principle of reciprocity (1959) emphasizes the rewarding character of conformity—individuals conform to norms first and foremost because conformity is beneficial, gratifying, profitable, pragmatic, etc. Similarly, LaPiere (1954) depicts conformity as a means of maintaining status. Parson's theory (1951) of social order is more inclusive; it places greater emphasis on normative consensus, attributing deviational tendencies to ineffective socialization, and describes social control largely in terms of checking deviational tendencies that were not eliminated through socialization. Despite the contrasts, all of the positive theories of social order assert that *effective* social control lies in everyday interaction (e.g. between parent and child, husband and wife, employer and employee), where each party has the capacity to control the other by terminating reciprocity or otherwise withholding rewards. As such, the positive theories tacitly deny that the exercise of social control is limited to a particular category of individuals, and they tacitly reject the focus of social control studies on any particular category of individuals (e.g. a propertied class, elites, legal officials, etc.). But Malinowski, LaPiere, and Parsons stop short of denying that there are social units in which legal officials are essential agents of social control.

The foregoing brief survey compels the recognition that no theory of social order supplies a compelling rationale for any particular answer to the fourth question (Who exercises social control?). So the challenge in conceptualizing social control is to avoid a definition that would arbitrarily limit the exercise of social control to a particular category of individuals, but at the same time realize a definition that permits *demonstration* of a widely accepted assumption: Some categories of individuals exercise more social control than others.

Fifth Question: By What Means Can Social Control be Exercised?

A listing of all the more obvious and specific means of attempts to manipulate behavior would occupy considerable space; so a few illustrations must suffice: corporal punishment, flattery, promises, psychosurgery, pleas, fines, execution, incarceration, blackmail, gifts, and contracts. Given such diversity, it is not surprising that none of the illustrative definitions (supra) or the tentative definitions even suggest that social control is necessarily limited to one or even a few specific means; and not a great deal of significance can be attached to such phrases as "putting forth directive stimuli" (Lumley), "process by which stimuli are brought to bear effectively" (Bernard), and "the use of power" (Wood).

Doubts as to the feasibility of limiting social control to one specific means (e.g. incarceration) or even a broad class of means (e.g. punishment) increase upon recognition that the two major contending *classes of theories* on social order differ sharply in their emphasis on particular means. "Negative" theories emphasize punishment and coercion (especially punishment and coercion by legal officials), while "positive" theories emphasize rewards (insofar as that word applies to transactions in everyday interaction). Since the relative merits of the two theories are debatable, there is at present no rationale in the literature for focusing social control studies upon certain specific means to the exclusion of others. That conclusion would not be altered even by acceptance of the idea that social control is the counteraction of deviance.[21] There are all manner of means by which such counteraction is attempted (or "takes place," if intention is irrelevant), and the relative frequency of the various means is questionable.

The only conspicuous argument for limiting social control to certain means stems from the widely recognized point that social control is normative in one sense or another. That idea suggests that the means of social control are *socially approved* ways by which an individual may manipulate the behavior of others.[22] That conception would make the means of social control relative

[21]The prophylactic conception provides no rationale for restricting social control to particular specific means, and the point is not just that deviance can be counteracted by any one of seemingly infinite ways. Moreover, the very idea of "means" suggests something that is alien to the prophylactic conception—social control is intentional; and obvious attempts to manipulate behavior are hardly indisputable evidence that the behavior is deviant, let alone that the attempts are in some sense socially approved. Consider the great interest in "behavior modification" techniques (aversive conditioning in particular) that became conspicuous some ten years ago (Bandura, 1969; Campbell and Church, 1969; and London, 1969). Whatever the purpose of the development of such techniques, it is pointless to assume that the techniques will be used only to prevent deviance, insofar as that notion has anything to do with widely shared evaluations of conduct. Indeed, even now, critics of behavior modification regard it as deviant (Kittrie, 1971; Mitford, 1973).

[22]It is significant that the prophylactic conception of social control does not speak to the question, which is to say that the means employed to counteract deviance are conceptually irrelevant (evidently). The point is significant because it bears on what most candid sociologists would admit to—that they regard social control as distasteful at best and inherently dangerous. Only someone who is supremely indifferent to the notion of human liberty would regard social control as benign, and that is reason in itself for reservations about the prophylactic conception of social control. In making the *means* of counteracting deviance conceptually irrelevant, it also makes a concern for due process and the justification of punishments irrelevant. Yet, unsurprisingly, those concerns loom very large in studies of or thoughts about social control and crime (Bedau, 1978; Grupp, 1971; Kittrie, 1971; Skolnick, 1966). Perhaps it is a mistake to mix value judgments (e.g. defending due process) and conceptual issues (in this case, defining social control), but they are mixed nonetheless. It is as though someone were told: "Look, a Gestapo agent and a British bobby are both agents of social control; so forget about differences between them that are conceptually irrelevant."

to particular social units, but that is not the problem with the conception (indeed, it might well be one of its merits). The problem is that the formulation of criteria of *social approval* entails all of the problems in defining and identifying norms,[23] and for that reason it will not do to refer to means of social control as "sanctions." The point is not just that conceptualizations of sanctions are ambiguous as to the question of social approval; additionally, no one has formulated criteria of social approval that are empirically applicable but not arbitrary.

Sixth Question: What Are the Goals or Consequences of Social Control?

Consider the following: "Fred stopped smoking pot because his older brother moved into his apartment." If the statement is true, Fred *altered* his behavior in response to his brother's behavior; but that consequence may not have been intended by the older brother, who may not even know of Fred's habit. In any case, intended or not, the brother's behavior altered Fred's behavior in a particular direction or way. Whether that "direction" made the brother's behavior social control is another matter. If the direction in which behavior is altered by the actions of others makes no difference, then the definition of social control is certain to be very broad. Hence, one may limit a conception of social control to stipulate that the actions of one or more individuals must alter the behavior of other individuals in a particular specified direction.

When it comes to the ends or consequences of social control, only three of the illustrative definitions (supra) directly bear upon the question. Berndt speaks of "processes and procedures that exert pressure on persons and groups to conform to the norms"; Cohen speaks of "tending to reduce or prevent deviance"; and Parsons speaks of "mechanisms which counteract deviant tendencies." Despite the divergent terminology, it would not be a distortion to interpret all of those phrases as stipulating that someone's behavior is social control only if it promotes conformity to norms.[24] The immediate problem with such a stipulation is not that it admits the possibility of unintentional social control; rather, that the stipulation rests on a dubious assumption: that the term norm can be defined in such a way that the definition not only is empirically applicable but also is acceptable to an

---

[23] Witness, for example, the flood of protests over the use of behavior modification techniques, psychosurgery, and electronic surveillance in the criminal justice system (Kittrie, 1971; Mitford, 1973; Shapiro, 1972, 1973). Yet the major contemporary issue has little to do with such "corrective" techniques; rather, it centers on the morality and constitutionality of capital punishment.

[24] The stipulation reintroduces the prophylactic conception of social control, and it may well be that the conception enjoys a large following because it answers three of the six major conceptual questions in such a way as to distinguish social control from control in general. What is subject to social control? Deviant behavior. Who is subject to social control? Deviants. What is the goal or consequence of social control? Counteraction of deviance. The answer to the last question

effective majority of sociologists. The reasons why that assumption is dubious are discussed in Chapter 1, and note that the problem would remain even if the definitions of Berndt, Cohen, and Parsons were construed as stipulating that social control is the deliberate prevention of deviant behavior. So we reach a depressing conclusion: No existing conceptualization or theory provides a defensible answer to any of the six central questions about social control.

(footnote continued)
distinguishes the prophylactic conception of social control from a purely ''reactive'' conception, one which equates social control with reactions to deviance'' [see Wilson's definition (supra) and Clark and Gibbs (1965)]. The purely reactive conception of social control does not avoid any of the problems in defining deviance, and in implicitly denying the relevance of goals or consequences it makes social control even more heterogenous than does the prophylactic conception.

The Final
Definition
of Social
Control

4

As indicated in the pursuit of major conceptual questions (Chapter 3), there is no basis for modifying the tentative definition of social control such that only certain kinds of human behavior are subject to social control, only a few means of social control are possible, only particular categories of individuals are subject to social control, only particular categories of individuals can exercise social control, or attempts at social control have only a limited range of goals. Hence, while the major conceptual questions serve to describe problems in defining social control, only the question pertaining to "intentionality" has been answered. However, limiting social control to the intentional manipulation of human behavior does not emphasize the social quality of social control, distinguish it from what is loosely called normal or everyday human interaction, or attribute a normative quality to social control.[1] So there are compelling reasons for expanding the tentative definition along lines that have no direct bearing on any of the major conceptual questions.

Expansion of the Tentative Definition

The subsequent *final* definition of social control is narrower than the tentative definition, which essentially equates social control with the

[1] Only the prophylactic conception of social control does those three things, and were it not for problems with the notion of deviance that conception would be accepted.

manipulation (intentional) of the behavior of others. Unlike the tentative definition, the final definition does not treat social control as though it is one thing—a unitary, homogenous pheonomenon. Rather, *social* control is described as any one of five types of control behavior.

Social control is an attempt by one or more individuals (the "first party" in either case) to manipulate the behavior of another individual or individuals (the "second party" in either case) *by or through*:

I. the first party communicating to the second party some reference to a third party, still another individual or still other individuals; *or*

II. the first party punishing, rewarding, or rectifying a third party's behavior; *or*

III. the first party manipulating a third party's behavior by communicating allegations about the second party to the third party; *or*

IV. the first party using the presumed influence of a third party on the second party's behavior, without exclusive reliance on communicating an allegation about the second party to the third party or without exclusive reliance on communicating to the second party a reference to the third party; *or*

V. the first party (1) using a third party in gathering information on the second party, or (2) the first party directing a third party to limit the behavior of the second party to certain social contexts through coercion or the threat of coercion, or (3) the first party taking any action with a view to facilitating the manipulation of the second party's behavior through a third party.

Elaboration

The final definition is ponderous, and its constituent terms are alien to other definitions of social control; hence, readers are not likely to understand it fully. At this point no effort should be made to realize a complete understanding, as the terms employed in the definition denote very abstract notions and their meaning can be best clarified by illustrations. First, however, a commentary on the general features of the definition is necessary.

External Behavior Control and Social Control

The initial (unnumbered) section of the final definition pertains to externalistic control, *of which social control is a subclass*. Externalistic control is *not* defined in terms of *specific* kinds of behavior that individuals engage in when attempting to manipulate the behavior of others (e.g. blackmail, praise, corporal punishment). Rather, externalistic control takes place whenever someone engages in *any kind* of overt behavior with the intention of manipulating someone else's behavior, that is, attempting to prevent some kind of behavior, alter behavior in some particular direction, maintain on-going behavior, or terminate someone's behavior altogether.[2] As such, the *specific* means of externalistic behavior control are seemingly infinite.

What has been said of the specific means of externalistic control applies also to social control. However, since social control is a *subclass* of externalistic control, it must be distinguished from the larger class. That distinction is made in parts I−V of the final definition, each of which delimits a *type* of social control.

The considerations introduced in parts I−V have no bearing on *specific* means of social control (e.g. corporal punishment). Any specific means may or may not be employed in a particular instance of social control, but whether or not an instance of externalistic control is social control depends (inter alia) on the number of parties taken into account by the first party (i.e. the individual or individuals who attempt to manipulate the second party's behavior).[3] As indicated in all parts of the definition, the first party takes into account *at least* two other parties, which is to say that social control involves at least three parties (including the first party), and the rationale for that feature of social control should be made explicit.

Rarely in the history of human societies has one individual attempted to manipulate the behavior of everyone else in the society through coercion or the threat of it. The rarity poses no mystery, of course, because no human being is so strong, swift, and immune to injury that he or she can succeed in such an enterprise. Nor is any individual so blessed with charisma that through purely personal appeals (persuasion, requests, pleas, argumentation) or exemplary conduct he or she can manipulate the behavior of all members of a large social unit. Lack of time, insufficient means of communication, and inadequate knowledge of members alone limit the range of effective manipulation of behavior (both number of individuals and kinds of behavior) through requests or commands. True, authority and a "chain of command" appear to eliminate constraints on the manipulation of behavior, but there are two immediate questions. First, how do individuals come to realize authority? Second, what do they do when a command is disobeyed or a request not

---

[2] At least one goal of the first party is to manipulate the *overt* behavior of the second party. One may object that some controllers aim for nothing less than an alteration of the controllee's covert behavior (e.g. attitudes, drives, motivation, perception, values). The point is recognized, and that is one reason why the kinds of control (not all necessarily social control) described in *1984* (Orwell, 1949) and *Brave New World* (Huxley, 1946) is viewed with such horror by many readers. However, even when a controller, social or otherwise, is concerned with more than the manipulation of overt behavior, he or she looks for and seeks to produce an outward sign (the controllee's overt behavior) of a change in the controllee's covert behavior (e.g. genuine reform, remorse, rebirth, etc.). Hence, the present focus on overt behavior does not preclude recognition of the possible concern on the part of controllers with manipulating covert behavior.

[3] If one conceives of "means of social control" so broadly as to encompass the use of third parties, then the present definition does answer the fifth major conceptual question in Chapter 3 (By what means is social control exercised?). Yet the definition is a far cry from the usual concern with specific means of control (e.g. imprisonment, fines, corporal punishment), and for reasons indicated later none of those specific means are *necessarily* social control as defined here.

honored? The answer to both questions is that no individual (the first party) can effectively manipulate the behavior of a large number of individuals (the second party) without "using" other individuals (the third party) by one or more of the ways described in parts I—IV of the final definition of social control. Stating the argument another way, when individuals go beyond immediate coercion, direct punishments, promises, commands, and requests, externalistic control becomes social control. Hence, some instances of social control can be described, like politics, as the struggle of the few to control the many; but the present conceptualization of social control is not limited to the political sphere or to large social units. Rather, the definition stipulates only that at least three individuals are involved in each of the five types (I—V) of social control; and their involvement must be such that one or more individuals can be characterized (in light of the definition) as the first party, another as the second party, and still another as the third party.

Although the triadic character of social control—the manipulation of the second party's behavior by the first party through a third party—distinguishes it from externalistic control in general, critics are likely to demand further justification of the distinction. They are especially likely to question the *exclusion* of proximate control, as when a gunman disables a store clerk or when a customer asks the clerk for change or when the proprietor directs a clerk to close the store at noon. As stressed at various points in this chapter, the final definition makes social control less ubiquitous and more normative than other classes of externalistic control (e.g. proximate control, self-control). However, even if critics should grant that the final definition attributes normative qualities to social control and distinguishes it from everyday interaction, they may not regard those considerations as a compelling defense of the definition. As pointed out in the Preface, the ultimate defense of *any* definition is its use in impressive theories. Steps toward presenting theories of social control (in conjunction with the present definition) are taken in Chapter 6; but it would be grossly unrealistic to reject a definition until it is employed in fully developed and widely accepted theories. Moreover, one specific rationale for the definition has been given, and a brief repetition is in order: the Caesars, Cromwells, Ghandis, Hitlers, Lincolns, Luthers, Maos, and Roosevelts of the world cannot realize their goals without engaging in social control as defined here. The point is that there are definite limits as to what can be accomplished through proximate or even sequential control (e.g. a chain of *command*). To be sure, the rationale is an argument that actually *could be* false. But it does not lack theoretical significance, especially since the definition of social control is not limited to would-be national leaders, to the political sphere, or to large social units. Stating the rationale more broadly, there are all manner of objectives in social life (the organizational sphere particularly) that can be realized only through social control as defined here.

Referential Social Control: Part I of the Definition

In all instances of referential social control the first party attempts to manipulate the second party's behavior by communicating some *reference* to a third party. Thus, as indicated in the first row of Table 4-1, should a child say to a sibling "Give me back the candy or I'll tell mother," with the idea of making the sibling return the candy, the child (first party) has attempted to manipulate the behavior of the second party (the sibling) by reference to a third party (the mother). As such, the event would be an instance of referential social control (henceforth, referential control).

Observe that in the illustrative instance it would not be a distortion to say that the child had some appreciation of what social scientists think of as *authority*. It is as though the child has said: "I can't make you return my candy, but we know someone who can." However, as the other illustrations in Table 4-1 indicate, not all instances of referential control entail what social scientists would recognize as an appeal to authority. Yet in all instances the third party is someone perceived by the first party as respected, hated, feared, esteemed, loved, or valued *by the second party*; otherwise, the first party has no basis for anticipating that the reference to the third party will have any impact on the second party's behavior.[4] An attempt at social control may fail precisely because the first party has misperceived the *normative relevance* of the third party for the second party; but successful social control requires expertise, and some people are simply better at it than others.

A reference to a third party is always something extrinsic (though crucial), meaning not simply part of the goal that the first party is attempting to realize. Consider the following excerpt from a hypothetical telephone conversation: "Ted, pick up Jim on your way over to work." In a sense the speaker has made reference to a third party (Jim), but "pick up Jim" is simply the goal of the speaker; as such it would not be referential control or, for that matter, any type of *social* control. Rather, it would be proximate (purely interpersonal) control.[5] To further appreciate the distinction, consider how this attempt at

---

[4] If the reference alludes to what the third party has done, is doing, will do, or may do, credibility is another concern of the first party; and the same is true of references to what has happened, is happening, or may happen to the third party (e.g. what someone has or will do to the third party). The truth of the reference is conceptually irrelevant; but the first party can hardly be indifferent to this question: What is the second party prepared to believe? That question makes *perceived expectations* (Chapter 1) all the more important as a normative property.

[5] Defined in general terms, proximate control is an instance where an individual manipulates the behavior of one or more other individuals without making use of a third individual or category of individuals (real or fictional). Although commands and requests are two principal means of proximate control, the range of means is seemingly infinite; and typologies of proximate control in the social and behavioral sciences are extremely primitive. For example, the notions of "pressure" and "influence" are so broad as to blur the distinction between proximate control and social control. The development of a typology of proximate control is beyond the scope of this work, but the omission is not a tacit denial of the importance of proximate control (if only because of the connection with the notion of authority and charisma).

Table 4-1. Some Illustrations of Referential Social Control[a]

Row No.	Central Point Communicated to the Second Party by the First Party	Parties			Designation of the Subtype of Referential Social Control
		First	Second	Third	
1	"Give me back the candy or I'll tell mother."	Child	Sibling	Mother	Commensalistic
2	"My enemy is Germany's enemy; always and only, the Jew." Quoted in Waite (1977:367)	Hitler	Other Germans	Jewish Germans	Disassociational
3	"Warning: The Surgeon General has determined that cigarette smoking is dangerous to your health."	Officials of a governmental agency	Smokers	Surgeon General	Authoritative
4	"Keep on producing like that and I'll ask the boss to promote you."	Supervisor	Worker	Employer	Promissorial
					(continued)

[a] In all instances of referential social control the first party attempts to manipulate the second party's behavior by making some reference to a third party.

proximate control could fail and the failure give rise to an attempt at referential control. Suppose that Ted refuses to pick up Jim and the speaker says: "If you don't do it, the boss will hit the roof." The crucial point is that the first party (the speaker) has now resorted to invoking a third party that the first party perceives as *normatively relevant* for the second party (Ted) and not just part of the goal that the first party is attempting to realize (that Ted pick up Jim). Invoking the "boss" is hardly an extreme measure; nonetheless, it illustrates the point that referential control is typically not a feature of normal or everyday interaction. Rather, social control commonly comes into being when the first party's request or command has been rejected or, stated more broadly, when the first party's evaluation and/or expectation of someone's conduct has been violated.

Returning to the illustrative case of the child engaging in referential control (row 1, Table 4-1), more than an appeal to authority has been made. The child also presumably made a judgment about something that social scientists designate as *normative qualities* of a situation. The judgment can be summarized as though the child is saying to the sibling: "You know that

Table 4-1. *(continued)*

Row No.	Central Point Communicated to the Second Party by the First Party	Parties			Designation of the Subtype of Referential Social Control
		First	Second	Third	
5	"I have taken French hostages, and I will shoot them if a German soldier is killed in this city."	Gestapo agent	French partisans	French hostages	Intimidational
6	"The President has assured me of his support."	Local politician	Electorate	Popular President	Associational
7	"Cease your political activity for the public will be told that you are an adulterer."	Legal official	Popular black dissident	Public	Degradative
8	"Your Honor, my argument is based on the Supreme Court's ruling in Furman vs. Georgia."	Attorney	Trial judge	Supreme Court Justices	Juridical

mother would view your possession of the candy as wrong." Of course, the attempt to manipulate the sibling's behavior may fail because the first party and the second party simply do not agree in their perception of the normative qualities of the situation—even though they may agree as to the implied designation of an authority.

Now consider a quite different illustrative instance of referential control, one described in row 2 of Table 4-1. No writer on 20th century German history appears to doubt that one aim of Hitler in his violent denounciation of Jews was the control of non-Jewish Germans, especially to gain their electoral and/or financial support.[6] As in the case of the previous illustration (row 1, Table 4-1) there were three parties; but in the case of Hitler's referential control, millions of individuals constituted the second party (non-Jewish Germans) and hundreds of thousands of individuals constituted the third party (Jewish Germans in particular). Unlike the child, Hitler was not threatening the intervention of the third party, nor did he appeal to an authority. For that matter, a would-be dictator is playing a dangerous game in recognizing a higher authority, especially an identifiable, living person. Yet, like the child, Hitler evidently assessed the normative qualities of a situation, in his case

[6] See Allen (1965), Bullock (1962), Grunberger (1971), and Waite (1977).

Germany in the 1920s and 1930s.[7] One of those qualities was an intense negative evaluation of Jews by non-Jewish Germans; viewed in that light, Hitler simply adopted a Machiavellian principle: To control individuals, attack their enemies or praise their friends. Since there are several principles of social control that could be aptly characterized as Machiavellian, a more distinctive label for Hitler's "Jew-baiting" is *disassociational* (a subtype of referential control). By contrast, the child's referential control (row 1, Table 4-1) was *commensalistic*, with that label suggesting "mutual respect for at least one particular authority."

The subtypes of referential control that one chooses to recognize is a matter of theoretical or research interests and, above all, one's *guess* as to their relative importance. Nonetheless, the illustrations in Table 4-1 may suggest a much more limited range of behavior than is actually delimited by part I of the final definition of social control. Accordingly, with a view to denying that suggestion, four points should be made.[8] First, the subtypes of referential control in Table 4-1 by no means exhaust the possibilities (which are seemingly infinite); hence, no particular significance should be attached to these subtypes, nor to the labels chosen to identify them. Second, the perception or overt behavior of the third party is in no sense a criterion of referential control; indeed, the third party may never be aware that reference has been made to him or her.[9] Third, the attitude of the first party toward the third or second party is irrelevant (e.g. Hitler's "Jew-baiting" would have been referential control even if he had really admired Jews and held non-Jews in contempt), and the *ultimate* goal or goals sought by the first party in attempting to manipulate the second party's behavior is not relevant *conceptually* (e.g. Hitler's *ultimate* goal beyond increasing electoral or financial

---

[7] In one passage after another of *Mein Kampf*, Hitler unwittingly acknowledges the social origins of his antisemitism. Like anyone else, Hitler learned it, and it appears that he may have learned how to use Jews in social control from Austrian politicians. If Hitler contributed anything novel to German culture other than genocide, it was to the pathological fear of communism; and he exploited that fear by the frequent use of "Marxists" as a third party in referential control. The general point is that it would be naive to dismiss Hitler's Jew-baiting or rabid anticommunism as mere ranting (i.e. nothing more than expressive behavior). Unfortunately, he was an artist at referential control.

[8] For the most part, these points apply also to other types of social control described subsequently.

[9] The point is best illustrated by instances where the third party is deceased. Thus, in a suit filed by the American Civil Liberties Union the claim was made that the F.B.I. not only failed to warn Mrs. Viola Liuzzo, a civil rights worker murdered in Alabama in 1965, that her life was in danger but also waged a slander campaign against her to aid in the "cover-up." If the accusation is valid, then the F.B.I. agents (as the first party) sought to dampen protests of influential persons and/or the public at large (the second party in any case) by making slanderous reference to the deceased Mrs. Liuzzo (the third party). Such defamatory referential control is especially likely when legal officials seek to justify their dubious actions against someone; they attempt this by making it appear that the object of the action "deserved it." For a brief account of the suit, see the July 6, 1979 edition of *The Tennessean* (Nashville), p. 5.

support of the Nazi party is not relevant in characterizing his Jew-baiting as referential control). And, fourth, the third party may be a particular individual, a definite and finite category of individuals (e.g. Carter's cabinet officials), a definite but seemingly infinite category of individuals (e.g. blacks, whites, police officers), an indefinite but seemingly finite category of individuals (e.g. all Americans who oppose legalization of abortion), or an indefinite and seemingly infinite category (e.g. "communists").

Of the four points just made, the last one is the most complicated. The distinction between definite and indefinite or between finite and infinite is not crucial for conceptual purposes. While the illustrations in Table 4-1 suffice to indicate how the third party may be something more than one particular individual, they do not indicate how that may be the case for the first party and/or the second party. Consider a war party attempting to provoke the defenders of a fortified village to leave the fortification and attack, thereby surrendering an advantage. The members of the war party may in concert taunt the defenders, shouting that they are "like children." As such, the war party as a whole can be rightly spoken of as the first party, all defenders of the village as the second party, and "children" as the third party. Then consider an instance where, in order to manipulate the voting behavior of stockholders (second party), a corporation president orders a vice-president to direct the supervisor of the public relations division to prepare a press release that announces the severance of economic relations between the corporation and the Republic of South Africa (third party). If all three of those individuals are privy to the goal of that press release, they are among the first party in that attempt at referential control; and there is a rationale for considering them so even if only the president is aware of the goal. Given the president's proximate and sequential control (stemming from authority) of the other two individuals, the two and the president form what is, sociologically speaking, a real unit.

When reference is made to a category of individuals as the third party, the first party and/or the second party may be a member of the third category, as when a platoon officer admonishes novices before a battle: "If you lay back when the attack starts, just forget about the men in this outfit treating you with any respect." Then note that the third party may actually comprise two or more distinct categories of individuals, as when a candidate for an office says to a prospective supporter: "My opponents have been bribed time and again by the oil companies." A reference may allude to what others have done, are doing, or may do *to, for,* or *with* the third party; but in such a case the others (the "oil companies" in the illustration) may appear to be the third party along with someone else (the candidate's opponents in the illustration) or a distinct fourth party. For that reason, social control has been described as involving *at least three parties*. However, for purposes of classifying control behavior, all individuals or categories of individuals referred to by the first party can be taken as the third party, even though distinctions among them may loom large in the first party's perception and even though such distinctions may be recognized for one reason or another in particular studies of social control.

Although the illustrations in Table 4-1 suggest that reference to a third party is explicit and verbal, that need not be the case.[10] A nonverbal and implicit reference is well illustrated by the discovery of a Belgian administrative officer in the Congo (Hallett, 1968:15) that the lens of glasses worn by his native (black) assistant were simply clear glass. On being asked by the officer, "Do things really look different to you when you put them on?," the assistant replied, "No, monsieur. I look different. These *bashenzi*—those ignorant natives—this way they have more respect for me." It appears obvious that the wearing of glasses was intended to prompt other blacks to identify the wearer with Europeans and thereby make them more compliant. Hence, in this "associational" subtype of referential control, the assistant was the first party, the Europeans the third party, and all other blacks in the region were the second party.

Of all of the parties involved in social control (whether referential or any of the other types), the sheer variety of instances is much greater as regards the identity or "nature" of the third party. The point is not just that the third party may be an indefinite and infinite category of individuals (e.g. "no decent person would act like you have"); additionally, the third party may be deceased ("What would your mother think about you if she were alive?") or a supernatural being (a god, a spirit, etc.).[11] While the diversity of the third

---

[10] The present conceptualization calls for a close integration of sociolinguistics and social control as fields of study, and a step in that direction has been taken by Cook-Gumperz (1973). Note also that the conceptualization can be used in the study of "impression management" (Goffman, 1959, 1961b). Referential control is a strategic tactic in impression management, because the would-be "manager" commonly communicates this message to his audience: I am a member of such-and-such *category* of individuals. Consider one of Goffman's observations (1959:4): "Since a girl's dormitory mates will glean evidence of her popularity from the calls she receives on the phone, we can suspect that some girls will arrange for calls to be made. . . ." (Goffman subsequently documents such instances.) When a girl communicates an identification with the category "popular girl," she makes reference to a third party. Such instances would be identificational referential control, even though both the identity of the second party and the exact goal of the first party may not be obvious.

[11] While the first party could literally invent a third party (i.e. make reference to a fictional individual or category of individuals), such an invention is not likely to be relevant for the second party. However, the first party may make reference to a category of individuals without having any particular individual in mind. Consider Rock's observation (1973:23) on a tactic of creditors in England: "One mail order firm invented a debt-collector because the word 'debt collector' flourishes a threat." Granted the devious quality of the threat, debtors are likely to believe that "debt collectors" do exist. Similarly, since most individuals are inclined to believe that there are mentally ill people, both of the following statements could be referential control: "He is mentally ill, and if you give him money it will be wasted in a week." "You know that you are mentally ill, and there is no telling what will happen to you if you leave me." The general point is that any term which denotes a type of condition or a type of behavior implies a reference to a category of individuals—vague and indefinite though it may be.

party is not peculiar to referential control, it is most conspicuous for that type, the simple reason being that the first party need not assume the third party will take any action or even actually exist.

Despite the enormous range of behavior delimited by the conceptualization, referential control hardly constitutes normal or everyday interaction. Thus, in hailing a cab, inviting a friend over to dinner, ordering an employee to perform some task, or requesting a pack of cigarettes in a store, no reference is made to a third party, the simple reason being that the related expectations or evaluations of conduct are seldom violated. Yet it should be obvious that virtually anyone can engage in referential control; that virtually anyone can be the second or third party; that reference can be made to a third party in all manner of ways; and that the variety of goals that may be sought through referential control defies description.

Vicarious Social Control: Part II of the Definition

In all instances of vicarious social control the first party attempts to manipulate the second party's behavior by punishing or rewarding a third party, or rectifying the third party's behavior. Suppose that the third party has committed some type of act, and the first party seeks to discourage the second party from also committing that act. To that end the first party may take some action toward the third party on the presumption that the second party will perceive the action as punitive and hence a threat.

Whatever its empirical validity, the deterrence doctrine is a theory of vicarious social control. The doctrine makes two claims: that a severe punishment of an individual convicted of a crime will deter that individual from repeating the offense; and that the publicization of such a punishment will deter *others* from committing the type of crime in question. The second claim suggests a basis for identifying legal punishments as social control. Insofar as legal punishments are intended to deter potential offenders (not just potential repeaters) there are three parties involved—those who prescribe or administer punishments (the first party), the object of an actual punishment (the third party), and all others potentially subject to such punishment (the second party). Advocates of the deterrence doctrine do not presume that *general* deterrence is realized by a chain of command (i.e. sequential control) in which the third party (the individual who has been punished) subsequently manipulates the behavior of the second party by ordering or admonishing the second party to refrain from the type of crime in question. If all instances of manipulation of behavior through a chain of command (which necessarily involves three or more individuals) were taken to be social control, then much of normal or everyday interaction in corporations or military units would qualify.

It is not the infliction of pain that makes the administration of legal punishments social control. If a gunman should pistol-whip a clerk to force the bartender to open a safe, the act is punitive and an attempted manipulation of behavior; but no one is likely to argue that such an act is therefore social control. Yet it would be dubious to argue that the gunman's behavior was not social control because it violated a norm, a criminal law in particular. Any such *criterion* of social control would ignore all of the problems and issues in defining norms (assumptions about normative consensus in particular), or it would simply leave the determination of social control to those who enact criminal laws. In particular, the criterion would exclude the acts of terrorists, but some of their acts are vicarious control. Unlike the typical offender, terrorists may rob banks that are known for providing financial support of a political regime, thereby warning owners of other banks of the consequences of supporting the regime.

While the actual legal punishment of individuals is social control if undertaken to promote general deterrence, one can argue, as Durkhiem (1949) did, that in some legal systems (especially those of ancient societies) the "purpose" of criminal law is retribution, not deterrence. Those who make that argument have yet to present evidence that no legislator or sovereign in such legal systems contemplated deterrence as a rationale for the prescription of legal punishments.[12] Moreover, there is a basis for questioning even the existence of a *purely* retributive criminal justice system, one in which each legal punishment is prescribed or administered as an *end in itself* (i.e. criminals are punished only because they deserve it). If a legislator or sovereign senses that the public or a particular social division, such as a class or caste, demands a harsh punishment for a particular type of crime, then prescribing such a punishment is hardly an end in itself. Advocates of the retributive doctrine [see critiques in Bedau (1978) and Grupp (1971)] argue that a punishment should be prescribed as an end itself. They make that argument not only to oppose utilitarianism (the deterrence doctrine in particular) but also because they appear reluctant, given their concern with justice, to equate punishments with vengeance. Perhaps legal punishments should be prescribed as ends rather than as means, but that is not to grant that legislators or other sovereigns prescribe penalties without regard to deterrence. Even the notion of vengeance itself suggests a utilitarian consideration, which is to say that legislators may actually prescribe penalties with a view to satisfying some "audience" (e.g. an electorate), and that such action is manipulative. The general point is that the prescription or administration of legal punishments may reflect no concern whatever for "just deserts"; rather, it may reflect only a keen sensitivity to public opinion—the views of the powerful in particular—and a determination to maintain or enlarge political

---

[12] For that matter, deterrence has been the rationale for penal law in agrarian or feudal societies. Deterrence was the dominant rationale for legal punishment at various times in Imperial China, and the debates of Chinese scholars and elites over penal policy are ample evidence of their sensitivity to deterrence (Bodde and Morris, 1967).

support. In such a case, the punished individuals are the third party, and the second party is a constituency or a particular interest group. Legal punishments may also be prescribed and/or administered with a view to preventing or reducing private vengeance of crimes; and the same may be said of any attempt by a legal official to *rectify* the behavior of a defendant in a civil case (e.g. to compensate the complainant). However, the purpose of such rectification is not necessarily limited to "doing justice." An additional or perhaps distinct alternative purpose may be simply to terminate the complaints of the plaintiff or other actions by the plaintiff to realize satisfaction. As such, the first party (a judge or other legal official) manipulates the behavior of the second party (the complainant) by rectifying the behavior of the third party (punishing the defendant or accused).

While vicarious control includes legal punishments, it is by no means limited to the legal sphere. Many a weary mother knows all too well that a child may be disciplined to deter the child's siblings or to *placate* them.[13] Moreover, just as an individual may be punished with a view to deterring or placating others, so may they be rewarded with a view to prompting others to emulate their conduct. Yet the idea is not that social control is little more than punishments or rewards. Neither term—punishment or reward—enters into the definition of referential control, and not all instances of punishments or rewards are social control. When pistol-whipping a clerk in a store, the typical gunman is engaged in proximate control, not social control, even though the act is clearly punitive. Similarly, if a woman rewards a man with sexual favors for his lavish gifts, it is not likely to be social control.

Numerous instances of normal or everyday interaction are not vicarious control, some examples being hailing a bus, ordering a meal in a restaurant, and making a signal for a left turn. It is particularly important to recognize the distinction between vicarious control and the manipulation of behavior through a chain of command, for a chain of command may be part of normal, everyday interaction in some types of social units. When X orders Y to order Z, X attempts to manipulate Z's behavior by manipulating Y's behavior; X's presumption is that Y will in turn manipulate Z's behavior through an order. No such presumption is entailed in X's firing Y with a view to maintaining discipline over Z or other subordinates (e.g. employees) or with a view to maintaining the support of W (a still higher official in the organization). The point is not just that commands may be a part of everyday interaction in certain types of social units (e.g. a corporation or infantry regiment), or that commands are neither punishments nor rewards. There is the additional idea that social control commonly occurs after a command has been disobeyed.

---

[13] Consider this account of Anthony Grey (1970:85) of his interrogation by Chinese officials (a Mr. Chi and Chi's superior) prior to Grey's prolonged detainment in his Peking house. "Mr. Chi was glaring at me and emphasizing his words vehemently in a fashion calculated to convey revolutionary antagonism towards the class enemy—a show, I reflected later, designed as much to impress his [Chi's] superior of his correct political orientation as to impress me."

Commands are attempts at externalistic control, but social control is special in that it may be used to *reinforce* commands. While numerous writers have referred to norms as social control, the identification is dubious. Insofar as norms actually exist, social control may take the form of *enforcing* them.

Those who engage in vicarious control may be no less sensitive to normative qualities of situations than those who engage in referential control. The idea of punishing some individuals with a view to manipulating the behavior of *other* individuals entails some belief as to what those other individuals regard as desirable, undesirable, pleasant, painful, good, or bad. Further, as for rectifying the behavior of a third party with a view to manipulating the behavior of a second party, there is always this question: What will it take to "satisfy" the second party? Yet the first party may not always make the correct assessment of the normative qualities of the situation; indeed, social control may fail because the first party's assessment was incorrect.

The kinds of vicarious control designated in Table 4-2 (rows 1 and 3) as "deterrent" and "advancive" are important in that punishments and rewards may well be the principal tactics of control (social or otherwise). However, it is essential to recognize that vicarious social control is not limited to the promotion of deterrence or the promotion of emulation (as in row 3 of Table 4-2). What is designated here as "hypocritical" referential control (row 2, Table 4-2) is distinct from deterrent or advancive control, and recognition of hypocritical control is contrary to the image of social control conveyed by the literature prior to the 1960s. Several books and articles in that literature suggest that social control agents somehow automatically enforce "society's norms" (thereby implying normative consensus) in an impersonal, disinterested manner. That image ignores more than instances where social control agents (i.e. the first party) enforce the evaluations of conduct of a small but powerful minority (e.g. legislators, a dominant economic class). It also ignores instances where social control agents act in that capacity to further their own personal well-being or interests, as when a judge issues an injunction to terminate a strike but does so to gain electoral support. However, there is a normative quality even in hypocritical control, because accurate knowledge as to what the second party (e.g. the electorate) desires in the way of reactions to the third party (e.g. homosexual school teachers) is a basis for manipulating the second party.[14] In acting consistent with the perceived

---

[14] Grunberger's account (1971:53) of an attempt by the Nazis to appear more egalitarian and thereby gain support from the lower class and *genuine* socialists: "On one occasion Goebbels . . . stage-managed the arrest of a director of the *Reichsbank* who had made use of a perfectly valid interpretation of the law to evict a difficult tenant from a house he owned. While the arrest of this 'plutocrat' was given maximum publicity, his subsequent release remained a non-event as far as the public was concerned." The illustration suggests a point that is too cumbersome to be recognized in the definition of vicarious social control. Rather than actually punish or reward the third party, the first party may only create that impression. Indeed, general deterrence might be furthered by media reports of punishments of individuals who (though perhaps named) never existed. That is one reason why advocates of the retributive doctrine in criminal justice have an abiding distrust of the deterrence doctrine—it is conducive to dubious practices.

Table 4-2. Some Illustrations of Vicarious Social Control[a]

Row No.	Situation, Action of First Party, and Rationale or Expectation of First Party	Parties			Designation of the Subtype of Vicarious Social Control
		First	Second	Third	
1	A judge sentences a convicted felon to prison in the belief that others will be deterred.	Judge	Others	Felon	Deterrent
2	A judge sentences a person to the maximum sentence for posession of marijuana, in anticipation of gaining electoral support.	Judge	Electorate	Person	Hypocritical
3	An employee makes far more sales in a year than do others; and the employer gives the employee a two-week vacation, presuming that other employees will increase their sales efforts. efforts.	Employer	Other employees	Employee	Advancive
4	A man of clan X has allegedly raped a woman of clan Y. The head of clan X executes the man to prevent vengeance by clan Y.	Head of clan X	Clan Y members	Alleged rapist	Placative

[a] In all instances of vicarious social control the first party attempts to manipulate the second party's behavior by punishing or rewarding a third party, or rectifying the third party's behavior.

desires and expectations of the second party, the first party seeks to increase the probability that the second party will support or at least heed the admonitions of the first party.

Allegative Social Control: Part III of the Definition

In all instances of allegative social control, the first party attempts to manipulate the second party's behavior by communicating allegations about the second party to a third party. As the first step toward clarification, the distinction between allegative and vicarious control warrants careful consideration.

Previous reference to the rectification of behavior may bring to mind the notion of tort law; but tort law becomes operative only when someone makes an *allegation* about the behavior of someone else. In making that allegation the plaintiff engages in social control as the first party, and the defendant is the second party. The plaintiff attempts to manipulate the behavior of the defendant (e.g. payment of damages) by manipulating the behavior of legal officials, such as a judge (the third party). Observe that the manipulation of a legal official's behavior is attempted by making allegations about the second party in the presence of the official. However, the situation is different from a chain of command in a hierarchical organization, as when X orders Y to order Z. In a tort action the first party (the plaintiff) has no basis to order the third party (a judge) to manipulate the behavior of the second party (the defendant).

Tort actions are not the only instances of allegative control, and punishment is not the distinguishing feature of that type of control.[15] With a view to manipulating the behavior of the second party, the first party may initially manipulate the third party's behavior in such a way that the third party bestows a reward on the second party (perhaps merely praises the second party). But how can the first party realize the reward or punishment of the second party by the third party if the first party cannot command or request that action? The first party does so by bringing allegations about the second party to the attention of the third party; and those allegations may be either negative (e.g. an expressed or implied condemnation) or positive (e.g. a laudatory commendation), depending on the end sought by the first party.

Allegative control is ordinarily more normative than other types of social control. To realize success, the first party must appeal to the perceived normative standards of the third party, for what the third party will do depends not just on the credibility of the allegation about the second party but also on

---

[15] A "tort action" does not reduce to one and only one type of social control. In the same action, the plaintiff engages in allegative control, while the judge engages in vicarious control (with a view to placating the plaintiff and/or deterring others from the conduct attributed to the defendant).

how the third party evaluates the alleged behavior of the second party—
positively, negatively, or indifferently. Equally important, while the first
party may perceive the third party as having authority over the second party,[16]
the third party may perceive his or her authority differently. Indeed, the
outcome of allegative control may well depend on how all of the parties
perceive the authority of the third party, and the notion of authority is a
normative notion.

Even though allegative control is especially conspicuous in the legal
sphere, everyday human interaction is not free of allegations by one party to
another about still another party (e.g. gossip). However, when such allegations are made in the context of everyday interaction, those making them may
not anticipate any particular consequence. In any case, allegative control
apparently takes place in some types of social units more than in others.
Because children in the same family are rarely of the same age and strength,
the younger and/or weaker commonly resort to allegative control (with a
parent as third party), especially when referential control has failed. Allegative control is also fairly common in large, highly organized social units (e.g.
corporations, universities, military units). In such social units subordinates at
the middle level (e.g. supervisors, department heads) often resort to allegative
control because their authority is stringently limited, especially when it comes
to administering severe negative sanctions and dispensing major rewards.
Insofar as subordinates at the middle level manipulate the behavior of
subordinates at the lower level through *recommendations* of promotion or
salary changes, those recommendations entail allegations (positive or negative) made to superordinates (e.g. owner, employer), who are the third party.

Although allegative control may appear simpler than vicarious control, the
sheer variety of allegative control defies description, and Table 4-3 is only
suggestive. For that matter, no particular significance should be attached to
the labels employed in that table (or any of the previous tables) to denote
particular subtypes of control. Again, the subtypes of social control (allegative or otherwise) that one chooses to recognize are a matter of theoretical or
research interests; hence, a definition of the subtypes is not essential.

There is a possibility that allegative control will be confused with
referential control. When the first party brings an allegation about the second
party to the attention of a third party, the allegation itself entails *reference* to
the second party. However, in the case of referential control the first party
communicates *nothing* to the third party; hence, the first party's manipulation

---

[16] The first party assumes that the third party can and will manipulate the second party's
behavior either through proximate control (e.g. a command or request), sequential control, or
some type of social control. Exactly what the first party expects the third party to do (e.g. punish
the second party, issue an order to the second party, reward the second party) is conceptually
irrelevant. For that matter, the third party need not perceive his or her action as "manipulative,"
let alone know of the first party's machinations.

Table 4-3. Some Illustrations of Allegative Social Control[a]

| Row No. | Central Point of the Allegation Made by First Party to Third Party | Parties | | | Designation of the Subtype of Allegative Social Control |
		First	Second	Third	
1	"Mother, John took my candy."	Child	Sibling	Mother	Appellative
2	"She attempted suicide."	Father	Daughter	Psychiatrist	Ameliorative
3	"This is the third day in a row that he has missed work."	Supervisor	Worker	Employer	Hierarchical
4	"King is under the influence of communists."	F.B.I. official	Martin Luther King	One of King's supporters	Stigmatizing
5	"A robbery is taking place across the street."	Bystander	Unidentified individual	Police	Universalistic
6	"The defendant was careless when performing surgery on me."	Plaintiff	Defendant	Judge	Adversarial
7	"Senators, I urge passage of this bill requiring the registration of everyone who opposes U.S. involvement in the Vietnam war, because they should be held responsible for their careless charges."	"Expert" on subversion	War protestors	Senators	Censorial

[a] In all instances of allegative social control the first party makes allegations known to a third party about the second party, on the presumption that the third party will then attempt to manipulate the second party's behavior.

of the second party's behavior is not predicated on the assumption that the third party will "do something."[17] By contrast, in the case of allegative control, the first party attempts two or more manipulations of behavior in a

[17] Of course, the classification of a particular event as to type of social control (or whether social control at all) may be made difficult by the lack of information in an account of that event. To illustrate, Pospisil (1958:21) gives an account of an exotic practice among the Kapauku Papuans—a mourner burying a deceased relative (head above the ground) facing the home of someone who has purportedly wronged the mourner, and admonishing the spirit of the deceased

sequence, the first (manipulation of the third party's behavior) is direct by the allegation itself and the second (the manipulation of the second party's behavior) is indirect. That is the case because when the first party communicates allegations about the second party to the third party, it is done in the expectation or hope that the third party will *do something*, thereby manipulating the second party's behavior.[18] The allegation itself is thus an attempted direct manipulation of behavior (of the third party); but the first party's expectation or hope is that the third party will respond to the allegation by doing something that alters the behavior of the second party, which is to say that the first party attempts to manipulate the second party's behavior indirectly.

The distinction between allegative and referential control is illustrated by a child's statement: "Mother, John took my candy away from me." If the child intended to manipulate *only* the mother's behavior, the type of social control would be referential, for a reference is made to another party (John would be the third party and the mother the second party). However, insofar as the child has some hope that the mother will in turn manipulate John's behavior forcing him to relinquish the candy, it is allegative control, with John as the second party and the mother as the third party. So, while in allegative control there is always some reference to the second party, the party referred to is the ultimate object of the anticipated sequence of manipulations of behavior. Specifically, in referential control the party referred to is *not* the object of the attempted manipulation of behavior. (Again, in the case of referential control nothing need be communicated, directly or indirectly, to the third party).

Returning to the illustration, it may be that the child resorted to allegative

---

(footnote continued)

to revenge that wrong. If the mourner truly believes that there is a spirit and one that will respond to the admonition, it would be allegative social control (albeit perhaps unsuccessful). However, in the one case described by Pospisil, the loud voice of the mourner and the proximity of the accused could be significant. If the mourner perceived the accused as believing in a vengeful spirit and inclined to rectify the wrong to placate the spirit, then the mourner's action would be referential control (or, perhaps, both allegative and referential control). Another possibility is that the mourner announced the accused's misdeeds in the hope that some living third party (another villager) would take action against the accused; if so, it would be allegative social control. Still another possibility is that the mourner was saying to the accused "Look what others will think of you," in which case it would be referential social control. Unfortunately, as is so often the case in anthropological reports, not enough information is given to decide among the alternatives. It is not trivial that such exotic behavior can be described as "allegative and/or referential control," meaning that it can be "placed" in the conceptual scheme.

[18] To help understand the distinction, reconsider the accusation by the American Civil Liberties Union made against the F.B.I. in connection with Mrs. Viola Liuzzo (see footnote 9). If the F.B.I. did engage in a slander campaign, it entailed allegations about Mrs. Liuzzo; but the F.B.I. agents would have been concerned with manipulating the behavior of the public (to stave off or dampen protests of the murder), not the behavior of Mrs. Liuzzo (perhaps not even if she had survived the shooting). If the accusation of the American Civil Liberties Union about the F.B.I. is valid, the F.B.I. agents engaged in referential control rather than allegative control in launching the slander campaign. The accusation itself is allegative social control on the part of the American Civil Liberties Union representatives, with the F.B.I. as the second party and judges or jurors as the third party.

control after failing at referential control, having said to John: "Give me back the candy or I'll tell mother."[19] That statement may be construed as a threat of allegative control, but in itself the statement is not an attempted manipulation of the mother's behavior. Indeed, a threat to manipulate behavior is not even an essential feature of referential control. The child could have said: "You know that mother said that taking things away from me is wrong." Of course, it could be argued that the ultimate goal of all such statements would be the same and hence the referential-allegative distinction is irrelevant; but such an argument would ignore the real possibility that only one of the two types of social control, allegative or referential, may be effective in certain situations.

Allegative certain control is not likely to be confused with vicarious control, because the latter does not *necessarily* entail any allegations. Nonetheless, allegations are not completely alien to vicarious control. The essence of vicarious control is that the first party does something to the third party on the presumption that the "something" will have an impact on the behavior of the second party. That something may be an allegation about the behavior of the third party, aimed to intimidate the second party. The second party may be intimidated (as expected by the first party) for fear that the first party will make a similar allegation about him or her, if he or she does not recant, remain silent, or otherwise placate the first party. Such a case would be an instance of the deterrent subtype of vicarious social control. When vicarious control entails allegations, they are made about the third party on the presumption that the second party will fear becoming the object of a similar allegation and modify his or her behavior to avoid that allegation. By contrast, in all instances of allegative control some assertions about the second party are made known to the third party on the presumption that the third party will do *something* to the second party.

---

[19] Such a situation would pose no problem in attempting to count the frequency of instances of the various types of social control in some social unit, whether through direct observations or through soliciting accounts of members of the social unit about past events (e.g. disputes). The events in question (the child first attempting referential control and then resorting to allegative control) would be symbolized as "referential→allegative." For purposes of a frequency count, one instance of referential control and one instance of allegative control would be recorded; but that symbolization would be a more accurate representation of what took place. Of course, it could be that a child attempts both types of social control simultaneously, as when he or she says to the mother, within earshot of the brother: "Mother, John took my candy." If the circumstances were such as to justify inferring both types of social control simultaneously, then it should be recorded as "allegative-referential control." Should the circumstances justify only the inference of one or the other but not both, the symbolization could be "allegative/referential"; and should the circumstances justify the inference of one or the other and possibly both, then it could be symbolized as "allegative and/or referential control." The point is that in gathering data on the frequency of the various types of social control, there are bound to be events that cannot be typified with confidence. Such cases can be recorded as indicated, and in the frequency count each ambiguous identification (e.g. allegative/referential) would be counted as one-half or .5 rather than one or 1.0 to the total frequency of each type. Similarly, in the "and/or" situation, each of the two possible types would be counted as .67 rather than 1.0. What has been said of multiple or ambiguous identifications of referential and allegative control applies to any combinations of types, even combinations of more than two types.

Modulative Social Control: Part IV of the Definition

In all instances of modulative social control the first party attempts to manipulate the behavior of the second party by using the presumed influence of a third party on the second party's behavior. Modulative control differs from allegative control in that the second party does not rely exclusively (if at all) on allegations about the second party to the third party. It differs from referential control in that the first party does not rely exclusively (if at all) on a reference to the third party.

The present conceptualization of social control depicts the first party as acting on presumptions that are consistent with some general sociological principles, even though the first party may be only dimly aware of those principles. As previously pointed out, when engaging in referential, vicarious, or allegative control, the first party tacitly subscribes to normative determinism. When it comes to modulative control, the presumptions of the first party entail the notions of power, authority, and charisma, all of which reduce to the idea that some individuals are distinguished by their perceived influence over others. In undertaking *modulative* control, the first party recognizes that idea and attempts to manipulate the second party's behavior by using the presumed influence of the third party over the second party's behavior.

As suggested by the illustrations in Table 4-4, modulative control can take place in all manner of ways;[20] however, the illustrations only suggest a distinction which should be made explicit. In all instances the first party attempts to use the *perceived* influence of the third party; but such use may take the form of either an endeavor to increase that influence (e.g. row 3, Table 4-4) or an endeavor to decrease it (e.g. row 1, Table 4-4),[21] as well as instances where the first party assumes that the third party's influence need not be increased or decreased. Moreover, although not suggested by the illustrations

---

[20]The illustrations are misleading in that they suggest that the third party is always a particular individual or a definite, identifiable, and finite category of individuals. Consider an unusual and widely publicized action by the Lakehead Board of Education, Thunder Bay, Ontario, Canada. The Board let it be known that they would give the student body any money left from an annual fund of $35,000 used to repair damages from vandals, and the students could use the remaining money for any *collective* enterprise (e.g. an organized trip, financing a dance). Although the Board's actions were not described in sufficient detail [see *The Tennessean* (Nashville), June 16, 1979, p. 8], it appears that the Board's strategy was to use peer influence, meaning that nonvandals would be prompted to check the behavior of vandals. If so, the Board engaged in modulative control.

[21] As still another tactic for decreasing influence, Goffman observes (1959:215): ". . . filling station managers used to be shifted periodically from one station to another to prevent the formation of strong personal ties with particular clients. It was found that when such ties were allowed to form, the manager sometimes placed the interests of a friend who needed credit before the interests of the social establishment." Modulative control was also a common practice in the South during the period of slavery, notably in the passage of laws that limited the spatial movement of slaves and prescribed their illiteracy, one purpose being to reduce the influence of "outside agitators" (Genovese, 1974; Stampp, 1967).

Table 4-4. Some Illustrations of Modulative Social Control[a]

Row No.	Brief Description of Some Individual's Activities and Related Goals	Parties			Designation of the Subtype of Modulative Social Control
		First	Second	Third	
1	The director of a city's youth services department arranges for a popular professional athlete to visit city recreational facilities, on the presumption that juveniles will be prompted to participate more in organized sports and less in delinquent activities.	Director	Juveniles	Athlete	Identificational
2	A judge orders the detention of a juvenile on the presumption that the juvenile's siblings and friends will be further removed from the "bad" influence of the juvenile and hence less likely to engage in delinquency.	Judge	Other juveniles	Juvenile	Isolative
3	An advertising agent pays a movie star to endorse some product in a television commercial; the presumption is that the commercial will increase sales of that product.	Agent	Consumers	Movie star	Testificatory

(continued)

Table 4-4. (continued)

Row No.	Brief Description of Some Individual's Activities and Related Goals	Parties			Designation of the Subtype of Modulative Social Control
		First	Second	Third	
4	A dictator orders the deportation of a Marxist writer and lecturer, assuming that it will reduce the propensity of workers to strike.	Dictator	Workers	Writer	Insulative
5	An incumbent prevails upon a bishop to publicly characterize an opposing candidate as immoral.	Incumbent	Voters	Bishop	Denigrative

[a] In all instances of modulative social control the first party attempts to manipulate the second party's behavior by using the presumed influence of the third party on the second party's behavior, without exclusive reliance on communicating an allegation about the second party to the third party or making reference to the third party in communicating with the second party.

in Table 4-4, a first party may literally attempt to create an influential person with a view to subsequent use of that influence.

As in other types of social control, in the case of modulative control the first party does not attempt to manipulate the second party's behavior by directing commands to the second party.[22] The point is not just that the manipulation of behavior through commands is part of everyday interaction in some social units (e.g. infantry regiments, corporations). No less important, social control commonly comes into being when commands fail, and in that sense social control is a special kind of externalistic control.

Unlike the control exercised in a chain of command (e.g. employer−supervisor−worker), modulative control does not entail commands by the first party to the third party *and* commands by the third party to the second party. Yet that stipulation does not preclude commands by the first party to the third party *or* commands by the third party to the second party (but

[22] Modulative control may be only one type of control in a sequence. Thus, creditors (first party) may initially request payment from a debtor (proximate control), threaten the intervention of a "debt collector" (referential control), hire a lawyer to warn the debtor (modulative control), and finally bring suit in court (allegative control) as a last resort [see Rock (1973) for a wealth of illustrative observations on tactics in debt collection]. Whether there is a distinctive sequence of types of control in certain spheres of human activity (e.g. debt collection, socialization of children) is one of many questions that are beyond the scope of this work.

not both command sequences) in modulative control. Indeed, when the first party attempts to use the influence of the third party, the attempt may be based on the presumption that the third party has authority over the second party, which is to say that the third party can command the second party to do certain things and that such commands will be obeyed. So if two male employers are friends, one may call the other and say: "Look, my car will not start; so send that fellow who works for you, Fred's his name, over to fix it for me." The employer making the *request* has recognized that he does not have the authority to order Fred or a personal relationship with him that would justify asking a favor, but he presumes that he can manipulate the behavior of someone who does have that authority. Observe, however, that the first party does not command the third party (the other employer) to command the second party (Fred).

Here is another illustration of modulative control, one in which the first party in effect commands the third party to manipulate the second party's behavior. Suppose that with a view to preventing a union shop an employer commands a popular, hence influential, worker to speak among other workers against voting for unionization. The control is not sequential (i.e. chain-of-command), for the employer does not presume that the popular worker has the *authority* to command other workers as to voting.

The most pressing problem is the possibility that modulative control will be confused with allegative or referential control. Reconsider the case of the employer engaging in modulative control through a request to a friend, another employer. The request entailed *reference* to another individual, Fred; but the ultimate goal of the first party in making the request of the other employer, the third party, was to manipulate the behavior of Fred, the second party. Hence, it would not be referential control, because reference is made to the *second* party, not the third party (insofar as social control takes the form of a process or sequence of manipulations, the last party is the second party). Nor would it be allegative control, the reason being that no allegation is made about the behavior of the second party (Fred), let alone so as to elicit approval or disapproval of that behavior by the third party (Fred's employer) and a corresponding reaction by the third party (which is essential for allegative control).

Now reconsider the other illustration, in which an employer commands a popular worker to speak among other workers against voting for unionization.[23] Reference is made to the other workers, but they are the *second party* in this attempt at social control; and the employer may not even communicate with the other workers. To attempt referential control of the other workers, the employer could speak to the other workers and make reference to the popular worker in question (e.g. "Jim has told me that he is opposed to unioniza-

---

[23] The employer's actions would have been no less modulative control had he or she paid or requested the popular worker to speak against unionization.

tion.''), but that is not the case in this instance. Then consider that in commanding the popular worker the employer makes no allegation about the behavior of the other workers, let alone in such a way as to elicit the approval or disapproval of the popular worker and a corresponding reaction. However, one can imagine an employer resorting to allegative rather than modulative control in such a situation. If commanding the popular worker to speak against voting for unionization is viewed by the employer as improper, dangerous, or ineffectual, the employer could (as an alternative) communicate an allegation to the popular worker—that a majority vote for unionization will lead to a ''communist-dominated union.'' Such a statement would surely be an allegation about the behavior of the other workers (what their voting behavior will produce); and if the statement were made with a view to prompting the popular worker to speak in opposition to unionization and to sway the vote, the employer would have engaged in allegative control, not modulative control. Since the goal of the employer is the same in either case (i.e. to realize a majority vote against unionization), the distinction may appear to be unimportant; but to ignore it would be to ignore the employer's assessment of the credulity and ideological orientation of the popular worker.

Commands have been emphasized throughout the foregoing because of their bearing on notion of authority, and because they are seemingly essential in large social organizations. However, when it comes to proximate control, there are other alternatives to commands, such as punishment, the threat of punishment, rewards, and the promise of rewards. But those means of proximate control are not conspicuous alternatives when it comes to sequential control, and even when they are employed in sequential control the means do not have the transitive quality of commands. The logic of a chain of command is this: If X can command Y to command Z, then X could command Z directly. Of course, in actual practice X may seldom command Z directly; but that is the case because of spatial-temporal considerations, meaning that X finds it physically difficult if not impossible to issue commands to Z (especially if the chain of command is long and/or of the ''branching'' type). Because of the transitive quality of a chain of command, sequential control is defined exclusively by reference to commands. Consider, for example, the dubious validity of this argument: If X requests Y to request Z to do something and Z does it, then Z would have done it had X made the request directly to Z. To the contrary, X may have made the request to Y in recognition of a purely personal relation between Y and Z. It may well be that X offers money to Y to offer money to Z to do something on the assumption that Z would not do it for the same price (if at all) should X make the offer directly.

The general principle in modulative control is that the first party perceives the third party as having an influence over the second party that the first party does not have, but the first party prompts the third party to act by something other than or in addition to an allegation about the second party. The principle is illustrated by a story in the *Honolulu Advertiser* (May 30,

1978, p. A-4) about Dolan Hoo, a Taiwanese student at the University of Hawaii. Hoo campaigned to become President of the Chinese Students Association, without approval of the Honolulu consulate for Taiwan. Officials of the Kuomintang Party, which rules Taiwan, were described as "furious." According to the newspaper account, Hoo's mother flew to Honolulu after being visited by agents of Taiwan's Investigation Bureau, and she told her son that she would commit suicide if he did not "stay out of trouble." Hoo's brother, a pilot for China Airlines, reportedly was told that his job might be jeopardized by Hoo's behavior—which was possibly an instance of referential control, with the agents as the first party, Hoo's brother as the second party, and China Airline officials as the third party. While the newspaper account left many questions unanswered, it appears that the Taiwanese agents went beyond allegations about Hoo's behavior and engaged in modulative control, with Hoo as the second party and Hoo's brother and/or Hoo's mother as the third party.

The previous observations should not be construed as meaning that in all instances of modulative control, the third party intentionally manipulates the second party's behavior. The third party may not be aware that the first party is using him or her, and the ways that the third party can influence the second party seem infinite. Thus, if a dictator orders the deportation of a leftist writer on the assumption that the workers will be less inclined to strike, the third party (the radical writer) is obviously not intentionally manipulating the workers to cease striking. Rather, the third party is used only in the sense that his or her assumed influence has been terminated.[24] Then consider the conniving wife who covertly encourages a bachelor's flirtations on the assumption that her husband will become jealous and hence more attentive. In such case, the third party (the bachelor) is surely not intentionally manipulating the behavior of the second party (the husband); but it would hardly be a distortion to say that the first party (the wife) is using what she perceives to be the influence of the third party's behavior on the second party, and it is the first party's perception of influence that is crucial in modulative control.

Prelusive Social Control: Part V of the Definition

The illustrations of prelusive control in Table 4-5 and the definition of it (see table note) are sufficient to clarify the notion. However, because prelusive control is much rarer than the other types of social control, a commentary on the rationale for recognizing it is necessary.

---

[24] For various reasons, the first party may attempt to conceal his or her connection with the third party when engaging in modulative social control. Consider the resignation of Johannes Vorster as Prime Minister of South Africa following a report of a government commission (*Time*, June 18, 1979, p. 42): "The most important finding of the commission . . . was that Vorster was fully aware of a covert operation by his former Minister of Information . . . to spend tens of millions of dollars in an illegal and secret effort to influence the news media."

Table 4-5. Some Illustrations of Prelusive Social Control[a]

Row No.	Identification of First Party	Activities and Goals of First Party	Designation of the Subtype of Prelusive Social Control
1	A police official in a "subversive activities" squad or section	The first party encourages a university student to report statements made by students or by faculty that are indicative of "disloyalty," with a view to manipulating the behavior of those students or faculty.	Informative
2	Owner of a company	The first party makes inquiries about the "character" and employment history of an individual who has applied for a position in the company. The owner's policy is to deny employment to anyone whose honesty is questioned or who has ever been fired, on the assumption that such individuals must be supervised too closely.	Preemptive
3	A senator	The first party directs a secretary to search arrest and mental hospitalization records for names of contending candidates for the senatorial position. The senator contemplates using such records in subsequent referential or allegative social control.	Facilitory
4	Legislators	The first party enacts a law which instructs police officials (third party) to bar all "communists" from entering the country.	Exclusionary

[a] In all instances of prelusive social control the first party attempts to manipulate the behavior of the second party by (1) using a third party in gathering information on the second party or (2) directing a third party to limit the behavior of the second party to certain social contexts through coercion or the threat of coercion or (3) taking any action with a view to facilitating the manipulation of the second party's behavior through a third party.

Social control is not ubiquitous if only because it is commonly the case that when two individuals (e.g. a customer and sales clerk) engage in a transaction (or simply interaction) the outcome is so consistent with the expectations and evaluations of both individuals that neither perceives a need to manipulate the behavior of the other beyond that realized in the transaction itself. (Indeed, the transaction may be so routine and habitual that neither individual construes the transaction as the manipulation of behavior.) Again, social control commonly takes place when one party acts contrary to the expectations or evaluations of another party. Yet there are situations where the first party has an interest in the conduct of so many prospective second parties that the first party cannot observe the conduct of each second party, let alone acquire the information necessary for a successful attempt at manipulating the behavior of those second parties. Thus, generals, presidents, wardens, executives, police officers, priests, dictators, and would-be dictators are continually faced with what they perceive as a need to know more about numerous individuals. So much information on so many individuals may be needed that the first party resorts to the use of a third party in gathering that information.

Although the first party can use a third party as a source of information without the third party's knowledge, there are situations in which the first party commands the third party to engage in surveillance of prospective second parties. Third parties may engage in surveillance through unobstrusive observations (as when they are "planted informers"), or they may be sources of retrospective information (as when F.B.I. agents interview professors about particular college students). In any case, when using third parties the first party may strive to ascertain not just whether the behavior of the second party has been contrary to the first party's expectation or evaluation of conduct, but also to detect the inclination or predisposition of the second party to engage in such behavior. In using a third party to gather information on a prospective second party, the first party is not manipulating the second party's behavior. However, when the prospective second party is any one of numerous individuals, the first party is never indifferent to this question: Whose behavior should be manipulated? In using a third party to answer that question, the first party engages in prelusive social control, for the first party perceives the answer as necessary for the manipulation of behavior.

The first party never engages in social control without some presumption as to what the second party and/or third party fear, whom they respect, the behavior they condemn, etc. Rather than base such presumptions on intuition, the first party may use a third party as a source of information to answer this question: For any given prospective second party, what kind of attempt to manipulate that party's behavior is most likely to succeed? When the first party uses a third party to that end, the use is no less prelusive social control than when the third party is used to identify those who have committed some type of act.

When first parties engage in prelusive social control they commonly compile dossiers on numerous individuals, presuming that the dossiers can be used in referential, vicarious, allegative, or modulative control. One extensive effort in that direction during this century was made by Rheinhard Heydrich, a major S.S. official in Nazi Germany (Wighton, 1962). Heydrich directed his subordinates (third parties) to compile information on prominent Germans (political figures, military officers, and members of the Nazi party). There is no doubt that he made frequent use of that information in social control, especially in allegative and referential control (e.g. allegations to Hitler about the homosexuality of a general).

One need not look to Nazi Germany for examples of prelusive social control. Numerous authors have asserted that for years C.I.A. and F.B.I. agents compiled dossiers on Americans that were subsequently used in extralegal if not illegal forms of control.[25] The initial and exact purpose for having compiled a particular dossier may be disputable even today, but much of the information in the dossiers could be used to facilitate social control, especially the allegative variety. Thus, even a rumor that an entertainer or writer attended a particular political meeting can be used to make an allegation that the second party is a "red" appear more credible to a third party (e.g. a sponsor of radio or TV shows, a publisher).

Prelusive control is the most complicated type of social control in that the first party may direct a third party (e.g. an employee) to engage in research that bears on one of two questions. First, of all prospective second parties, who is acting contrary to a standard stipulated by the first party? Second, given any individual or category of individuals designated by an answer to the first question, what would be the most effective way to manipulate their behavior? Prelusive social control in the form of research is by no means peculiar to the political sphere; advertisers engage in it frequently.

Described in general terms, prelusive control is much more proactive than reactive (especially in comparison to the other types of control). The proactive quality of prelusive control is more conspicuous when the first party takes steps to exclude particular individuals or entire categories of individuals from certain social contexts (e.g. entry into a country) on the assumption that such individuals would be difficult to control.[26] Such 'exclusionary'' prelusive control is not limited to the political sphere, but it is particularly conspicuous in that sphere because agents of the state can readily use coercion or the threat of it to restrain a second party.

[25] Prelusive control is not limited to officials and political purposes. It may well be that in all highly urbanized countries records on all manner of people are maintained by all manner of individuals (Wheeler, 1969). To be sure, not all such records are maintained as a venture in prelusive control, but it is difficult to imagine records that could not be used in that enterprise. For that matter, one need not keep records to engage in prelusive control. As Rowan observed (1978) in a comparison of President Carter and former President Lyndon Johnson: "Carter doesn't know where 'the bodies are buried' on the Hill, so he can't extort any votes out of lawmakers. Johnson knew who was sleeping with whom, who was taking money from which lobbyist, who would be in trouble if the post office in his district suddenly was closed." Accepting Rowan's observations, to the extent Johnson "collected stories" about people with a view to using that information in allegative or referential control, he engaged in prelusive control.

[26] In his classic study of "total institutions," Goffman (1961a) failed to emphasize the absence of what is designated here as exclusionary prelusive control. For all practical purposes the personnel of prisons and state mental hospitals cannot exclude "members," and it may well be that many features of control (social or otherwise) reflect negligible exclusionary control. In particular, prison or hospital personnel (guards, nurses) are not inclined to take an inmate's "outside" associates (relatives, friends) as the third party in allegative, referential, or modulative social control. They assume (and perhaps with some justification) that those associates have no influence over the inmate or that such influence is "bad." Hence, it is not particularly surprising that personnel of total institutions appear to rely extensively on proximate control (coercion in particular), vicarious social control (the deterrent variety especially), and surveillant prelusive control.

Bearing on Conventional Terminology

The final definition of social control departs from convention, and the divergence is made all the more conspicuous by the exclusion of numerous terms (e.g. formal, legal) that writers commonly employ in analyzing social control.[27] However, a conceptualization may be less radical than it appears, and that is the case here.

Control and Social Control

The present departure from convention stems largely from the persistent failure of social scientists to distinguish social control from control in general. As suggested by the following typology, numerous major classes and subclasses of control should be recognized.

I. Material
   A. Transformational (e.g. making a knife blade from a bone)
   B. Locational (e.g. diverting a stream, moving an object)

II. Biological
   A. Cultivable (e.g. growing corn)
   B. Animate
      1. Nonhuman (e.g. training a horse to pull objects)
      2. Human
         a. Internalistic or self-control
         b. Externalistic
            (1) Directorial
               (a) Proximate (e.g. hailing a cab)
               (b) Sequential (e.g. through a chain of command)
            (2) Social
               (a) Referential
               (b) Allegative
               (c) Vicarious
               (d) Modulative
               (e) Prelusive

Most social scientists would recognize that social control excludes all classes of control preceding IIB2, but it does not follow that all "human control" is social control. If it so argued, then the class of phenomena denoted by social control is very broad, and there is no rationale for such an inclusive

---

[27] Some of the terms (e.g. formal) are vague, and none of them are useful in defining social control. Thus, no one is likely to argue that all "formal control" (whatever that may mean) is social control and that all social control is formal control. However, some of the terms can be used to designate subtypes of social control. Thus, when state officials incarcerate individuals with a view to furthering general deterrence, such acts can rightly be designated as legal-deterrent-vicarious social control.

class. By contrast, recall the earlier emphasis on the ostensible effective limits of directorial control—proximate and sequential.

Even if the present conceptualization of social control is narrower than conventional thinking on the subject, that does not preclude work toward a theory of human control or, for that matter, a theory of control in general. However, to pursue a theory of human control or control in general at the outset would be only another chapter in the history of "grand theory," which is to say a theory that ostensibly applies to everything but actually applies to nothing. A more realistic strategy would be to pursue special or limited theories, and such theories require distinctions like those in the foregoing typology.[28] That is even more the case given dissensus as to the specific questions that a truly general theory of control should answer. However, if distinctions as to classes of control are accepted and treated seriously, fairly specific questions about the empirical interrelations among classes of control can generate and direct field studies in the natural history tradition. Thus, it hardly strains credulity to suppose that there is some empirical relation between the character of "material control" and "social control" in a society. The exact nature of the relation cannot be postulated at present, but surely it is reasonable to assume that the efficiency of material control limits the amount of time, energy, and technology that can be devoted to social control, especially the prelusive variety.

As for distinctions between types of human control, even descriptive research would be constructive if aimed at answering two questions. First, under what conditions do attempts at directorial control, proximate or sequential, tend to fail? And second, given such failures, under what conditions do would-be controllers commonly resort to social control? The argument is not that those questions are necessarily the most strategic. Rather, without distinctions such as those introduced here, social control studies will have no *manageable* questions and the conventional question as to the nature of the relation between social order and social control is anything but manageable.

Control and Power Reconsidered

Social scientists seemingly presume a conceptual relation between control and power, but the nature of that relation remains vague and disputable. Nothing can be said for the widespread practice of defining power or control by reference to the other term and leaving the other term undefined or defined only vaguely. However, a conceptualization of power *or* control should be

[28] No claim is made that the typology is sufficiently detailed, not even in the case of "human control." In particular, various types of self-control should be recognized; and some thought should be given to the possibility of recognizing "cultural control" as a major division of externalistic control and distinct from proximate, directorial, and social control.

such that it readily extends to a definition of the other term without a radical departure from convention. In that connection, it is hardly radical to think of one person, ego, as having power over another person, alter, if and only if ego controls alter's behavior to some extent. That conceptual link is consistent with common and proper use of the term ''power'' as a *noun*. One has or does not have power over someone else; by contrast, ''control'' is a verb, and one does not ''have it.''

The immediate problem is that any answer to the following question would be unrealistic or arbitrary: How much must ego control alter's behavior before ego has power over alter? The only way to avoid the question is to make power a *perceptual* phenomenon, meaning that ego has power over some stipulated component of alter's behavior if and only if ego, alter, and/or some other member of the social unit in question perceives ego as (1) capable of controlling alter's behavior and (2) doing so without being subject to the control of someone else as a consequence. Summarizing with an explicit definition: Power is the perceived capacity of one individual (or more than one individual acting in concert) to control some behaviors of another individual or other individuals and remain free of control by others as a consequence, with such capacity perceived by at least one member of the social unit in question.

The definition is consistent with two characteristics commonly attributed to power: it is neither an exclusively psychological phenomenon nor an exclusively behavioral phenomenon. As for the first characteristic, ego may have power over alter without ''knowing it,'' provided that alter or some other member of the social unit perceives ego as having some capacity to control. The second characteristic is a recognition that by occupancy of a particular status (e.g. President) ego may be perceived by himself, herself, or others as having the capacity to control the behavior of individuals in other particular statuses (e.g. generals, admirals), even though ego has never actually controlled their behavior.

The present definition is not consistent with all conceptualizations of power or even with common practices. For one thing, it is conventional to speak of one individual as having power over another individual without reference to behavior, and that practice cannot be justified. Even though power is conceptualized here as a perceptual phenomenon, individuals with power are perceived as having the capacity to control someone's *behavior*.

The present definition also differs from the common practice of speaking of power as though the only relevant consequence is success in control. Yet virtually any determined and able adult can control the behavior of all manner of individuals by the threat or actual use of violence (e.g. assassination). Such control is not power because those who engage in it are perceived as subject to countercontrol as a consequence, meaning that they are perceived as liable to punitive or disabling reactions.

For each type of control there is a corresponding type of power. Thus, the *lay* conception of ownership entails the notion of "material power": The owner of an object is perceived by others as having the capacity of "material control" over that object. Then individuals in particular occupations (e.g. locksmith) are perceived by others as knowing how to control material objects but not always being immune to countercontrol, while the owner enjoys all manner of immunities but may lack the expertise to realize various kinds of material control. Both notions, ownership and expertise, also touch on cultivable power and nonhuman power; and the connection with "perceived capacity to control" is especially conspicuous in the case of nonhuman power, notably in the liability of owners for the behavior of animals. Even "internalistic power" corresponds to conventional notions, especially in the legal sphere, where the rationale for civil commitments and other deprivations of legal powers is the subject's lack of control over his or her behavior. Finally, virtually all laws and lay conceptions pertaining to statuses or status relations are studies in externalistic power, which is to say that certain categories of individuals are perceived as having the capacity for proximate, sequential, referential, allegative, vicarious, modulative, or prelusive control. The related distinctions as to the types of power and even the distinction between social and directorial power may not be important for some purposes, but that is largely a matter of substantive interest. In any case, the present conceptualization permits additional distinctions as to types of power, such as the kinds of behavior that are perceived as controlled (political, economic), the level of control (national, dyadic), or the identity of those who perceive the capacity for control and immunity from countercontrol.

A Concluding Qualification

The immediate rationale for defining social control in terms of five types of behavior is to make the definition as clear as possible. However, as often happens in conceptualization, the price of clarity is complexity; but a simpler definition can be realized without reference to the five types of social control. Stating that definition briefly: Social control is an attempt of one party to manipulate the behavior of another party through still another party by any means other than a chain of command.

Since social control can be defined without reference to particular types, the present conceptualization does not stand or fall on the claim that the five types identified in this chapter are exhaustive. Should it be discovered that the five types of social control are not truly exhaustive, then additional types can be recognized. The alternative would be to speak simply of "residual social control," meaning any instance of social control that is not referential, vicarious, allegative, modulative, or prelusive. That alternative is all the more feasible because of the anticipation that there are few if any instances of social control that cannot be classified as referential, vicarious, allegative, modulative, or prelusive.

In Defense of the Final Definition

5

As suggested in the Preface, the dilemma of conceptualization is that not a great deal can be done to defend any definition. No one can demonstrate that a definition is right or wrong, true or false. A definition may appear conventional or unconventional, arbitrary or meaningful, but such judgments tend to reflect personal opinion. Since major theories commonly rest on what were conceptual innovations (i.e. new terms, new definitions), it would be foolish to dismiss a definition because it is unconventional; and what initially appears to be an arbitrary or radical definition of something may eventually come to be regarded as the only possible definition.

Although no definition is right or wrong, true or false, definitions are not beyond rational assessment. If a term is part of a field's empirical language (i.e. it is used to describe or classify particular events or things), then the empirical applicability of that term's definition is the immediate consideration. Only attempts to use a definition provide a basis for a truly systematic assessment of its empirical applicability; nonetheless, it is often the case that certain problems in applying a definition can be anticipated.

While nothing short of the actual use of a definition in stating and testing theories can *demonstrate* its utility, speculation as to utility is justified and desirable.[1] That is especially so when the definition

---

[1] Utility is not the only consideration; there also is the question of compatability with

pertains to the subject matter of a field of study, as is the case for "social control." [2] If the definition is alien to all well-known theories and lines of research in the field, then the definition is likely to be rejected (perhaps rightly so) as excessively radical. However, if a new definition is accepted, it can serve to identify gaps in the field—facets of the field's subject matter that have been ignored.

Intentionality Reconsidered

The terms "attempt" and "manipulate" in the final definition implicitly attribute an intentional quality to social control. Specifically, the first party's overt behavior is an attempt to manipulate the second party's behavior if and only if (1) the first party anticipates that the overt behavior will prevent, terminate, alter, or maintain the *second party's* behavior and (2) the first party perceives that such a consequence is desirable. A simpler and perhaps more conventional conception of intention can be expressed like this: If an individual anticipates a particular consequence of his or her behavior, that behavior is intentional. Note, however, that in performing surgery a physician may anticipate that the patient will suffer some pain; yet that consequence would not be the physician's intent even though anticipated. So intention is construed here as both *cognitive* (anticipating a consequence of one's behavior) and *affective* (perception of the anticipated consequence as partially or wholly desirable).

The designation of a behavior (control or otherwise) as intentional is in no sense an explanation of it. Thus, although it is pointless to presume that the meaning of "robbing a bank" has nothing to do with intention, it is equally pointless to presume that the intentional quality somehow explains that behavior. That point is stressed in recognition that sociologists avoid reference to intention in definitions, evidently because they view it as the road to reductionism (resorting to psychological explanations of what sociologists take to be sociological phenomenon).

While definitions never explain anything, a definition of a type of behavior may be formulated with a view to realizing consistency between the definition and some explanatory principle—one that purportedly explains numerous

---

(footnote continued)

other notions in the field. Observe that the final definition of social control is not only consistent with the traditional emphasis in sociology on "social action" [stemming largely from Weber (1968)] but also an extension of it (i.e. the first party in social control takes *into account* at least two other persons).

[2] If someone wishes to question the identification of social control as a field or subfield of sociology, they should make their criteria explicit. After all, courses on social control are taught, textbooks on the subject are published, and some social scientists (sociologists in particular) identify social control as one of their specialties.

types of behavior. That strategy takes on special significance in contemplating the definitional attribution of intention to control behavior. The explanatory principal is that the frequency of an individual's engagement in some type of externalistic behavior control is a direct function of previous success.[3] Control is successful only if the would-be controller anticipates or hopes for some consequence of that behavior and perceives that consequence as having been realized. Accordingly, the distinction between successful and unsuccessful control is lost if an intentional quality is not attributed to control behavior; and that loss would preclude utilization of the explanatory principle, which could have far-reaching implications in the study of social control.

The validity of the explanatory principle in question is not beyond dispute, but it is entirely consistent with everyday experience and with the research findings on operant conditioning. As for everyday experience, consider an instance where an individual asks a store clerk to give change in one dollar bills. Who would deny that such behavior is intentional or that previous control behavior of the individual could be relevant in explaining that particular instance? That instance would not be explained merely by inferring that the behavior was intentional; rather, the behavior would be explained by subsuming it under the general explanatory principle.

Some sociologists might cringe at the reference to operant conditioning, viewing it as the road to reductionism; and others will question the relevance of operant principles in the present context, knowing that Skinner, the leading figure in the history of operant conditioning studies, eschewed such terms as intention.[4] Indeed, Skinner might point out that a similar explanatory principle can be formulated without reference to intention: The frequency of engagement in some type of behavior is a direct function of previous reinforcement of that behavior. To illustrate, suppose that members of an audience enter into a conspiracy to applaud a speaker only when the speaker's statement is preceded by the speaker raising his or her arm. Conceivably, such an audience response could markedly increase the "arm raising rate" without the speaker ever being aware of the association, meaning that the speaker never *intended* the gesture to elicit applause.[5] It would not follow that the

[3] The principle is consistent with the so-called "law of effect" in psychology, even though that law is commonly stated in such a way as to be ambiguous with regard to recognition of intention and covert behavior in general. For an elaborate treatment of the principle's implications and a sociological interpretation of the "law of effect," see Homans (1974).

[4] Since numerous sociologists and numerous psychologists (Skinner in particular) join forces, so to speak, in eschewing or ignoring the notion of intention, one must surely wonder as to how the notion necessarily opens the door to reductionism or, more specifically, the surrender of sociology to psychology.

[5] Intended or not, the case would be an illustration of operant conditioning; and neither the existence nor the significance of operant behavior is questioned here. However, the principles of operant conditioning in no way justify a denial of intention as a quality of human behavior. For that matter, the principles of operant conditioning are a study in ambiguity as regards recognition of intention and other facets of covert behavior.

explanatory principle in question (one that implicitly refers to intentional behavior) is somehow invalid. Had the speaker employed the gesture intentionally, repetition of the gesture would have been even more closely associated with the "response of the environment" (applause by an audience). Hence, the principle rests on the argument that those engaged in intentional behavior are especially sensitive to "responses of the environment." Recall that in the previous illustration the members of the audience entered into a conspiracy, the *intention* being to increase the speaker's "arm raising rate." Suppose that for some reason the rate did not increase as anticipated. Is it not plausible that the *failure* in control would lessen the audience's inclination to *control* a subsequent speaker in the same manner? Indeed, how can one speak meaningfully of a "failure in control" without attributing intention to the control behavior?

The general point is that the use of principles of operant conditioning in the study of externalistic behavior control does not preclude the attribution of intention to control behavior. Although Skinner does not describe experimenters as attempting to control the behavior of pigeons (Skinner's favorite animal), it is surely the case; hence, the present version of operant conditioning would apply to the experimenters, not to the pigeons. It should also be noted that Skinner's attempts to avoid recognition of covert behavior (e.g. the notion of intention) creates more problems that it solves.[6] Granted that the emission of some type of behavior is a direct function of the frequency with which that behavior has been reinforced, what is a reinforcer? Skinner cannot answer "a reinforcer is a reward" without implicitly recognizing covert behavior (e.g. perception, intention), especially in the case of human behavior. However, if a reinforcer is defined as any event that is *followed* by an increase in the emission of some type of behavior, then what appears to be an explanatory principle is actually a *definition* of a reinforcer and cannot be proven false.

Whatever the rationale for attributing an intentional quality to control behavior, some critics will persist in questioning that attribution. The most likely question can be introduced by reconsidering a previous illustration of referential social control: If Hitler actually received greater electoral and/or

---

[6] The problems are secondary to a general issue—Skinner's seeming determination to cleanse the vocabulary of the human sciences (not just psychology) of terms that denote covert behavior. In *Beyond Freedom and Dignity* Skinner (1971:10) quotes this statement by Karl Popper: "What we want is to understand how such nonphysical things as *purposes, deliberations, plans, decisions, theories, tensions,* and *values* can play a part in bringing about physical changes in the physical world." Skinner's commentary on Popper's quest fairly drips with disdain, but Skinner does not speak directly to three questions. First, are we to assume that the covert behavior alluded to by Popper is a fantasy? Second, if such behavior does take place (i.e. not just Popper's private hallucination), is it insignificant for the social and behavioral sciences? And, third, is there an a priori basis for knowing that the questions suggested by Popper's statement can never be answered? Skinner's failure to speak directly to such questions is not puzzling, for an affirmative answer to any of them would be incredible.

financial support through his castigation of Jews, what difference does it make whether he intended to manipulate the behavior of non-Jewish Germans to that end? A similar "what difference" question could be posed about all previous illustrations of social control, and all such questions tacitly deny either the purposive quality of human behavior or its significance.

Since the purposive quality of human behavior is recognized by virtually any adult, a denial of it would be grotesque. As for its significance, the most important consideration is the previously stated principle—individuals engage in a type of behavior to the extent that they have some cognitive basis for anticipating consequences perceived as desirable. Hitler did not engage in the public castigation of Jews on one isolated occasion; and whatever his mental aberrations may have been, it strains credulity to suppose that Hitler was indifferent to the consequences. Perhaps he would not have engaged in the castigation of Jews as a kind of referential social control had there been no German tradition of virulent antisemitism, and such socio-cultural factors should be recognized even though they have no bearing on the intentional quality attributed to social control.[7] However, it would be incredible to reject the possibility that Hitler baited Jews in part (if not wholly) because he perceived it as effective.

The argument is not that the success or failure of attempted control is somehow objectively given. Success or failure is a matter of the perception of would-be controllers, and it is not presumed that one instance is necessarily decisive as to the continuance of control attempts. The presumption is that of *some kind* of relation between previous success in some sort of control behavior and repetition of that behavior, with the exact nature of the relation left to theoretical speculation and research findings. However, the very idea of success in attempts at control is illogical unless an intentional quality is attributed to control behavior.

If critics persist in using the aforementioned "what difference" question as a rationale for ignoring the intentional quality of control behavior, they should confront the full implications. The "what difference" question affects all manner of terms, both in natural languages and in the social science vocabulary. Consider, in designating a case of death as suicide, "what difference" does it make if the deceased intended to take his life? The point is that asking the "what difference" question would obliterate the distinction between suicides and deaths in general. Similarly, what difference does it make if revolutionaries intended to overthrow a regime by violence? What difference does it make if a migrant intended to remove himself or herself from a place of residence for more than one night? What difference does it make if executives or owners intend to drive up the price of gasoline when

---

[7] Social control can be and should be the field of study where the perennial debate over "individuals versus socio-cultural factors" as forces in human history occupies center stage.

they order tankers to delay port entry? What difference does it make whether a husband intended to kill his wife when poison "fell" from his hand into her cocktail?

True, numerous terms in the sociological vocabulary apparently have nothing to do with intention, some instances being social integration, class conflict, and alienation. But the meaning of those terms is notoriously vague, and in the attempt to clarify their meaning no one has been able to avoid using words or phrases in natural languages (e.g. French, English) as *primitive terms* in definitions. Yet the meaning of the vast majority of those words or phrases entails the notion of intention. Think of, for example, fighting, kissing, driving, reaching, robbing a bank, eating, greeting, requesting, rejecting, buying, and voting. The meaning of those terms surely has something to do with intention, and "technical" definitions of them that exclude the attribution of intention appear ludicrous. The general point is that extension of the "what difference" question would strip the vocabulary of the social sciences.

Implications of the Definition

Any new definition is a departure from convention, and the extent of that departure has implications at least in contemplating its short-run utility, especially when the definition delimits the subject matter of a field of study. A distinct and radical break from convention may be necessary for progress in a field; but it inevitably entails a loss of things associated with the older definition, such as related terms (e.g. a definition of control or social control could make "coercion" irrelevant), research findings, and even entire theories. Yet a new definition may be less of a radical break with convention than it appears, and that is the case for the final definition of social control.

Social Control and Deviance

As pointed out in Chapter 3, current definitions of social control typically reflect the "prophylactic conception," for they pertain one way or another to counteracting deviance. Since the definition proposed here makes no reference to norms or to deviance, it may indeed appear radical.

"Counteracting deviance" may suggest conscious and deliberate attempts at prevention, but the definitions set forth by Berndt, Cohen, and Parsons allude to "processes" or "mechanisms" that exert pressure on individuals to conform to norms or that otherwise counteract deviant tendencies. Such terminology admits the possibility that social control may be unintentional, unplanned, crescive, etc. By contrast, insofar as norms exist, the final definition of social control admits the possibility that the first party may manipulate the behavior of the second party in such a way that the second party's behavior becomes consistent or remains consistent with some norm; but the manipulation itself must be intentional. More exactly, the first party's behavior must be such that one can justifiably *infer* the intention to alter the second party's behavior.

The contrast between the final definition and a typical contemporary definition would be reduced if the latter were reworded as "attempts to prevent deviance," which would imply the attribution of an intentional quality to social control.[8] However, one may attempt to prevent deviance by resorting to proximate or sequential control. A father may whip his son with the idea of preventing the son from smoking again; but since the father's action involves only two parties (including the father), it would not be social control. The immediate reason is that social control cannot be defined defensibly by enumerating specific means (whipping) or enumerating particular status designations (e.g. father—son), for any such "enumerative list" is bound to be incomplete and/or peculiar to particular cultures. However, since an enumerative definition of social control is avoided both by the final definition and by the prophylactic conception, more should be said about the rejection of the latter, especially as regards the hypothetical case of the father whipping his son.

This case would not qualify as social control in accordance with the prophylactic conception without an affirmative answer to two questions: Is the son's smoking deviant? Did the son cease smoking or reduce his smoking because of the whipping? An answer to the second question is bound to be conjectural, and an answer to the first question leads us into a conceptual mire. If one answers the first question affirmatively because the father's reaction was punitive, the answer is a tacit acceptance of a *reactive* criterion of deviance (an act is deviant if and only if reacted to punitively); and such a criterion will not bear examination. Thus, if a gunman beats a clerk in a store when the clerk denies knowing how to open the safe, then the clerk's behavior was deviant. Punishment surely is not the only reaction that identifies a particular act as deviant, and one problem with the reactive conception of deviance is that the relevant kinds of reactions remain unstipulated. Even if a punitive reaction is a *sufficient* criterion of deviance, then the clerk's behavior was deviant; but no one is likely to accept that designation.

Of course, one may reject the reactive conception of deviance and cling to the older, normative conception, according to which an act is deviant if contrary to some norm. But what is the norm in the case of a "smoking son"? It cannot be solely the normative opinions of the father, as no one questions the idea that a norm is a property of a social unit and not of an isolated

---

[8] Even if the prophylactic conception should be so modified, a troublesome question would remain: Is an attempt to prevent some type of behavior social control only if the individual *correctly* perceives the behavior as deviant? Since the final definition of social control makes no reference to deviance, it can be applied without confronting that question.

individual. But that idea gives rise to a difficult question: In the case of the "smoking son," what is the relevant social unit? If one answers "the father, the son, and other family members," what if the father and one daughter agree that the son should not smoke, while the mother and the son have a different opinion? Indeed, what if all of the son's friends approve of smoking, while all of the son's relatives disapprove of it? Since the normative opinions of the son's friends could have a great impact on his behavior, what rationale would justify ignoring those opinions? Moreover, since the father is not the only person who may react punitively to the son's smoking, why exclude school teachers from the relevant social unit? Indeed, why exclude police and court officers; and if such officers are relevant, what of those who enact laws and ordinances?

As the foregoing questions suggest, there are all manner of justifications for expanding the boundary of the relevant social unit in the determination of a particular norm; but with expansion doubts grow as to how the normative opinions of one member have an impact on another when the two never interact or have a social relation (Denzin, 1970). That is the principal reason why advocates of reference group theory question the reality and/or significance of even "community norms." [9] Yet advocates of that theory solve no problems by arguing that individuals govern their behavior largely in terms of the perceived normative opinions of their friends, fellow workers, teachers, family, etc.[10] Even if those designations (e.g. friends) had a perfectly clear meaning and even if the "etc." could be ignored, reference group theory provides no directions whatever for drawing the boundaries of social units independently of a particular individual (in this case, a particular son *or* father). For that matter, if a particular individual must be the point of departure in identifying the norms that are relevant in each particular situation, purely practical considerations (money, time) would virtually preclude systematic research on "attempts to prevent deviance." That is the case because even if one individual consciously and deliberately tries to prevent another individual from engaging in a certain kind of behavior, it

[9] Equally important, there is no justification for assuming that the consensus problem in defining and identifying norms is somehow avoided by limiting social control studies to social units that are smaller than communities, and that point gains special significance in the case of organizations. Granted that organizations may be the most strategic unit for social control studies, the existence of "rules" in an organization does not necessarily signify normative consensus. For that matter, while research on certain types of behavior (e.g. drinking) and reactions to such behavior (e.g. punishment) in an organizational context would ostensibly qualify as a social control study according to the prophylactic conception (Bensman and Gerver, 1963; Habbe, 1969; Gersuny, 1973), that conception appears patently alien to several "organizational aspects" of social control as identified by Etzioni (1968).

[10] Whatever the merits of the argument, advocates of reference group theory are all too prone to describe social control as somehow "automatic" (no less than followers of Durkheim and Sumner). Specifically, "heroes, villains, and fools" are agents of social control (Klapp, 1954) only insofar as the first party *uses* such terms or individuals in social control.

would not be the prevention of deviance even though intentional unless it could be shown that the behavior would be a violation of some assumed norm.

But suppose that someone formulates an acceptable rationale and method for identifying relevant social units in research on norms. Other problems would emerge immediately. If a norm is a collective evaluation of conduct, as most definitions clearly suggest, then the only systematic way to assess evaluations of conduct in a social unit is to ask members normative questions, such as whether they approve, disapprove, or have any opinion about people smoking cigarettes. Such a question is all too simple, but no rewording of the question would come to grips with this realization: Human beings rarely (if ever) evaluate actual acts solely in terms of the acts themselves. To the contrary, the approval or disapproval of a particular act is commonly contingent on the social identity of the actor (e.g. age, sex, ethnicity, race), the identity of the object of the act (if any), the social place, the social time, etc. No such contingencies are incorporated in the illustrative normative question about smoking, and it is inconceivable that all possible contingencies can be known and stipulated in an intelligible normative question. Taking an actual act as point of departure (e.g. a particular son smoking) and describing that act as part of a normative question would not be a solution, for the *total context* of that act (e.g. the age of the smoker, the sex of the smoker, where, when, etc.) cannot be described in posing a normative question about the act.

Let us assume that the "contingency" problem is somehow solved; even so, what proportion of members of the relevant social unit must voice disapproval of a type of act or a particular act to justify identifying it as deviant? Requiring absolute normative consensus (i.e. all members must agree) would be unrealistic in that such a condition may be extremely rare (especially among social units larger than a family). However, any standard less than absolute normative consensus (e.g. only 67% of the members need agree) would be arbitrary and ignore differential power. Suppose that the relevant social unit in the illustrative case comprises the son, his residential family, and his friends. Then suppose that 80% of that social unit voice approval but the son's father and mother are opposed. How can one justify giving "equal weight" to the normative opinions of the son's friends and the son's parents? The parents can impose all manner of sanctions on the son (e.g. deprivation of an allowance), including recourse to legal authorities. Nonetheless, there is surely no obvious, systematic way to take differential power into account.

The foregoing problems are largely ignored by sociologists, who persist in an uncritical usage of the two terms, norm and deviance. Yet it is an illusion to suppose that conventional definitions make it possible to identify norms systematically, or that the designation of particular acts as being either deviance or conformity can avoid seemingly insoluble problems.

Perhaps the notion of a norm has utility even if left vague; but should that argument be accepted, the present conceptualization makes it possible to interpret instances of social control as *attempts to prevent deviance*. The point is not just that those who engage in social control judge the "normative qualities" of situations, including the authority of third parties; additionally, the first party manipulates behavior in accordance with his or her evaluations of conduct. As such, social control entails evaluations of conduct, the central notion in defining a norm. The first party's evaluations of conduct may or may not be shared by other members of the social unit; but the very idea that a norm is a "shared" evaluation of conduct creates seemingly insoluble problems. Moreover, the contingency problem is reduced in the study of social control because the decision of the first party to manipulate the behavior of the second party surely reflects recognition of the relevant contingencies *in that particular situation*. When the first party engages in referential or allegative social control, some judgment about the authority or power of the third party is implied by the action itself. Similarly, vicarious social control cannot take place unless the first party attempts to manipulate (i.e. reward or punish) the behavior of a third party, and that consideration bears on the power of the first party. So, far from ignoring differential power—as is often the case with a definition of a norm—the study of social control in the context of the present conceptualization virtually presumes it.

Only one qualification of the foregoing argument is needed. If the notion of norm and/or deviance is left vague, social control can be construed as attempts to prevent deviance; but not all attempts to prevent or counteract behavior are social control.[11] As suggested previously, should a father inflict corporal punishment on his son with a view to deterring the son from smoking again, it is proximate control, not social control. However, the study of social control is concerned with (inter alia) what people do when "things go wrong" in dyadic interaction, and surely things have gone wrong when an attempt to prevent behavior through proximate control (including authority) fails. No less important, human beings do not typically engage in attempts at control, social or otherwise, without contemplating prospects for success and making a choice among alternatives. Try to imagine, for example, legislators attempting

[11] Yet it is difficult to imagine any definition of deviance that would make "attempts to prevent deviance" a subclass of social control (as defined here) unless the definition of deviance stems from a conception of norms that makes any individual's evaluation or expectations of conduct in any particular situation a norm. Moreover, some instances of social control (e.g. some cases of extortion and *all* cases of blackmail) would be deviant in itself by virtually any definition of deviance. So the present argument is really that of some empirical association between social control (as defined here) and attempts to prevent deviance, not a logically necessary association, especially if the more conventional definitions of deviance are accepted. As such, the present argument makes it possible to formulate an *empirical* question: Under what conditions will attempts to prevent deviance take the form of social control?

to prevent crimes solely through proximate control.[12] They commonly aim for a penal policy that furthers general deterrence (Morris, 1966), a subtype of vicarious social control. Yet attempts to prevent deviance are not limited to vicarious social control (especially outside of the legal sphere), and that type of control encompasses far more than deterrence.

To summarize, social control is not conceptualized here in such a way that it has nothing to do with the prevention of deviance, but at the same time the conceptualization does not entail all of the seemingly insoluble problems in defining norms or deviance. More specifically, whatever the definition of deviance, social control is *one* way that an attempt may be made to prevent deviance.

Terms Excluded

The final definition of social control is not consistent with all things or events that sociologists identify (often uncritically) as social control, and most of the terms in the definition are largely alien to some conventional ideas about social control. As for the things or events, no list of them would constitute a definition of social control, or even necessarily suggest a definition. Nonetheless, the literature suggests some agreement among writers as to instances of social control, and no definition of social control should be alien to that literature.

Social scientists often identify the speeches of well-known or infamous leaders (e.g. Hitler) as exercises in social control, and that characterization is consistent with another convention—the designation of propaganda as social control. That convention is not disputed, but it does not suggest a definition of social control. The reason is not just that "propaganda" is subject to all manner of interpretations. Even if consensus could be realized on a very precise definition of propaganda, two questions as to the nature of social control would remain unanswered. First, what are the other subclasses of social control? And, second, in what sense is propaganda social control? The final definition of social control makes an answer to the first question unnecessary; and particular communications (e.g. speeches, publications) commonly regarded as propaganda (Lowenthal and Guterman, 1970) are

[12] Although Hart (1961) does not speak of proximate control, sequential control, and social control, time and again he argues that law is a means for controlling large numbers of individuals. Hence, law is a means of social control (both by convention and as defined here) because there are (as Hart recognizes) definite limits as to the number of individuals who can be controlled effectively by exclusive reliance on proximate or sequential control. But the illustrations in Chapter 4 should make it obvious that the final definition of social control does not equate it with legal control. For that matter, the argument about "size" and the limits of proximate or sequential control does not rest on arguments by Hart or other prominent figures in jurisprudence. The insights of Simmel (1950) and the traditional concern in organizational sociology with the "span of control" (Entwisle and Walton, 1961) are perhaps even more relevant.

virtual studies in referential and allegative social control. Accordingly, the present definition supplies a rationale for the identification of propropaganda as social control.

What has been said of propaganda applies to virtually all of the various terms commonly used to describe means, types, or kinds of social control, such as punishment, reward, coercion, blacklisting, censorship, ostracism, degradation, banishment, cooptation, and stigmatization. The utility and shortcomings of such terms are not examined at length because they are not directly relevant for the present conceptualization; but two things should be noted briefly. First, no list of those terms would amount to a defensible definition of social control. Second, no one has been able to construct a *typology* of social control that encompasses even a majority of the terms in the social control literature, let alone define the terms so that they denote mutually exclusive classes of social control. (For example, what is the distinction between degradation and stigmatization?) Nonetheless, the vast majority of those terms are not alien to the present conceptualization; indeed, they can be used to identify *subtypes* of social control. To illustrate, censorship could designate a subtype of *modulative* social control, provided that all instances of that subtype are cases where censors have attempted to repress or alter a communication (e.g. speeches, publications) with a view to eliminating the influence of the communicator (e.g. lecturer, writer) on some audience. But censorship is *vicarious* social control if the censor silences a speaker or writer with a view to intimidating other speakers and writers.

Not all behavior denoted by the kinds of terms in question can be taken as social control—at least not as conceptualized here. Thus, "punishment" may be a means of proximate control rather than social control, as when a parent spanks a child; and identifying punishment in general as social control would be questionable (recall the pistol-whipping of the clerk in a typical robbery).[13] Questions also arise when some phenomenon is explicitly excluded from social control. Thus, Janowitz to the contrary, in light of the final definition,

---

[13] While numerous commonly recognized types of acts can be *loosely* characterized as either being social control or not being social control, that is the case only for *typical* instances of those types. The typical instance of legal imprisonment is probably social control, because it implements a penal policy to promote general deterrence, and the typical spanking of a child is probably proximate control. However, the claim is not made that all instances (past, present, and future) of legal imprisonment are vicarious social control, nor that all spankings are proximate control. Perhaps Durkheim is at least partially correct (i.e. not all punishments in all criminal justice systems are applied to promote general deterrence), and few would question that parents have been known to spank a child to placate a complaining neighbor or a "law and order" grandparent. So *general* observations as to what is and what is not social control cannot be taken as categorically valid, but a conceptualization that does not permit general observations would be crippling. However, a phenomenon may be conceptualized or described in such a way that it is difficult to judge whether or not typical instances of it are social control. That is especially the case for "stigmatization" when the phenomenon is described from the perspective of those who are stigmatized rather than those who stigmatize [see Goffman (1963)].

coercion can be employed by those engaged in social control.[14] Specifically, some punishments in vicarious social control are coercive (e.g. imprisonment), and coercion (or the threat of it) may be employed to administer punishments that are intended to deter or placate the second party.

Still another qualification is that a few terms used by writers in describing means of social control are largely alien to the present conceptualization. For example, some writers identify gossip as a means of social control [e.g. Ambrose (1975:37)] Such an identification would be consistent with the prophylactic conception of social control if it could be shown that gossip counteracts deviance; but those who identify gossip in general as a means of social control do not defend the identification, let alone recognize the need to demonstrate that it counteracts deviance. The point is not that gossip cannot be social control. Some human beings are clever, conniving creatures; they may engage in gossip with a view to manipulating behavior, in which case it would be social control (most likely allegative or referential).

The literature is also a study in terms that denote strategic statuses in social control. Consider the following list of complementary statuses: bourgeoisie−proletarian, parent−child, employer−employee, leader−follower, supervisor−worker, and master−slave. Such status relations are essentially control relations; however, whether all of them are social control is another matter. No claim to that effect is made in connection with the present conceptualization, but the conceptualization would not terminate the concern with strategic statuses in social control. Even if the kind of control that enters into a status relation is predominantly proximate (commonly the case for parent−child) or sequential (commonly the case for employer−employee), the present conceptualization of social control is nonetheless relevant. When proximate or sequential control fails in such status relations, the would-be controller often resorts to social control, as when parents abandon commands, admonishments, pleas, or corporal punishments and turn to juvenile au-

---

[14] See Janowitz (1975:84) and commentary in Chapter 3 (note 16) on his exclusion of coercion from social control. Given the divergent conceptualizations of coercion (Pennock and Chapman, 1972), it would be dubious to use that term in defining social control. Nonetheless, a legion of social scientists (Goode, 1972) have attributed so much importance to coercion (or force) that to exclude it from social control *by definition* borders on the incredible. For what it is worth, coercion is conceived of here as the use of mechanical or biological principles to restrain or terminate behavior, instances being incarceration, shooting, and injection of disabling drugs. There is a more conventional definition (Pennock and Chapman, 1972), something like this: Coercion is the threat of inflicting punishment on someone with a view to controlling his or her behavior. That definition and the present definition differ primarily in that the present definition *excludes* the use of cultural symbols in coercion. The present definition is preferred to what may be the more conventional definition because the latter obliterates the distinction between "coercion" and "sanction threat" and is a conceptual mire. For example, if a graduate student threatens to terminate his or her sexual relation with a professor unless he or she receives a grade of "A" in some course, is that threat coercion in light of the conventional definition? The question would be difficult even if the putative conventional definition should refer to the threatened infliction of an "evil" rather than a "punishment."

thorities, in which case they have shifted to an attempt at referential or allegative social control of the child. Similarly, when employees defy their authority, owners or managers may solicit the aid of legal officers *or* threaten such solicitation, in which case they have turned from proximate or sequential control to referential or allegative social control. In large companies or corporations, however, social control is not just something resorted to when commands fail. The control of hundreds of employees poses all manner of organizational problems, and to solve those problems employers promulgate rules that stipulate sanctions and organize the enforcement of those rules, all of which is referential, vicarious, or prelusive social control.[15] In small companies or corporations proximate or sequential control may be predominant. The same is true of control in the context of the master−slave relation; but when the status relation is one of class or caste, proximate or sequential control is less common. Thus, when Marxists allege that in capitalist societies the bourgeoisie control the proletariat, they are not speaking only of control in particular work places; they are speaking also of control that is national in scope and aimed at inculcating acceptance of prevailing economic relations among proletarians *in general* and the repression of dissent. Whatever the validity of the Marxist theory, such a control system could not be based on proximate or sequential control alone. Rather, capitalists would have to support the candidacy of conservative political candidates, bribe members of regulatory agencies, provide financial support for reactionary religious leaders, discourage the appointment of dissenting educators, and dominate the mass media. Those activities are predominantly social control (especially the modulative kind), not proximate or sequential control.

While the present conceptualization is not alien to the emphasis in the literature on particular means of social control and key statuses, it also permits recognition of phenomena that have heretofore been slighted in the study of social control, advertising in particular. That institution or behavior complex cannot be readily identified as social control within the context of the prophylactic conception, because it would be questionable to characterize advertising as counteracting deviance. However, virtually all American advertising is referential and/or modulative social control. No manufacturer

---

[15] The *actual* administration of a sanction (whether perceived by those who prescribed it as a punishment or a reward) is vicarious control if intended (by those who prescribed it) to promote general deterrence or emulation. The prescription itself (i.e. the enactment of a law or the formulation of a rule) is referential and/or prelusive control, depending on the perception of those who prescribe the sanction. If they view the prescription itself (including the promulgation of the law or rule) as promoting general deterrence or emulation, it is referential social control (i.e. reference to what a third party, such as a judge or supervisor, will do given certain types of conduct). However, a sanction may be viewed as promoting general deterrence or emulation only when actually applied, in which case its prescription is prelusive social control (i.e. it *facilitates* vicarious social control). Of course, the two alternatives are not mutually exclusive: the prescription of a sanction may be both referential and prelusive social control.

can command the owners of mass media technology (e.g. television networks, radio stations, newspapers) to run advertisements, but their services can be purchased. In such a case, the first party (the manufacturer) uses the influences of the third party (e.g. personnel of a television network or newspaper) in an attempt to manipulate the behavior of the second party (all potential consumers of the product in question). If there is an intermediary in such a transaction (e.g. an advertising agency), it is nonetheless modulative social control, though a more complicated kind; and modulative control can be combined with referential control, as when a TV announcer informs us about the consumption habits of a movie star.

Institutions and Social Control

Prior to the emergence of the prophylactic conception of social control, the literature reflected a preoccupation with institutions as the locus of social control. Thus, Ross's conceptualization of social control (1901) is primarily a list of institutions (e.g. law, religion) that supposedly contribute to social order. The prophylactic conception of social control does not amount to a rejection of the "institutional perspective," because it can be argued that particular institutions counteract deviance. That argument is entirely consistent with what Lemert (1972:53, 95) rightly and critically characterized as the "assumption of automaticity in the control process." Specifically, the assumption is that social control flows from institutions (or "social structure") without conscious and deliberate attempts to manipulate behavior.[16] American husbands who are faithful to their wives do so because that behavior is simply part of the institution of monogamy (including "norms"), the counterpart to the "invisible hand" in *laissez faire* economic theory. The assumption ignores the fact that wives in great numbers engage in all manner of activities to check a husband's roving eye, that in many jurisdictions adultery remains a felony, or that the employers of husbands may admonish them to curb their sexual communism. The point is that insofar as norms exist, the norms themselves do not ensure conformity. Stated otherwise, rather than blithely assume that social control automatically stems from institutions, sociologists should entertain the possibility that certain kinds and amounts of social control are necessary for institutions.

The present conceptualization of social control does not use the term institutions, but the reason is not just that the term is vague. It is feckless to attempt a definition of social control by merely listing institutions. The list is bound to be incomplete and ethnocentric (e.g. peculiar to Anglo-American countries), and such a definition would not indicate the sense in which the listed institutions are loci of social control. If it is implied that the institutions

---

[16] This view is commonly attributed to Sumner, but it stems no less from Durkheim.

counteract deviance, then the list would only be an inferior and questionable version of the prophylactic conception of social control. It would be inferior because no one is likely to argue that *only* institutions counteract deviance, and it would be questionable because it rests on the dubious assumptions that each institution listed actually counteracts deviance. To the contrary, if religion is one of the institutions, during 200 years (circa 1500–1700) of European history (Kamen, 1967) religion was the primary locus of ideological deviance (i.e. far from counteracting deviance, religion generated heresy). Furthermore, the claim that institutions are the loci of social control implies that institutions exist and function without social control. Assume evidence that confession in the Roman Catholic religion somehow counteracts certain kinds of deviance; even if this is so, it strains credulity to suppose that priests and parishioners participate in confessions automatically, without conscious and deliberate promptings from others.

Most important of all, an "institutional" definition of social control rests on a disputable assumption—that regardless of place or time the designated institutions contribute to social order. Even if one is willing to tolerate the vagueness of most terms that denote institutions (e.g. religion), to ignore the distinct possibility that the list of institutions in question is incomplete, and to equate social control with "that which contributes to social order," the assumption at issue is functionalism in its most vulgar form.

Despite the foregoing reservations, the present conceptualization does not preclude an "institutional perspective" in the study of social control. As a case in point, if religious beliefs are widely accepted in a social unit and religious leaders venerated by the bulk of members, then religion may well be the core of various kinds of social control, the allegative and referential types in particular. Since the third party is not necessarily a temporal human being, pronouncing the threat of a god's condemnation or the promise of a god's reward is referential social control. Moreover, if one is inclined to speak of "religious" social control, it need not be limited to the referential type. In one instance after another in the history of Western Europe, individuals have made allegations to the Pope or to a bishop about the behavior of someone else; and it would be remarkably naive to deny the possibility that those making the allegations were engaged in social control. It would be no less naive to suppose that the Pope has never used excommunication to deter others, which is vicarious social control.

Law as a Strategic Institution

The present conceptualization offers advocates of the institutional perspective a language to use in demonstrating what they now merely assume—that certain institutions are the primary loci of social control. If only because such a demonstration calls for research and not just conceptualization, no effort in that direction is made here. However, some comment should be made on a convention that appears to be accepted by all social scientists, including scholars in jurisprudence: Law is an institution and a means of social control.[17] That convention is not an assumption or empirical assertion; rather, it is commonly accepted as *true by definition*. The convention does not clarify the meaning of social control. Nonetheless, if the convention is accepted (as it is here), then all conceptualizations of social control should be consistent with commonly recognized features of law.

Consider the problems posed in defining a criminal statute. It will surely not do to characterize a criminal statute as "something enacted by a legislative body," for legislators "enact" all manner of things.[18] Nor is it entirely satisfactory to characterize criminal statutes as literal prohibitions. A criminal statute is more nearly a prediction as to what will happen (e.g. imprisonment for five years) to individuals who are convicted of engaging in designated types of conduct (e.g. robbery). Since criminal statutes are not *literally* prohibitions, the last major figure in analytical jurisprudence, Hans Kelsen (1967), seemingly argued that statutes are directed not to the citizenry at large but to legal officials (i.e. statutes "instruct" officials, not the citizenry). However, even that quality of a criminal statute is not literal, nor does the term punishment or sanction appear in all criminal statutes, even though criminal statutes are commonly construed as being a "threat."

Once it is recognized that a definition of a criminal statute cannot be literal, the only alternative is a functional definition: one that describes what a criminal statute does *or* is intended to do. No one denies that the control of *someone's* behavior is one function of all criminal statutes, and that control is social control despite divergent conceptions of "law." Thus, if one argues that a criminal statute is directed to the citizenry in general, it is as an implicit *reference* to what legal officials will do given the kind of behavior stipulated in the statute, hence, referential social control. On the other hand, if one argues that a criminal statute is directed to legal officials, it is prelusive social control, having been enacted to facilitate the punishment of individuals and thereby further general deterrence or placate some party.

---

[17] See Black (1976), Litwak (1956), Parsons (1962), Pound (1968), Raz (1970), and Stone (1961). Far from clarifying either notion, the identification of law as a means of social control gives rise to another doubt about the prophylactic conception of social control. If by definition social control actually counteracts deviance, a law or its enforcement is social control only if it does actually counteract some kind of behavior. So the prophylactic conception of social control recognizes law as a means of social control only if law is efficacious, but the efficacy of law is one of the perennial disputes in jurisprudence and in the sociology of law (Ball et al., 1962; Blumstein et al., 1978; Gibbs, 1975; Jones, 1969; Lipton et al., 1975; Stone, 1961). As for phrases in definitions of social control (Chapter 3) such as "tendency to prevent or reduce deviance" (Cohen), "tend to counteract" (Parsons), or "exert pressure . . . to conform" (Berndt), they are little more than troublesome dodges, meaning that they vaguely attribute efficacy to social control. By contrast, Lemert (1972) argues that social control leads to deviance.

[18] Including recognition by the Massachusetts legislature of the chickadee as the official State bird (Fuller, 1969:91).

The foregoing should not be construed as suggesting that law is nothing more than a body of statutes. No authority in jurisprudence, the sociology of law, legal anthropology, or political science would accept that suggestion, if only because it ignores common law and is ethnocentric to the point of denying the possibility of law among nonliterate peoples. For that matter, legal realists in jurisprudence resist the idea that law can be described in terms of anything *akin* to statutes, written or unwritten. Instead, they argue that law is found in the *actual* behavior of legal officials, especially the decisions of judges in particular cases.[19] This is not the place to assess the merits of or objections to legal realism; so it will suffice to say that law is a means of social control in light of the present conceptualization, whether legal realism is accepted or rejected. Thus, when it comes to the actual behavior of officials, an instance of a legal punishment (e.g. execution, incarceration) is vicarious social control unless one is prepared to argue that it has nothing to do with general deterrence or placation. To be sure, a legal punishment is the outcome of a judicial process; hence, one can understand the emphasis in legal realism on the decisions of judges. Yet one would be hard pressed to find in criminal law *or* civil law a judge who will admit to deciding a case without regard to either deterrence or placation.

There are arguments about the nature of law other than those advanced by major figures in analytical jurisprudence (Kelsen, 1967) or legal realism (Llewellyn, 1951). H.L.A. Hart (1961) questions Kelsen's conception of law by arguing that it reflects a preoccupation with criminal law and fails to recognize how law enables citizens to realize their desires, as when they enter into contracts, get married, or make wills. The "enabling function" (not Hart's term) of law is overlooked also by legal realists in their concern with case law or dispute settlement, which necessarily excludes instances where individuals have used law effectively and thereby avoided litigation. We are not concerned here with whether wills, contracts, and marriages are actually components of law, nor even with the sense in which they are. Insofar as they are components of law, they are *prelusive* social control.[20] Should scholars in jurisprudence (followers of Hart in particular) dispute that identification, they should contemplate this question: Why would anyone follow "legal directions" when entering into a contract, getting married, or leaving a will if not to facilitate the manipulation of the behavior of others in disputes, should they arise, by making allegations to legal officials (including jurors)? If Hart's defenders should reply that people enter into contracts, get married, and make wills uncritically, it is a tacit admission that they attach no significance to the

---

[19] See Gibbs (1972) for illustrative definitions of law in the tradition of legal realism.

[20] Although H. L. A. Hart is much admired by this author, it must be said that he wrote as though everyone knew what a contract is and as though contracts are unquestionably legal phenomena. To the contrary, the notion of contract is one of the conceptual quagmires of jurisprudence, and that becomes all the more evident when one contemplates testing empirical propositions about contracts or simply gathering data on instances of contract (Macaulay, 1977).

"legality" of their actions. If that is so, one must wonder not only as to the sense in which those actions are components of law but also why the enabling function is important. It would be as though one argues that the alleviation of pain is the principal function of medicine but only to admit that people do not know why they visit hospitals or physicians.

There are various contending conceptions of law, and the divergence is even greater than suggested by the contrasts in definitions. The contrasts are not surprising if only because an astonishing variety of acts and practices are identified as components of law even in one Anglo-American country. The variety is such that no definition of law is likely to satisfy anyone truly; but the definitional problem cannot be ignored in conceptualizing social control because of an unquestioned convention—that law is a means of social control. Accordingly, there is a real need for a conceptualization of social control that facilitates the description of what would qualify as components of law by virtually any definition of law, regardless of country, culture, jurisdiction, or historical period. The extent to which the present conceptualization meets that need cannot be ascertained without attempts to use it; however, previous comments should not be construed as implying that law (including its enforcement) is limited to vicarious and prelusive social control. Regardless of the kind of law in question (e.g. criminal, tort, contract), the judicial process (litigation, prosecution, etc.) is a study in allegative social control and attorneys (prosecutors or otherwise) also engage in referential social control in that process. Observe that participants in the "operations" of law (whether law enforcement or litigation) other than officials (i.e. litigants, defendants, complainants, parties, plaintiffs, etc.) are necessarily engaged in referential, allegative, or prelusive social control.

The foregoing should not be construed as a claim that all behavior of individuals acting in the capacity of legal officials is social control. Proximate and sequential control does take place within each *organization* of legal officials. Thus, police chiefs issue commands to subordinates, and police officers issue orders to private citizens. Yet law is the most complex and organized sphere of social control, in that commands by legal officials may be backed by statutes or rules, which in themselves constitute referential and/or prelusive social control.

Empirical Applicability

No one uses the term social control as though it is a purely theoretical construct (i.e. that the term does not denote observable events or things). Consequently, any definition of social control should be regarded as empirically applicable, and contrary evidence would be sufficient grounds for rejecting the definition. Yet an assessment of the empirical applicability of any term in the social sciences is extremely difficult, and the reasons transcend two obvious considerations.

The first obvious consideration is that it would be grossly unrealistic to demand absolute empirical applicability, meaning no instances in which independent observers disagree in applying a definition to identify a particular event or thing. That criterion would virtually eliminate the social science vocabulary; hence, empirical applicability must be treated as a matter of degree. Even so, it is difficult to determine the degree to which any definition is empirically applicable (if only because no one can know the outcome of future attempted applications), and there is no clear-cut criterion as to the necessary degree of empirical applicability.

The second obvious consideration is that in assessing empirical applicability there can be no satisfactory substitute for actual attempts to apply the definition in question—having two more independent observers apply the definition to particular events or things and ascertaining the amount of agreement. Nonetheless, definitions can be assessed in a general way if only to anticipate problems in attempted applications. For instance, many of the definitions of social control considered in Chapter 3 (especially those formulated by Landis, Hollingshead, Parsons, and Sites) encompass terms so vague that doubts as to their empirical applicability are justified.

Turning now to less obvious considerations, most social and behavioral scientists think of empirical applicability (insofar as they use the term at all) in connection with ''the reliability of measures.'' But the ultimate criterion of reliability is *concordance,* meaning the amount of agreement among independent observers in the observations they report about the same events or things, whether those observations pertain to the application of a definition, a formula, or an instrument. Although concordance is the most important facet of empirical applicability, there are three others—intelligibility, universality, and feasibility. Some of those facets are not completely distinct from concordance, but they should be examined separately.

Intelligibility

Empirical applicability is precluded altogether if independent observers regard the definition as unintelligible. Whether a definition is so regarded commonly depends on the primitive terms in the *definiens* (meaning terms that are left undefined). For example, if a definition of social control includes the term ''power'' and that term is left undefined, then it is a primitive term in that context. Some terms in the *definiens* may be defined, and such ''supplementary'' definitions have a crucial bearing on the empirical applicability of the definition as a whole. Since an infinite series of definitions is impossible, some of the statements (primary or supplementary) that enter into a definition must comprise primitive terms.

No claim is made that everyone will understand the final definition of social control, but it is more intelligible than contending definitions *if* all definitions are studied carefully. In particular, while definitions that reflect the prophylactic conception of social control appear simpler (hence, more intelligible) than the final definition, application of those definitions presumes an understanding of "deviance" and requires judgments as to whether particular behaviors, practices, or institutions actually counteract deviance.

The foregoing claim about the superiority of the final definition is not a denial of problems in applying the definition. The immediate problems center on the notion of "manipulation of behavior" and the intentional quality attributed to manipulation. The notion is not difficult to comprehend if only because it has such an inclusive meaning—any alteration or termination of someone else's behavior. Moreover, inferences of intention *do not* require an identification of ultimate goals. For example, in examining Hitler's statements about Jews, one need not infer whether he intended to further electoral support of the Nazi party, increase financial contributions to the party, expand the party's membership, or solidify his authority within the party. Hitler may have anticipated any or all of those things, and perhaps even something else. Yet those statements would be referential social control regardless of Hitler's ultimate goal or purpose, as long as one infers that Hitler viewed them as contributing to the alteration or termination of someone's behavior. Even the exact identification of the "someone" (the second party) is not essential, nor need it be presumed that Hitler acted with a precise idea as to the identity of the second party. Briefly, the identification of the second party, the particular kind of behavior that Hitler anticipated altering, or the ultimate end sought would not be necessary to designate his Jew-baiting as social control. For that matter, the designation would not rest on the assumption that Hitler viewed *each* of his statements about Jews as being necessary or sufficient to manipulate someone's behavior; all that one need infer is that Hitler viewed such statements as contributing to that manipulation.

Despite all of the foregoing, one may understandably long for specific rules of inference (i.e. a stipulation of the conditions that justify inferences as to intention). Frankly, such rules cannot be formulated at present, and attempts to formulate them will be feasible only after extensive attempts are made to apply the definition of social control. Yet, even now, three *general guides* can be formulated.

First, while intention has a cognitive component and an affective component,[21] the latter can be ignored, because only rarely do individuals manipulate behavior to ends that they perceive as partially undesirable (e.g. when a surgeon anticipates gain as a consequence of an operation). Hence, in designating behavior as social control, one must be prepared to justify the inference that the first party anticipated the alteration or termination of someone's behavior; but one need not justify the inference that the

---

[21] Specifically, the first party anticipates that his or her behavior will have a consequence that he or she perceives as desirable. Since the word "anticipates" is used in the sense of "some perceived possibility," both notions (anticipation and desirability) reduce to the idea that the first party "hopes" for some consequence of his or her behavior.

party perceived that consequence as desirable. For that matter, the word "anticipated" should be construed as the perceived *possibility* of some particular consequence rather than some exact level or range of probability (e.g. 1.0, .5).

Second, one need not infer the intention of each act in a series of the same general type. To illustrate, no claim is made here that preliminary to each derogatory statement about Jews Hitler contemplated a particular possible consequence. It is necessary to assume only that at some point Hitler anticipated altering someone's behavior by making such statements. It may well be that the second party was not the same in all instances of Hitler's Jew-baiting (e.g. fellow Nazis in the early days of the party but, later, nonparty members), and it need not be assumed that Hitler's precise goal never varied (e.g. in some instances he may have anticipated expansion of party membership but increasing financial contributions to the party in other instances). Such distinctions could be relevant for certain research purposes, but they need not be recognized in designating Hitler's Jew-baiting as referential social control.

Third, there are five bases for inferences of intention, *and any one is a sufficient justification* for designating behavior as social control. The first is *unilateral*; a social scientist (or anyone working under his or her direction) infers intention through direct observation or accounts of overt behavior but without reference to anyone's interpretation of the first party's behavior. The second is *subjective*; the first party's interpretation (solicited or otherwise) of the behavior in question is the basis for inferring intention.[22] The third is *authoritative*; it is based on judgment of an expert (e.g. a historian of Nazi Germany) as to the first party's intention. The fourth is *social*; it is based on statements of a member of the social unit in question as to the first party's intention (e.g. statements by Goebbels, the chief Nazi propagandist, as to Hitler's intentions in making derogatory statements about Jews). The fifth is *cultural*; it is a judgment by the social scientist about what inferences the typical member of the social unit would have drawn as to the first party's intention had the member witnessed the behavior in question and known the circumstances.

---

[22] When it comes to the first party's interpretation (or that of anyone subsequently designated), there are two specific rules for inferring intention. First, if an individual expresses surprise at all of the *perceived* outcomes (including none at all) of his or her behavior, that behavior was intentional and the goals were all outcomes expected but not subsequently perceived as realized. Observe that the rule applies only in failures at control, and the surprise of the individual is *sufficient* but not necessary for inferring intention (the reason being that a hoped-for consequence is no less indicative of intention than an expected consequence). Second, if an individual perceives certain events as consequences of his or her behavior and voices *no* surprise to at least one of them, then that behavior was intentional and each such perceived outcome was a goal. The second rule pertains to successful social control and, like the first rule, it supplies a sufficient criterion for inferring intention. Again, one may hope for a consequence but be surprised by its realization.

The last basis of inference entails considerable conjecture; but it is no different from the reliance in Anglo-American law on the notion of the "reasonable man." Of course, jurists and lawyers are supposedly familiar with the reasonable man; but it is an illusion to suppose that social scientists can competently analyze social control (or virtually any phenomena, for that matter) in a social unit without first becoming familiar with the culture of that unit.

Needless to say, in any particular case the alternative bases for inferring intention may lead to divergent conclusions. For example, Hitler's statements as to the anticipated consequences of his ordering the execution of storm-troop leader Roehm in a major purge of the Nazi party and a historian's inferences as to Hitler's intentions could be quite different (Gallo, 1972). When there are divergent conclusions as to the first party's intention, any one of them can be a sufficient justification for designating the behavior in question as social control; but all instances of divergent conclusions should be recorded.[23] Although limited research resources or other circumstances may preclude more than one basis for inferences, the number should be maximized whenever possible, with all divergences and convergences reported. The immediate purpose is to ascertain the amount of divergence. It may be discovered, however, that some theories of social control are supported only when tests of them are limited to a particular basis (or strategy) for inferring intention.

Universality

Suppose that a definition of a metropolitan area (or related procedures for applying the definition) makes reference to automobiles and telephones. Because of that reference alone, the definition could not be applied in any country prior to the 19th century, and it might well be of limited utility in

---

[23] The situation becomes complicated when conclusions as to the type of social control are divergent (i.e. depending on which of the five bases for inferences are considered). To illustrate, if a historian's interpretation of one of Hitler's acts justifies inferring that the act qualified as referential social control but an interpretation of a member of the Nazi party justifies inferring that the act was allegative social control, then the act must be recorded as both referential and allegative. However, with a view to a frequency count of instances of the various types of social control, the act would be assigned the value of ".5 referential" and ".5 allegative." If some act is social control in accordance with only two of five bases of inferences, its value would be .4 (i.e. 2/5) in a frequency count and .33 if only one of three bases (i.e. only three bases were considered). Such a strategy is defensible primarily because sociologists are rarely interested only in particular acts or even particular agents of social control, not even a prominent figure like Hitler (though one might want to compare, say, Hitler and Roosevelt as instances of *types* of agents of social control). Rather, the concern is with characteristics of social control as properties of a social unit (whether a family or a country), and sociologists should concern themselves first and foremost with differences among social units as to major features of social control (e.g. the relative predominance of vicarious control). For that purpose, the prescribed strategy for frequency counts is defensible.

identifying metropolitan areas in contemporary developing countries, where the number of automobiles and telephones per capita is far less than in the United States. As such, the definition would not be universally applicable.

While the demand for universally applicable definitions in the social sciences may appear unrealistic, without them theories cannot transcend particular cultures and historical periods. Moreover, no one would seriously dispute that a definition which can be applied in any culture or historical period is superior to one limited to, say, the U.S. as of 1980.

All of the definitions of social control in Chapter 3 and the final definition appear to be universally applicable; and with the exceptions of those that make reference to "society" (e.g. Landis), it appears that the definitions could be applied to any type of social unit, whether a family or a country. Hence, universality is not particularly relevant in judging the merits of contending definitions of social control. Yet it is one thing to assert that a particular definition of social control can be applied in any social unit at any time and quite another to assert that social control itself is universal (i.e. present in all social units, past, present, and future), or that it occurs with approximately the same frequency in all social units. Differences among social units as regards the frequency of social control should be treated as a matter of discovery. Accordingly, a definition should not preclude the possibility of a social unit in which there is no social control; and that possibility is virtually precluded if social control is not somehow distinguished from normal or everyday interaction. Yet no significance should be attached to the seeming infrequency of social control in some of the social units or locales that have been studied intensely by social scientists and analyzed in a well-known publication, such as Whyte's *Street Corner Society* (1955), Llewellyn and Hoebel's *The Cheyenne Way* (1941), Liebow's *Tally's Corner* (1967), Howell's *Hard Living on Clay Street* (1973), and Pospisil's *Kapauku Papuans and Their Law* (1958). Inspection of those works will suggest few instances of social control as defined here. This may be due to all too general descriptions of behavior in those social units of locales (e.g. an author reports that someone "persuaded" someone else to do something without indicating how the persuasion was accomplished), or it could be due to the reluctance of the authors to make inferences about intention.[24] Nonetheless, for reasons to be indicated in the subsequent chapter, sociologists should entertain the possibility that social control occurs much more frequently in some social units than in others, and

---

[24] It is unfortunate that such "in-depth" accounts of particular social units or locales report only isolated, illustrative instances of social control; but that is the case regardless of the definition of social control. For that matter, it is an illusion (though widespread in sociology) that truly useful data can be gathered independently of any particular conceptual scheme. As a manifestation of that illusion, the reliance of sociologists on published data (e.g. census statistics) gives rise to a great deal of purely descriptive (atheoretical) research precisely because the data were not gathered in the context of any particular conceptual scheme that is peculiar to sociology.

definitions of social control should facilitate descriptions of such differences.[25] Few of the illustrative definitions (Chapter 3) facilitate the description of social control if only because in most cases it is not clear what would constitute an *instance* of social control. In the case of Hollingshead's definition, "organization of a people" hardly denotes events that can be classified and enumerated. And if social control is any process or mechanism that counteracts deviance (the prophylactic conception), what is an *instance* of social control?

Feasibility

Even if maximum agreement is realized when independent observers apply a definition, it may become obvious that its application requires enormous time and research resources. For that matter, regardless of the amount of time and research resources, some social phenomena (certain kinds of deviance being instances) are such that direct observation of instances borders on the impossible. The problem haunts all social and behavioral sciences that are primarily observational rather than experimental, and it certainly is the case in the study of social control.

Any definition of social control should be such that it can be applied in systematic research. The need is all the more pressing since contemporary data on social control (whatever the definition) comprise little more than isolated, casual observations by social scientists (historians and anthropologists in particular) in a few social units. Those observations could be a source for ideas that are steps toward theories of social control; but whatever their utility in that direction, the observations are too anecdotal and limited for tests of theories. Since this work is concerned primarily with conceptualization, it does not extend to a detailed treatment of research designs for gathering data on social control. However, at least one strategy should be described in general terms, if only because the study of social control suffers as much from a lack of research strategies as it does from inadequate conceptualizations (which is not surprising since a research design presumes a defensible conceptualization).

Assume that it is possible to select a representative sample of households, production organizations (companies, corporations), and churches (or equiva-

---

[25] Of course, it may well be that the most substantial and significant difference among social units has to do with the predominant type of social control, not its frequency. Hence, a definition of social control should facilitate the identification of types. In that connection, contemplate Kluckhohn and Leighton's commentary on the Navaho (1951:218): "The Navaho never appeals to abstract morality or to adherence to divine principles. He stresses mainly the practical considerations: 'If you don't tell the truth, your fellows won't trust you and you'll shame your relatives.' " A better illustration of referential social control cannot be provided. In addition, the commentary suggests a generalization: Among tribal, agrarian peoples, the predominant type of social control is referential.

lents) in each of three countries. Further assume that the countries are selected so that two of them represent extremes as regards the per capita use of inanimate energy (an indicator of complexity or development). Now assume that a representative sample of individuals can be selected from the three populations (households, production organizations, and churches) in each country. Finally, assume that questions something like the following are posed to each individual: When was the last time that two or more people in your (household, place of work, or church) got into a dispute? What was the dispute about and how did it develop? Who were involved? Who did anything in an attempt to settle the dispute? What did they do? What did they hope to accomplish? What was the outcome?

Such questions may appear far removed from the final definition of social control, but recall that social control is most likely to occur when something "goes wrong" in human relations (i.e. someone's expectations or evaluations of conduct have been violated), and that is the rationale for proposing a focus on disputes. However, the idea is not that all responses by individuals to the indicated kinds of questions will be reports of social control. It may well be that they report instances of proximate or sequential control. Indeed, some disputes may simply simmer, with no real attempt made by anyone to settle them. Nonetheless, accounts of disputes could be analyzed with a view to ascertaining differences among social units as regards the various types of externalistic control (social or otherwise) that enter into dispute settlement, and systematic descriptions of such variation could be strategic in speculation leading to theories about control (social or otherwise).

Far from being peculiar to the present conceptualization of social control, research along the lines just suggested would be useful in assessing the purported principal function of law: that it is a means of settling disputes. Yet there is actually very little *systematic* data on recourse to the law in dispute settlement, let alone data on different types of social units in different types of countries. Whatever the extent of recourse to law in dispute settlement and whatever variation there may be from one social unit to the next in that regard, it would bear on the study of social control; and accounts of the outcome of disputes would throw some light on the relative effectiveness of law and various types of control in dispute settlement.

The argument is not that all disputes result in social control, or that social control takes place only in the context of dispute settlement. Nonetheless, the kind of data just described would raise the quality of observations on social control from the anecdotal to that of systematic research.

Theories
of Social
Control

6

The sociological literature on social control suggests two major questions about the subject. First, why do the features or kinds of social control vary from one social unit or historical period to the next? Second, what is the relative efficacy of the various kinds of social control and why are some kinds more effective than others?[1] The two central notions, "features of social control" and "kinds of social control," are vague; but as subsequent observations indicate, those notions encompass such a wide variety of phenomena that a precise definition is neither feasible nor desirable.

It is most unlikely that any one theory can provide a complete answer to either of the two major questions. There are seemingly infinite features or kinds of social control, and the choice among them should depend on theoretical or research interests. Thus, one may or may not be interested in historical trends in the severity of legal punishments.

---

[1]The presumption is that some kinds of social control are more successful than others. It may well be that the differences among the various kinds of social control in that regard are so contingent on conditions (e.g. referential control is possibly more effective, overall, than is vicarious control but only in small social units) that an adequate answer to the second question cannot be in the form of a simple generalization. For that matter, the first question is also based on a presumption—that the features of social control vary a great deal among social units and over time. Both presumptions reflect a paucity of purely descriptive but systematic research on social control, and the present argument is that social control has never been conceptualized so as to facilitate such research.

Whether such interest bears on the first major question depends on one's conception of social control (i.e. whether the notion encompasses legal punishments). Differences of opinion on such subjects are beyond resolution; again, no definition is right or wrong, true or false. Yet certain conventions deserve recognition in assessing the merits of a definition, one being the designation of particular ideas as theories of social control. If the acceptance of a definition of social control entails a rejection of all such designations (i.e. there are no social control theories), critics would regard it as radical to the point of being unrealistic and perhaps rightly so. That is not to say that a definition of social control must be consistent with *all* conventional identifications of theories. In any case, a definition should serve to identify "gaps" in the literature, meaning specific questions about social control that have received little or no attention.

Punishment and Social Control

Before the widespread acceptance of the prophylactic conception of social control, several ideas about punishment were commonly designated as social control theories. That designation evidently stemmed from the early preoccupation with "means of social control" (Lumley, 1925) and the presumption that punishments (especially legal punishments) are means. The rationale for that presumption was never clearly articulated; but, accepting that presumption, the theories bear on the first major question about social control, as all of them imply an explanation of variation in the severity of legal punishment (e.g. why the death penalty is used more in some countries than in others).

The Labor Market

One of the theories is essentially Marxist. According to Rusche and Kirchheimer (1939), the character of legal reactions to crime depends on certain economic conditions. Given an excess of labor (as manifested in unemployment), the dominant economic class favors especially harsh penalties for crimes—ostensibly to repress dissent. The theory suggests that economic conditions determine specific kinds of penalties. To illustrate, the argument is that punishment tends to take the form of imprisonment given an excess of labor, whereas fines would be more common when labor power is in short supply.

Although Rusche and Kirchheimer's theory fits certain facts of European penal history, the merit is not surprising because their theory is essentially a summary of historical trends prior to World War II. For that reason alone, it is questionable whether the theory applies universally or even to contemporary

Western countries. In the case of the United States, for example, there has been a marked increase over recent years in the prescription of mandatory prison sentences but the increase ostensibly took place independently of changes in the unemployment rate.

Middle-Class Indignation

Whereas Rusche and Kirchheimer attribute harsh penal sanctions to a dominant economic class, Ranulf (1938) attributes them to the "middle class." The idea is that members of that class cling to their social position by conformity, so assiduously that they repress their libidinal (sexual) drives inordinately and suffer frustration as a consequence. That frustration is reflected in the moral indignation with which members of the class react to criminal acts and their demands for harsh punishment. It is as though members of that class are determined to use criminal law as a means of imposing their morality on everyone. So Ranulf's argument can be stated as a proposition: Legal reactions to crime are punitive to the extent that the middle class controls penal sanctions.

The meaning of "middle class" is debatable even in Western civilization, and outside that context the term is scarcely applicable. So systematic tests of Ranulf's theory are virtually precluded, especially since tests would require not only the identification of a middle class in each society being compared but also an assessment of that class's control over penal practices. (Ranulf tacitly assumed such control.) Finally, if the theory is evaluated by general observations, two historical societies are likely exceptions. Among the Aztecs and the Incas, reactions to crime were evidently severe (Davies, 1974; Moore, 1958); yet it would be dubious to argue that a "middle class" controlled penal practices in either society.

The Scapegoat Theory

In a sense, Ranulf's argument is a psychological theory of punishment, even though it focuses upon a particular social class. Psychological considerations are stressed even more in the "scapegoat" theory of punishment. The theory is an amalgamation of various ideas (Sutherland and Cressey, 1974); but all of those ideas seem to stem from a psychoanalytic perspective. So a brief summary is defensible. Rigid social proscriptions result in the repression of sexual and aggressive urges, with the consequence being guilt feelings. Punishment is one means of expiation, but those suffering guilt avoid punishing themselves by demanding (though they may not consciously recognize the connection) harsh punishment of criminals. In making such a demand the citizen in effect says to the criminal: You must suffer for having done what I unconsciously yearn to do.

If the scapegoat theory is intended only to explain why reactions to crime are punitive, then it ignores a significant phenomenon—the punitiveness of reactions to crime appears to vary greatly among social units and historically. However, if it is assumed that the repression of sexual or aggressive urges is of greater intensity in some social units than in others, then variation in punitiveness is consistent with the theory. Given that assumption, the theory can be reduced to a proposition: The more rigid the social proscription of sexual or aggressive acts, the more punitive the reactions to crime.

The most conspicuous defect of the theory is that, even when reduced to a proposition, it defies any systematic test. Each test would require (inter alia) that investigators somehow measure the rigidity of social proscription of aggressive and sexual acts (or measure their actual repression) in each of several social units, and for practical reasons alone such an undertaking is not feasible. Moreover, even if tests were undertaken, negative results would not be surprising, as the theory rests on the precumption that some "psychological need" of the general populace determines penal practices (e.g. statutory penalties). That presumption ignores the possibility that the elites of a social unit determine penal practices, and those practices may reflect largely political considerations [reconsider Rusche and Kirchheimer (supra)]. Even if the practices should reflect the "psychological needs" of the elites, it does not follow that such needs of the elites and those of the general populace are congruent.

Social Heterogeneity and Antagonism

According to Sorokin (1937:523), the punishment of crime reflects so-cio-cultural differences (more specifically, "ethicojuridical" heterogeneity) and antagonistic relations among the social divisions in a society; the greater the differences and the greater the antagonism, the more severe the punishments. The underlying idea is that a dominant social division (e.g. a caste) uses harsh penalties for crimes when it is culturally distinct from and in an antagonistic relation with the other divisions. The use of harsh penalties is essentially a strategy to maintain dominance, but Sorokin's theory is not limited to economic considerations. Conceivably, given marked religious factionalism in a society, reactions to crime would be harsh even if none of the religious bodies were economically dominant.

Sorokin's theory is commendable, but it defies systematic tests. Such tests would require measurement of "ethicojuridical" heterogeneity and antagonistic group relations. Sorokin does not specify how such phenomena are to be measured, and it is doubtful if they are measurable.

Cultural Consistency

The most general theory on the subject can be summarized briefly: The character of reaction to crime in a society is consistent with the cultural features and basic conditions of life in that society. That summary statement suggests a unity in the "cultural consistency" theory, as it is commonly known; but the theory actually comprises diverse ideas and represents the thinking of various social scientists (Sutherland and Cressey, 1974). As such, it is realistic to speak of illustrative versions of the theory. One version is that legal penalties are especially harsh when the death rate is high and physical suffering is very much a part of life. In such a society, the death penalty and torture would be expected to apply to various crimes, for such punishments are consistent with the conditions of life. Another version of the theory asserts a relation between the character of reactions to crime and cultural values. Thus, if the notion of "liberty" is dominant in the prevailing political ideology, then imprisonment rather than corporal punishment is likely to be a common penal sanction. A third version of the theory links penal sanctions with the economic system, capitalism in particular. For example, when the economy is based on the price system, then legal penalties are likely to take the form of graduated fines, with the amount depending on the type of offense.

Not one of the diverse ideas in the cultural consistency theory is truly satisfactory. Capital punishment and physical torture have been abolished in numerous countries, and that change took place as the standard of living and progress in medical science increased substantially; but comparisons of some countries (e.g. Mexico and the Republic of South Africa) create doubts about the universality of the relation. Moreover, capital punishment and physical torture are not as common among nonliterate people (Sorokin, 1937:611; Hoebel, 1954) as the theory suggests. Certainly reactions to what might be construed as crimes among certain nonliterate peoples (hunting−gathering units in particular) appear much milder than in the societies of antiquity (e.g. ancient Greece) and even milder than those practiced in England as late as the 19th century.

As for the asserted relation between the cultural valuation of liberty and the use of imprisonment as a penal sanction, there appears to be some association in the history of Western civilization, an example of which is the increase in imprisonment after the American and French revolutions. However, it is difficult to make judgments about the cultural valuation of liberty, let alone to measure the phenomenon. If general observations are to suffice, then one can argue that the Plains Indians placed a high value on personal liberty (Ambrose, 1975) but imprisonment as a reaction to crime was alien to those peoples. Then consider Anglo-American jurisdictions, where from 1940 to 1960 there was a marked decline in the proportion of convicted felons who received a prison sentence. It strains credulity to argue that the decline reflected changes in valuations of liberty. As for the asserted relation between penal sanctions and the price system (a component of capitalism), graduated fines played a role in reactions to delicts among the Ifugao of the Phillipines (Barton, 1919); but the economy of those peoples was largely of the subsistence type and scarcely capitalistic.

The Division of Labor

Durkheim's theory (1949 implies an inverse relation between the division of labor and the punitiveness of reactions to crime, but several other variables enter into his theory. In societies where there is little division of labor, social solidarity is "mechanical" — meaning minimal socio-cultural contrasts among the members, especially as regards their normative beliefs. Hence, the bond that unites the members is likeness and consensus. Durkheim argued that when normative consensus is marked in a social unit, even those who are not victims react to crimes intensely and demand retribution, as though they have personally been harmed. That demand is reflected in "repressive" law, which is punitive in character. As the division of labor increases, solidarity becomes organic, meaning that social life comes to be based more upon functional interdependence than upon likeness and consensus. Although repressive law does not disappear, the penalties for crime become less punitive, and "restitutive" law gains predominance. The purpose of restitutive law is to regulate and restore order rather than to provide punishment for the sake of vengeance.

Although one may equate repressive law and criminal law as it is known in Anglo-American jurisdictions, that syntax does not clarify Durkheim's juridicial concepts. One purpose of criminal law in Anglo-American jurisdictions is deterrence (Morris, 1966), not retribution alone. Further, restitutive law cannot be described as simply noncriminal law, for tort law has a punitive quality. So it is difficult to designate any specific juridical "facts" that either support or refute Durkheim's theory. In Western civilization, from antiquarian societies (e.g. Roman) to the present, the *general* trend may have been toward less punitive criminal sanctions; but even that point is disputable (Sorokin, 1937). Moreover, even if the general trend were in that direction, it is precisely that trend that led Durkheim to formulate his theory; hence, outside of the context of Western history, the theory is questionable. As mentioned earlier, reactions to deviance among some nonliterate peoples appear to have been relatively mild, but in such social units the division of labor is minimal.[2] So, contrary to Durkheim's theory, it may be that reactions

[2]For extensive and systematic criticism of Durkheim's theory, see Sorokin (1937) and Spitzer (1975a).

to crime are most punitive where there is a *moderate* degree of division of labor (i.e. neither high nor low).

Further Commentary on the Theories

The foregoing commentary on particular theories of punishment is all too brief, and several additional criticisms apply to all of them. It is not clear whether the theories purport to explain variation in the severity of prescribed legal punishments (e.g. statutory penalties) or *actual* legal punishments; in any case, none of them encompass a stipulation of procedures for the numerical representation of severity. Such a procedure would be extremely difficult to formulate (especially in such a way that its cross-cultural application would be feasible), the primary difficulty being that judgments of severity tend to be subjective and ethnocentric. For example, among nonliterate peoples "gang rape" was a fairly common reaction to allegations of adultery by a married woman. Is such a reaction more or less punitive than, say, five years of imprisonment?

Given seemingly insurmountable problems in the numerical representation of the severity of legal punishments, in attempting to test the theories it may be necessary to take the prescribed generality of the death penalty and/or the frequency of executions as indicative of the severity of legal punishments in general. However, even if that strategy were defensible, doubts about the validity of all of the theories are justified if only because none of them stress the possibility that dramatic and extensive socio-cultural change itself is conducive to severe legal punishments.[3] During periods of such change, a great deal of conflict is inevitable. Some interest groups promote change, others resist it, and the politically dominant group use severe legal penalties because the members view their position as jeopardized (Hay et al., 1975). Thus, in the past 200 years of European history there were two periods in which the generality of the death penalty increased dramatically. The first period was the 18th century (the onset of the Industrial Revolution), especially in England, where the number of capital offenses increased from approximately 160 in 1765 to approximately 200 in 1820 (Radzinowicz, 1948:3−4). During the other period, circa 1920−1935, several countries (e.g. Germany, Italy) underwent a major economic depression and became fascistic (Rusche and Kirchheimer, 1939). What the two periods share in common (and little more) is simply rapid and extensive socio-cultural change.

---

[3]Sorokin's theory (1937) comes the closest to emphasizing change. Indeed, his theory is largely stated in the way of assertions about longitudinal relations (i.e. change), and it remains to be seen whether the theory extends also to sychronic (cross-sectional) variation in punitiveness (e.g. differences among countries). Be that as it may, it could be that any massive and sudden social change is followed by major increases in the punitiveness of criminal sanctions, with *or* without a large increase in "ethicojuridicial hetrogeneity."

No real purpose would be served by further commentary on theories of punishment, because the interest of sociologists in those theories has long since ended.[4] The reason has little to do with the difficulties of testing the theories, or with general observations that cast doubts on the theories. Sociologists habitually tolerate untestable theories, even those that appear inconsistent with general observations. More relevant, the prophylactic conception of social control now has a large following, and according to that conception a practice or institution is not social control unless it does counteract deviance. Legal punishment surely qualifies as a practice or institution; but, for reasons subsequently indicated, over the past 30 years sociologists have been skeptical about the preventive efficacy of legal punishments.

Revival of Interest in the Deterrence Doctrine

Commencing in the late 1960s, a few sociologists turned to this question: Do legal punishments deter crime? That issue had been posed about 20 years before, and after several studies (most concerned with capital punishment) the answers were uniformly negative. Today, in light of recent studies (many by economists), only incorrigible partisans regard the evidence as compelling one way or the other [see surveys in Blumstein et al. (1978) and Gibbs (1975)]. Since space limitations preclude a summary of that evidence, this commentary is restricted to the reasons for inconclusive evidence.

Although the point is seldom recognized, the deterrence doctrine is not a unitary theory. It comprises at least three independent theories: one pertaining to specific deterrence, the postulated impact of punishment on those who have been punished; another pertaining to restrictive deterrence, the postulated restraining influence of the threat of punishment on those who commit crimes with impunity; and the last one pertaining to absolute deterrence, the postulated possibility that the fear of punishment has prevented some individuals from ever committing the type of crime in question. The theories are independent in that evidence falsifying one of them would have no necessary bearing on the other two (e.g. even if there is no specific deterrence at all, it could be that the threat of legal punishment does generate a great amount of restrictive deterrence—many individuals substantially restrict their criminal activities to avoid punishment). Unfortunately, systematic statements of the theories are lacking; and no deterrence theory can be reduced to a simple proposition, such as:The greater the severity of legal punishments in a jurisdiction, the lower the crime rate of that jurisdiction. To the contrary, in

---

[4]The termination of interest in punitiveness is unfortunate, especially in the case of Sorokin's theory (1937). It is thoroughly sociological, and *general* observations (including those made by Sorokin) suggest that the theory has real merit.

stating a theory pertaining to general deterrence (absolute or restrictive) no less than nine properties of legal punishment could be relevant (Gibbs, 1975).

Whatever properties of punishment are recognized in a deterrence theory, two problems will persist in testing the theory. First, putative evidence of deterrence (e.g. an inverse relation among American states between the objective certainty of imprisonment and the crime rate) may only reflect one or more of nine nondeterrent mechanisms (Gibbs, 1975), the most commonly recognized being incapacitation (e.g. auto theft is difficult when incarcerated). Second, even if deterrence research could be designed so as to exclude the preventive effects of nondeterrent mechanisms, it would be further necessary to take into account *extralegal* conditions that inhibit or generate criminality (e.g. perhaps unemployment or the social condemnation of crime); but there is no accepted theory that identifies the relevant conditions (Gibbons and Jones, 1975; Reid, 1979; Rubington and Weinberg, 1973; Tittle et al., 1978; Traub and Little, 1975).

Granted all of the problems in assessing the deterrence doctrine, deterrence is nonetheless a strategic subject for social control studies. While social control is by no means limited to legal punishments, a deterrent penal policy is clearly an *attempt* at control; hence, deterrence studies have immediate policy implications. Yet the prophylactic conception of social control discourages a concern with deterrence. That is the case for reasons other than the idea legal punishments are not social control unless demonstrably efficacious and doubts about the efficacy of those punishments. Additionally, the prophylactic conception of social control reflects an assumption—that it is the crescive features of culture and social life which maintain social order. That assumption is a tacit belittlement of conscious and deliberate social control, including a deterrent penal policy.

Another Perspective on the Deterrence Doctrine

Whereas advocates of the prophylactic conception of social control tend to deny that the deterrence doctrine is a theory of social control, or simply attach no significance to the doctrine, it is clearly a theory of social control in light of the final definition of social control (Chapter 4). That is the case if only because any legal punishment can be construed as an instance of vicarious social control (i.e. an attempt to manipulate the behavior of a second party by punishing a third party). Insofar as legal punishments aim at general deterrence, then in each instance the individual punished is the third party and the public at large (i.e. anyone subject to the criminal laws in question) is the second party. However, some distinguished figures in jurisprudence and sociology (Durkheim, 1949) have belittled the utilitarian or instrumental quality of legal punishments, deterrence in particular. That belittlement runs contrary to Morris's conclusion (1966:631) that deterrence is a "primary essential postulate'' in all but one of the world's criminal law systems. Followers of Durkheim will point out that his argument at least holds for criminal law in the societies of antiquity (e.g. Babylonia); but Durkheim did not demonstrate that those who prescribed punishments for crimes in such societies were indifferent to deterrence. Even if retribution is the purpose of those who prescribe the punishments, retribution is not necessarily an end in itself. Advocates of the retributive doctrine are prone to create that impression, because they are opposed to utilitarianism, the deterrence doctrine in particular. They are reluctant even to suggest that punishment is or should be a means to an end, such as the prevention of crime (Gibbs, 1978; Bedau, 1978). However, insofar as punishments are prescribed with a view to satisfying someone's demand for vengeance or merely with a view to what others may do if alleged crimes are not punished, then punishment is vicarious social control (though not the deterrent subtype). Advocates of the retributive doctrine and followers of Durkheim may of course deny such intentions; but that denial is merely opinion, and it reflects a determination either to treat retribution as a purely metaphysical notion or to ignore the purposive quality of human behavior, that of legislators in particular.

The foregoing should not be construed as attributing validity to the deterrence doctrine. Whether or not the doctrine is valid, it does bear on one major issue: the relative efficacy of the various kinds of social control. Moreover, while the final definition provides a rationale for identifying the doctrine as a theory of social control, the definition also indicates why the doctrine is a narrow theory of social control. The doctrine focuses on legal punishments; but several types of social control have nothing to do with punishment, let alone legal punishments. Consequently, while work on the deterrence doctrine should continue because of its policy implications, the doctrine is far too narrow to guide research on social control.

The Misidentification of Theories

Although the point is never recognized in the literature, the prophylactic conception of social control blurs the distinction between theories of social control and theories of deviance. Once it is granted that any behavior, practice, or institution that counteracts deviance is social control, whether intended or not, then virtually all ''etiological'' theories about deviance bear on social control. Thus, if someone asserts that unemployment is a cause of robbery, then by implication that assertion identifies *employment* as social control.

Despite widespread acceptance of the prophylactic conception of social control for some 30 years, it has given rise to very few social control theories. For that matter, even identifications of social control theories are commonly misleading; most of the theories are actually theories about deviance. Two illustrations will suffice.

Regard for Status

LaPiere's work (1954) represents the first major theory on social control after widespread acceptance of the prophylactic conception. That theory can be summarized in one proposition: The amount of conformity to the norms of a social unit is a direct function of the regard for status in that social unit. The summary is a gross oversimplification, but elaboration would not reveal a defensible rationale for regarding the theory as bearing directly on the major questions about social control. Indeed, unless one denies that deviance is the obverse of conformity, then LaPiere's ideas clearly constitute a *theory of deviance*. If regard for status is the primary determinant of the rate of conformity, then it is the primary determinant of the rate of deviance; and if conformists differ from deviants primarily by their regard for status, then the distinguishing characteristic of deviants is given by implication (i.e. a lesser regard for status).

Stating the matter another way, if social control is a *subclass* of conscious and deliberate attempts to manipulate the behavior of others (i.e. if it is intentional), then LaPiere's ideas do not constitute a theory of social control. The point is not that regard for status is a psychological variable—hence, alien to sociological theory. Rather, regard for status is largely a crescive phenomenon, meaning one that is not deliberately created or manipulated to some end.

Control Theories of Juvenile Delinquency

Whereas LaPiere's theory is by *implication* a theory about conditions that inhibit deviance, several theories of juvenile delinquency that emerged in the 1960s explicitly purport to identify conditions that supposedly inhibit delinquency. Consistent with the prophylactic conception, those theories have come to be designated as "control" theories (Conger, 1976; Elliott et al., 1979; Short, 1979). The present survey is limited to Hirschi's version (1969), largely because it best illustrates the issue in question—the distinction between a theory of social control and a theory of deviance.

Hirschi's theory does not encompass a conceptualization of control or social control, and one is left with the impression that either term designates *any condition* that inhibits juvenile delinquency. The theory postulates four inhibitory conditions: (1) commitment to conventional goals, (2) attachment to conventional persons, (3) involvement in conventional activities, and (4) beliefs in conventional norms. To Hirschi's credit, he supplied illustrative procedures for the measurement of corresponding variables. Nonetheless, unless one accepts the prophylactic conception of social control and unless the four conditions do inhibit delinquency, there is no basis for identifying Hirschi's work as a theory of social control.[5] The four conditions may make a juvenile more subject to effective control by parents and other "conventional" persons; even so, outside the prophylactic conception, the conditions themselves are not social control. There is no evidence that Hirschi's four conditions are commonly created consciously and deliberately, let alone to prevent juvenile delinquency. Rather, the conditions are largely crescive.

Research Findings and Isolated Propositions

The prophylactic conception of social control has not been conducive to the formulation of theories, let alone fruitful theories; but to argue that the conceptualization in Chapter 4 will be superior in that regard would be conjecture. That is the case because no conceptualization literally gives rise to theories, for nothing can be substituted for the imagination of a theorist. It may be that some conceptualizations stimulate the imagination more than others, but the superiority of one conceptualization over another in that regard cannot be assessed a priori. Yet the *utility* of a conceptualization can be so assessed in connection with two other considerations.

The first consideration has already been alluded to: A conceptualization can be such as to identify certain gaps in a field as regards theories. The present conceptualization of social control (Chapter 4) serves to identify several such gaps. For all practical purposes, theories on social control are limited to *one subtype* of social control, deterrent vicarious. So it should be obvious that the present conception of social control is more useful than the prophylactic conception when it comes to identifying gaps in social control theories. The gaps in the case of the prophylactic conception are simply all possible social "things" that counteract deviance but have not been recognized in one theory or another, and the variety of those things is seemingly infinite.

The other consideration is more complex and more important. Theories rarely spring from pure intuitions; rather, they commonly grow out of systematic research findings and the pursuit of isolated propositions. However, if research findings and isolated propositions cannot be somehow ordered or integrated, they are not likely to give rise to a theory. So conceptualizations should play a role in theory construction over and beyond providing theorists with a language; they should also provide some basis for organizing and integrating research findings or isolated propositions. The argument then is that the present conception of social control provides a better basis than the prophylactic conception, and a detailed commentary follows on one particular line of research to support that argument.

[5]Hirschi himself often refers to his work as a "bonding theory" (i.e. the emphasis is on the strength of the social bond between juveniles and society), and that is a more accurate characterization than either a control theory or a social control theory.

The Role of Provocateurs in Social Control

In an unusual and interesting line of research, Gary Marx (1974) made numerous observations on instances where the police have employed agents to infiltrate the ranks of terrorists or dissidents and provoke them into illegal acts, especially acts of violence. As rightly suggested by Marx, the strategy is indicative of the autonomy of certain components of the organization of law enforcement, the judiciary in particular. When law enforcement is truly monolithic (i.e. completely directed by one absolute and central authority), the police do not have to resort to provocation. In that case, insofar as the police believe that certain unidentifiable individuals have *or* will oppose the government, they can simply apprehend those individuals and summarily punish or incapacitate them. However, when the police must cope with an independent judiciary, such unilateral action is likely to be negated and publicly condemned as illegal. Marx's statement (1974:433) illustrates the point.

> It is a measure of the relative weakness of the American social control apparatus and the constraints still upon it that evidence must be presented in court that people have actually committed (or plan to commit) the acts for which they are tried. . . . In such a society, however great its failings in some absolute sense, the legal repression of those seen as politically undesirable requires that authorities feel compelled to trick or aid them into actually carrying out illegal actions.

What Marx does not emphasize is that in employing provocateurs the police engage in a complicated process of social control, one that comprises at least four distinct steps, depicted as follows:

$$\begin{array}{cccc} (1) & (2) & (3) & (4) \\ \text{Police} \rightarrow \text{Provocateurs} \rightarrow \text{Dissidents} \rightarrow \text{Judiciary} \rightarrow \text{Dissidents} \end{array}$$

Step 3 in the process is not the control of the judiciary by the dissidents; rather, the judiciary responds to allegations of the police (or prosecutors) about the acts of the dissidents (the accused), and the police *may employ provocateurs with a view to making those allegations credible*. To be sure, the ultimate goal of the police is the punishment or incapacitation of the dissidents; but since the goal is sought through the judiciary,[6] the police must engage in allegative social control, with the judiciary as the third party in one of the procedural steps. To make their allegations more credible, the police

[6]Of course, the police may resort to direct punishment and incapacitation of dissenters (real or imagined) without the knowledge or concent of the judiciary, as when police officials form "death squads" to assassinate those who supposedly oppose the regime (e.g. alleged "communists" when the regime is conservative or fascist). Such actions are commonly social control (deterrent vicarious), but in resorting to them officials abandon the principle of "legality" and may reduce popular support of the regime as a consequence.

resort to "planting" provocateurs among dissidents, thereby inciting the dissidents to violate laws and facilitating their apprehension. Accordingly, the police actually engage in a sequence of distinct but integrated types of social control, the first being the modulative type (planting the provocateurs) and the second being allegative social control. While the dissidents are the second party throughout the process, provocateurs are the third party in the modulative control and magistrates are the third party in the allegative control. Actually, such a social control *process* may be even more complex than indicated. Insofar as the police engage in the surveillance of dissidents and/or gather information as to the most effective provocation, they have employed prelusive social control (prior to the modulative and allegative).

The strategy of the police is summarized dramatically by C. B. Zubatov, a Police Director in Czarist Russia [quoted in Marx (1974:402)]: "We shall provoke you to acts of terror and then crush you." Since Czarist Russia is commonly characterized as an autocratic society, one might assume that the use of provocateurs is alien to democracies. Yet is is in democratic societies that one of the necessary conditions for police employment of provocateurs is most likely to be found—an independent judiciary. (Even in Czarist Russia the police could not be absolutely certain that their actions would be routinely sanctioned by the judiciary.) However, since an independent judiciary is only a necessary condition, a simple generalization is precluded. The police or their superiors must be determined to eradicate dissent, and that determination typically reflects an enormous hatred or fear of dissidents. Such hatred and fear cannot be an individual phenomenon, true of only a few officials; it must be widespread, a largely collective phenomenon. And that occurs only when the status quo is perceived as threatened by internal conflict, class conflict in particular. Yet class conflict is only one condition in which police officers and the citizenry at large become convinced that the status quo is jeopardized by "an enemy within." Witness, for example, that during recent periods of American history the public and police officers have been gripped by the fear of "domestic communists," and in each period the police employment of provocateurs and informants flourished (Marx, 1974). A proposition is thus reached: The employment of provocateurs by the police as a means of social control is most likely when there is an independent judiciary in the criminal justice system and legal officials are convinced that status quo is jeopardized by domestic enemies.

While the proposition is a far cry from a theory, observe that its formulation was facilitated by the present conceptualization of social control. By contrast, Marx's observations have no obvious bearing on social control in light of the prophylactic conception. For one thing, it is difficult to see how the provocation of dissidents in Czarist Russia can be construed as "counteracting deviance"; it could indeed be argued that the provocation itself was deviant, especially since the police surely had some purpose for concealing their activities other than keeping the dissidents uninformed. If that point is disputed, it leads to sterile debates about the norms of Czarist Russia. Nor can advocates of the prophylactic conception productively argue that the ultimate goal of the police was to counteract deviance. Intention is irrelevant within that conception, and even if the behavior of the dissidents was truly deviant (a disputable contention in itself, for it depends on whose norms are taken as the criterion), the actions of the police could not be identified as social control without proof that those actions actually counteracted dissidence.

Toward a Theory of Social Control

While it would be grossly unrealistic to reject a conceptualization of some phenomenon (in this case, social control) until it is used in an impressive theory, that use is the ultimate defense of any conceptualization. It may be that some conceptualizations are simply more fertile than others, as they seem to generate more theories. However, while a conceptualization may somehow stimulate the imagination of theorists, there are no rules by which a theory can be deduced from a conceptualization (again, there is no substitute for a theorist's imagination); and a conceptualization of a phenomenon does not stipulate the questions that are to be asked about it (i.e. questions that theories are supposed to answer). Yet the two major questions about social control (supra) are not particularly meaningful without reference to some conceptualization of social control, and the prophylactic conception has had little utility in that regard. Since virtually all behaviors, practices, and institutions may somehow counteract deviance in one situation or another, the relevant "kinds" of social control are seemingly infinite. Moreover, the prophylactic conception casts doubt on the logical character of the second major question, for if counteracting deviant behavior is the criterion of efficacy, then any kind of social control is necessarily efficacious (i.e. if a behavior, practice, or institution does not counteract deviant behavior, it is not social control).

The two major questions are much more meaningful in light of the final definition of social control (Chapter 4). While a theorist may accept that definition and yet recognize kinds of social control other than referential, allegative, vicarious, modulative and prelusive, those five types could serve as a point of departure in contemplating the first major question. In other words, if it assumed that each of the five types of social control are more common in some social units or historical periods than in others, then that difference calls for an explanation—a theory. Similarly, given evidence that the ratio of successful to unsuccessful attempts at social control is greater for one type (e.g. referential) than another (e.g. vicarious) in a particular kind of situation, then that evidence is relevant in contemplating an answer to the second major question.

For reasons indicated previously, the deterrence doctrine is a theory about the efficacy of a particular subtype of vicarious social control. Work on deterrence would be much more fruitful (at least from the perspective of social control) if the research designs were to determine how much legal punishments prevent crimes relative to the amount prevented by other types or subtypes of social control. Nonetheless, the second major question about social control is now receiving considerable attention.

The same cannot be said for the first major question. Hence, at this point attention turns to *prospects* for additional social control theories. Two points should be stressed. First, the present definition does not preclude recognition of kinds of social control other than referential, allegative, vicarious, modulative, and prelusive. Second, the subsequent speculation about the correlates of the relative prevalence of those five types is only a step toward a theory, and it is freely admitted that a truly defensible theory may have to await descriptive studies of social control in a variety of social units.

Size and Socio-cultural Differentiation

The fundamental assumption is that human beings tend to employ those types of social control that are the most effective. But that does not imply that all attempts at social control are successful. Indeed, human beings experiment with social control; and regardless of their experience, they seldom have complete assurance of success. For that reason alone one can speak only of a tendency for the most effective type of social control to prevail.

Granted the foregoing assumption, under what conditions will each type of social control be the most effective? An answer as regards some particular type (e.g. vicarious social control) implies a generalization as to the condition in which that type will be the most prevalent (relative to other types). As shown in Table 6-1, the most relevant conditions are identified here as the size of a social unit and the degree of internal socio-cultural differentiation in that social unit. The arguments about size and differentiation are reduced to empirical generalizations in Table 6-1, and all the arguments are actually extensions of the foregoing assumption—that the most effective type of control is the most prevalent. Thus, one type of control (e.g. proximate) may be particularly effective only in small, relatively undifferentiated social units; if so, that type should become less and less prevalent as both size and differentiation increase. It is recognized that even if all research findings are consistent with the empirical generalizations in Table 6-1, those findings will not directly substantiate the basic assumption. Nevertheless, the assumption is central in the line of reasoning that led to the empirical generalizations.

The size variable is relatively simple: It pertains only to the number of members of the social unit in which control is attempted. Socio-cultural differentiation is a much more difficult notion; it encompasses so many factors (e.g. variety of occupations, the number of distinct languages) that the utility of the term is dubious. It is used here precisely because the generalizations about social control are exploratory; therefore, the use of terms that have a

Table 6-1. Postulated Relations Among Types of Social Unit[a]

Size of Each Social Unit (No. of Members)	Degree of Socio-cultural Differentiation Within Each Social Unit		
	Negligible	Moderate	Extensive
Large	*Type I Social Unit* RSC/DC >II ASC/RSC >II VSC/ASC >II MSC/VSC >II PSC/MSC >II	*Type IV Social Unit* RSC/DC >I or V or II ASC/RSC >I or V or II VSC/ASC >I or V or II MSC/VSC >I or V or II PSC/MSC >I or V or II	*Type VII Social Unit* RSC/DC:greatest ASC/RSC:greatest VSC/ASC:greatest MSC/VSC:greatest PSC/MSC:greatest
Medium	*Type II Social Unit* RSC/DC >III ASC/RSC >III VSC/ASC >III MSC/VSC >III PSC/MSC >III	*Type V Social Unit* RSC/DC >II or VI or III ASC/RSC >II or VI or III VSC/ASC >II or VI or III MSC/VSC >II or VI or III PSC/MSC >II or VI or III	*Type VIII Social Unit* RSC/DC >V or IX or VI ASC/RSC >V or IX or VI VSC/ASC >V or IX or VI MSC/VSC >V or IX or VI PSC/MSC >V or IX or VI
Small	*Type III Social Unit* RSC/DC:least ASC/RSC:least VSC/ASC:least MSC/VSC:least PSC/MSC:least	*Type VI Social Unit* RSC/DC >III ASC/RSC >III VSC/ARC >III MSC/VSC >III PSC/MSC >III	*Type IX Social Unit* RSC/DC >VI ASC/RSC >VI VSC/ASC >VI MSC/VSC >VI PSC/MSC >VI

[a] Each ratio is the *average* proportion of *all* instances of control that are of the designated type divided by the *average* proportion for some other designated type. Average proportions are the component ratio values because the presumption is that there are *at least* two instances of each type of social unit. The difference between types of social units as regards size or internal socio-cultural differentiation is a matter of degree. Both the size classes and differentiation classes are established by a trichotomization of values, such that the number of social units does not vary among the rows of the table, nor among the columns. The designated types of control are: DC = directorial control (proximate and sequential); ASC = allegative social control; MSC = modulative social control; PSC = prelusive social control; RSC = referential social control; VSC = vicarious social control.

broad meaning could be a constructive strategy. In any case, the arguments pertaining to Table 6-1 refer primarily only to two dimensions of socio-cultural differentiation: status differentiation and normative consensus. Status differentiation is conceived as being a direct mathematical function of two variables, the number of occupied status configurations (e.g. male, married, carpenter, 60 years of age) in the social unit and the "evenness" of the distribution of members among those configurations. Normative consensus for present purposes is conceived primarily as a matter of the amount of agreement among members of the social unit as regards their *perceived* evaluations of types of behavior.

Before advancing the principal arguments, a comment should be made about Table 6-1, which summarizes all of the empirical generalizations that are implied by the arguments. In testing those generalizations the frequency of instances of each type of control in a given social unit is to be expressed in relative terms—as a ratio to the frequency of some other type. Thus, if in a given social unit over a given period (e.g. a week) there are 20 instances of referential social control and there are 400 instances of directorial control (proximate and sequential combined), then the relative frequency of referential social control is .05 (i.e. 20/400). That illustration is not purely hypothetical. In any social unit (regardless of its size or socio-cultural differentiation), most attempts at control are probably directorial (proximate or sequential). Observe, however, that Table 6-1 predicts that the ratio of referential social control to directorial control (RSC/DC) reaches its greatest magnitude in the largest and most differentiated social units (type VII). Similarly, while referential social control may be more common than allegative social control in all social units, the ratio of the latter to the former (ASC/RSC) is predicted to reach its greatest magnitude in the largest and most differentiated social unit. While all five ratios are expected to be the greatest for type VII social units, predictions are made about each of the other types. Thus, it is predicted that the ratio of the frequency of modulative social control to the frequency of vicarious social control (MSC/VSC) for type IV social units will be greater than the MSC/VSC ratio for type I, type V, or type II social units.

For reasons indicated subsequently, it is presumed that each type of social control becomes frequent only as social units increase in size and/or differentiation. The order in which the types become frequent is asserted to be as follows: referential, allegative, vicarious, modulative, and prelusive. Stated otherwise, as size and differentiation increase, each type of control gives way, so to speak, to another type in the indicated order.

Principal Arguments

As long as a social unit is completely free of normative dissensus, any request (proximate control) by one member will be honored by the member to whom it is directed, for both parties will perceive the request as justified. In that

condition there is scarcely any occasion for social control. It is when normative consensus is less than maximum but substantial that members are especially predisposed to referential social control; and they are most likely to
succeed in small social units.[7] Since the first party knows the personal relations among all members of a small unit, he or she can readily identify the
prospective third parties that the second party respects, loves, hates, or fears.
Further, because of the high degree of normative consensus, the first party can
attribute a normative orientation to the third party that the second party is
likely to perceive as credible. Thus, when one brother says to another, "Give
me back the candy or I will tell mother!", he can rely not only on the brother's
attachment to and dependence on the mother but also on the brother's perception of the mother's evaluative standards.

The postulated direct relation between the size of a social unit and referential social control does not stem from the proliferation of prospective third
parties. Rather, in large social units individuals cannot maintain those kinds of
personal relations (e.g. friendship) with *all* members that promote success in
proximate control. Moreover, proximate control through coercion and
punishment becomes less and less feasible as the size of the social unit
increases, especially if a high degree of normative consensus is maintained,
for the members are likely to resist jointly what they perceive as unjustified
coercion or punishment. However, the direct relation between referential
control and size is not linear; eventually, sheer numbers limit the *range* of
effective referential control. In large social units prospective first parties find
it difficult to know the network of personal relations throughout the social unit
(e.g. who is the friend of whom). The success of referential control then
becomes particularly problematical, the principal reason being that the first
party cannot readily identify the most relevant third party for all prospective
second parties.

Referential social control is sustained by a principle of social organization—that the size of a social unit does not increase indefinitely without status
differentiation.[8] That differentiation may originate in selective interaction, for
in large social units it is impossible for everyone to eat, sleep, or work
together. Selective interaction (whereby each member interacts only with a
limited number of other members, or interacts much more with some

[7]Note, however, that several tactics in referential control are made less feasible in small social
units, one being "misrepresentation," as when the first party makes reference to a category of
individuals in such a way as to identify himself or herself with those individuals. Consider
Goffman's observation (1959:60): "Claims to be a law graduate can be established as valid or
invalid, but claims to be a friend, a true believer, or a music-lover can be confirmed or disconfirmed only more or less." Nevertheless, successful social control through false claims (whatever
they may be) are more difficult in small groups, because the members know more about each
other. Hence, in very small units there is at least one condition that is likely to make certain tactics
in the way of referential or allegative control ineffective.

[8]Truly systematic evidence (as opposed to casual observations and widely accepted assumptions) in support of the generalization is largely limited to the literature of organizational
sociology (Beyer and Trice, 1979).

members than others) gives rise to socially recognized divisions of the population (e.g. co-residents, work groups, extended families).[9] Those divisions come to be socially recognized in the sense that some term in the language of the social unit's population designates the members of each division as a *collectivity,* and those terms are status designations.[10] Equally important, status differentiation develops *within* each division, which is to say that for any of several possible reasons (e.g. differences in physical strength, charisma, skills in sustenance activities) certain individuals in each division come to be recognized as leaders, experts, or simply as someone to be reckoned with. Certain terms (e.g. father, shaman, *tohunga*) come to designate those individuals regardless of their divisional membership (i.e. the terms apply *across* divisions of the social unit). Such status occupants have an authority that promotes success in proximate control, and it gives rise to sequential control (e.g. grandfather−son−grandson) at least within particular divisions of the social unit (e.g. an extended family or clan). The statuses also sustain referential social control, because the occupants are likely to be particularly respected, feared, or valued by individuals in other statuses; as such, they are strategic third parties in referential social control and readily identifiable. However, for the same reason occupants of those statuses can be used in allegative control, and that type of social control has one advantage over referential control. In allegative control the first party can control the second party without interacting with the second party, and therefore the first party can control a greater number of individuals (as second parties).[11] Rather than interact with each individual, the first party communicates an allegation about them to a third party, and the first party need only know who supposedly has authority over those individuals (e.g. a grandfather, a clan head).

Although divisional statuses (e.g. a clan head) facilitate allegative control, at the same time they limit its range of effectiveness. Consider four individuals, two of which (X_1 and X_2) are members of the same division of the social unit (e.g. a clan within a tribe), while the other two (Y_1 and Y_2) are members of some other division (e.g. another clan within the same tribe).

[9]Of course, a socially recognized division of a social unit is a social unit in itself. The term "division" is employed here to designate a social unit that is a distinct component of a larger social unit.

[10]A status is a socially recognized category of individuals in a particular social unit (i.e. a division of that unit). Specifically, it is a division of the social unit's members that is designated by some term (e.g. barbers, parents) in the natural language of that social unit; and there is agreement between at least two members of the social unit (one in the division and one outside of it) that some evaluations or expectations of conduct apply to that division but not to others. Statuses may be ranked (e.g. physicians have more prestige than laborers) or unranked (e.g. widower and bachelor).

[11]If a statistical association does hold between the size of a social unit and the relative frequency of some type of social control, it does not stem from some logical (i.e. necessary) relation. It is logically possible for any type of social control to take place in a social unit with as few as three members. For that matter, in any given instance of social control the first, second, and third parties may not be members of the same social unit.

Suppose that the statuses of the four are such that X_1 has power over X_2, and Y_1 has power over Y_2. With a view to controlling Y_2, X_1 or X_2 can communicate allegations about Y_2 to Y_1; and with a view to controlling X_2, Y_1 or Y_2 can communicate allegations about X_2 to X_1. However, for attempts at allegative control to succeed, the third party (X_1 or Y_1) must view the allegation as credible and as describing something contrary to his or her evaluations of conduct (including conduct contrary to the third party's interests). Thus, should X_2 allege to Y_1 that Y_2 has been hunting on land that belongs to X_2, Y_1 may not view the complaint (allegation) as justified *even if credible*. If that is the case, it is unlikely that Y_1 will do anything to alter or rectify the hunting behavior of Y_2, and the attempt of X_2 at allegative control fails. Both the allegation and its failure are, of course, indicative of normative dissensus, and dissensus becomes all the more likely when there are several distinct divisions of a social unit. But a decline in normative consensus is not the only check on the effective range of allegative control; there are also "structural" limits. Returning to the previous illustration, if X_1 entertains controlling Y_1 by making allegations about the behavior of Y_1, to whom would X_1 direct the allegation? Since neither Y_2 nor X_2 have power over Y_1, there is no appropriate person to whom X_1 could direct the allegation.

The foregoing observations on allegative control are misleading in that they suggest that social control is only a way that disputes between individuals are settled. Yet once there are distinct divisions of a social unit, any one of several *perceived needs* can prompt action to promote integration of those divisions, some of the possible perceived needs being concerted military action by all adults regardless of their divisional membership, the settlement of disputes between leaders of the various divisions, and the promotion or preservation of economic relations (e.g. trading) among the divisions. Those perceived needs may stem primarily from the recognition of normative dissensus within the social unit as a whole, and the common solution is to enforce certain evaluations of conduct by the administration of punishments. With that step allegative control gives way to vicarious control. However, whatever the agencies or organizations that administer punishments, it is not assumed that they are created for the benefit of all members of the social unit. To the contrary, truly organized vicarious control may stem from conquest or the determination of one division of the social unit to impose its normative standards, exploit the other divisions, or otherwise further its interests.

Since punishment is unique in the antagonism and opposition that it promotes, those who prescribe its administration must be able to coerce all others. Hence, the idea that the State monopolizes the use of force. The immediate implication is that once something akin to the State comes into being, various divisions of the social unit (those in subordinate political positions) are severely restricted as to the kinds of vicarious control they can exercise, even though the members of those divisions may aspire to control the behavior of everyone in the social unit. Thus, even if capitalists control the State, it is significant that they do not threaten consumers with imprisonment and fines for failure to purchase certain commodities. Moreover, once the division of labor reaches that level (i.e. producers look to a national market), normative dissensus is so conspicuous that appeals to moral or ethical principles are not likely to be perceived as an effective way to control consumers. Once the division of labor (a dimension of social differentiation) reaches that level, contending economic interests gives rise to normative conflict (i.e. structural dissensus). Contrasts in the ideology of labor leaders and capitalists are examples. Capitalists may resort to indirect vicarious control of labor by (inter alia) promoting the criminalization of unions, strikes, and boycotts; but far from resolving the normative conflict, those measures commonly intensify it.

The alternative to vicarious control for those divisions of a social unit who do not monopolize coercion is modulative control. Even though a particular capitalist or retail proprietor may not own a television station or publish a newspaper, he or she can pay for the services of mass media personnel and *use* their influence to manipulate the behavior of consumers. And if a celebrity is paid a fee to testify that he or she uses the product in question or to extol its merits, that action is also modulative control.[12] As for reducing normative conflict (e.g. promoting a conservative ideology among employees), there are all manner of possibilities exemplified by the use of modulative control, such as financial support of fundamentalist preachers, subsidizing the works of reactionary authors, and underwriting the campaign expenses of conservative politicians.

The previous example should not be construed as suggesting that modulative control is peculiar to propertied classes. Indeed, those who stand in opposition to the propertied class are even more predisposed to modulative social control, if only because they have limited access to means for exercising vicarious control indirectly (e.g. influencing the enactment and enforcement of criminal statutes). However, when a "normative minority" has no assurance of success in either modulative control or indirect vicarious control, they may resort to direct vicarious control, as terrorists. Perhaps even more relevant, if one subscribes to the pluralistic model of democratic societies, then all manner of interest groups (not just capitalists) are engaged in an unceasing struggle to realize political influence; and modulative social control looms large in that struggle.

Granted that terrorism may be less important than pluralism, it is especially

---

[12]Here we see the role of money and wealth in social control, a role that it would be difficult to exaggerate, at least in some types of societies (capitalist in particular). Briefly, money or wealth makes it possible for the possessor to engage in all manner of modulative and prelusive social control.

relevant in contemplating how and why agents of the State go beyond vicarious control. In a large social unit characterized by marked normative dissensus, deterrent vicarious control (e.g. a penal policy aimed to promote general deterrence) may be ineffective because sheer numbers preclude close surveillance of all potential perpetrators of crimes[13] and normative dissensus precludes public support of Draconian penalties. While agents of the State do not view "ordinary" or "street" crimes (e.g. muggings, rapes, burglaries) as truly jeopardizing the system, they view political crimes (e.g. sedition, insurrections, instigation of riots) in a quite different light. Moreover, agents of the State commonly associate political crimes with publicly identifiable dissenters. Thus, throughout most of his career as Director of the F.B.I., J. Edgar Hoover evidently viewed such organizations as the Black Panthers and International Workers of the World ("Wobblies") as engaged in a vast *political* criminal conspiracy. Once agents of the State identify dissenters as political criminals or instigators, they focus their control efforts much more than in coping with "ordinary" crimes. Whereas attempts to prevent ordinary crimes are predominantly vicarious control (i.e. simple general deterrence), modulative control looms large in the strategy of State agents in coping with dissenters. As observed earlier, the agents commonly resort to planting provocateurs among dissenters. Another tactic is relentless prosecution of influential dissenters with a view to realizing their deportation or confinement. The most alarming modulative tactic is likely to be that combined with illegal deterrent vicarious control. By assassinating an influential dissenter, State agents (not excluding the military) hope to deter others; and, in any case, they eliminate what they perceive to be a dangerous influence.

As just suggested, in huge social units characterized by marked normative conflict, social control by State agents must be *selective*. It becomes unrealistic to contemplate controlling everyone, or even to enforce all laws equally; and given a large and heterogeneous population, it is difficult to imagine any one particular type of control (e.g. deterrent vicarious) being effective for all situations. Hence the agents of the State must confront this difficult question: Who should be subject to the greatest efforts at control and what types of control should be attempted? In seeking an answer, the agents engage in prelusive control.

Once political crimes come to be identified as the only crime that must be controlled, then the greatest concern is with detecting dissenters, and surveillance becomes the paramount focus.[14] Observe that the controllers are seeking an answer to the question: Which individuals should be subject to the greatest efforts at social control? Yet still another question must be answered:

---

[13]Surveillance is important if only because it supposedly furthers the objective certainty of punishments of crime, one of the major variables in the deterrence doctrine.

[14]The most common organizational manifestation is the formation of "subversive" squads in police forces, and such specialization is in itself indicative of a large social unit.

For any particular target of control (i.e. a prospective second party), what would be the most effective type of control? If referential control is contemplated, then it is advantageous to know whom the second party especially respects, fears, hates, and loves. If allegative control is contemplated, the controllers can ill-afford to be ignorant of strategic third parties or indifferent to the credibility of allegations. The controllers must recognize that the target is much more likely to be vicariously deterred by some kinds of punishments more than others (indeed, even the choice of the third party could be relevant). Finally, in contemplating modulative control, there is no assurance of success without knowledge of those who have influence over the target and how that influence is wielded. The general point is that in large social units with negligible consensus and marked status differentiation the effectiveness of referential, allegative, vicarious, and modulative control is highly contingent; and to identify those contingencies, would-be controllers must engage in prelusive control.[15] Other than surveillance (including the use of informers), the primary tool in prelusive control is the dossier, compiled to facilitate any of the four other types of social control.

Research Strategy

Even if the preceding arguments make the empirical generalizations in Table 6-1 credible, they do not suggest a strategy for testing those generalizations. Strategy is a major problem in undertaking research on social control because virtually any member of any social unit engages in social control and virtually any kind of behavior is subject to social control. So enormous resources would be required for a truly inclusive study of social control in even one small social unit. Therein lies the advantage of designing research solely to test a few specific empirical generalizations; the design limits the scope of the investigation and furthers its feasibility. Nonetheless, tests of the empirical generalizations in Table 6-1 will not be a simple matter; but there are several alternative strategies—some much more feasible than others.

Some of the previous arguments allude to change in social units, but the generalizations do not rest on any evolutionary assumptions that increases in size or socio-cultural differentiation are somehow inevitable. The only assumption is that social units can be selected in such a way that they differ substantially as to size and internal socio-cultural differentiation. Such variation may be manifested in the history of a particular social unit (i.e. through change in size and socio-cultural differentiation over time), and two or more social units taken at the same point in time may differ substantially as

---

[15]Prelusive social control is not limited to agents of the State. Advertising agencies spend vast sums of money to identify the most susceptible targets for a given kind of advertising and to estimate the effectiveness of each kind. Either line of research is prelusive social control.

to size and socio-cultural differentiation. While the generalizations may hold for both comparisons, it is much more feasible to test them through synchronic comparisons (i.e. comparisons of different social units at approximately the same point in time). Longitudinal comparisons would require research on change in a social unit over several years, and change in its size or socio-cultural differentiation could be negligible.

While the generalizations in Table 6-1 hopefully hold for all types of social units (e.g. countries, communities, companies, families), there is a rationale for testing each generalization by comparing social units *of the same type*. The arguments offered in support of the generalizations in Table 6-1 do not deny that features of social control in a social unit depend to some extent on the "organizational position" of that social unit relative to other social units and the "basic activities" in that social unit. To illustrate positional differences, employees of the Internal Revenue Service appear subject to far more vicarious social control (laws, regulations) originating outside that social unit than are employees of General Motors. Neither General Motors nor a particular family are governmental divisions and to that extent they are similar in position, but the basic activities of General Motors are such that the employees (executives in particular) are much more subject to vicarious social control by regulatory agencies than are members of a particular family. Finally, it may well be that the position *and* basic activities of custodial institutions (e.g. prisons) make the kinds and amount of control (social and otherwise) in such places virtually unique (Goffman, 1961a; Sykes, 1958).

When it comes to selecting social units of the same type, some types are neither desirable nor feasible. Households or nuclear families do not vary a great deal as to size, and countries are far too large. The most strategic social units would be retail stores in the same community (e.g. a particular metropolitan area). Such units may be too prosaic for the tastes of some sociologists,[16] but they can be selected readily in such a way that they differ appreciably as to size and internal status differentiation.

The scope of the proposed research can be reduced by excluding the attempts of members of a retail store (owner, manager, or employee) to control the behavior of customers; but that restriction is not a guide as to the procedure for making observations, and investigators need instructions beyond "observe and record attempts at control." The prescribed strategy is to interview each member, with the interview guided by a schedule that commences with a candid statement of research purposes and assurances of

---

[16]If so, investigators can select more interesting social units, such as law enforcement agencies or mental hospitals. However, those alternatives are likely to be located in different communities and differ as to organizational position. By contrast, all retail stores could be in the same community; and differences among them as regards organizational position can be minimized by selecting only stores that are locally owned and independent (i.e. not units in a chain store).

confidentiality.[17] The next items on the schedule would pertain to the age, sex, marital status, parental status, race or ethnicity, religion, occupation or position of the interviewee.

The following are illustrations of the questions directly pertaining to the research of social control.

During (year) what was the last time that someone who worked in this store accused someone else who also worked in the store of doing something wrong?[18]

What was the accusation?

Who was accused?

Who made the accusation?

Why was it made?

How was it made?

To whom was it made?

Why was it made to that person?

What did (he/she) do?

Why did (he/she) do that?

What did the person do after making the accusation?

Why did (he/she) do that?

Did any other persons who came to know of the accusation do something about it?

What did they do?

Why did they do it?

What was the eventual outcome?

Such questions would be posed in recognition that individuals are especially prone to engage in social control when their evaluations of conduct are violated. Such instances are likely to be reported when a member of a social

[17]If the stores are locally owned and independent, they may be small enough to interview each employee of each store, yet vary appreciably as to number of employees. Should it be necessary to resort to sampling, the sample design should be such that the owner or manager of each store is interviewed; otherwise, a great deal of modulative and prelusive social control might go undetected. In any case, at least 18 retail stores (social units) should be examined, two for each of the nine cells in Table 6-1.

[18]With a view to avoiding excessive duplication of reports about a particular dispute, the time period could be varied from one respondent to the next (e.g. January or Fall of 1980 for one respondent, but June or Summer of 1980 for another). However, some duplication (i.e. independent reports about the same dispute) is desirable.

unit is asked about "accusations of wrongs." Since proximate or sequential control is often not only successful but also very much part of everyday interaction, numerous instances of it are not likely to be reported in response to the question about accusations of wrongs. Accordingly, the interview data should be supplemented with data that stem from unobtrusive observations by at least one investigator during one week of physical presence in the store throughout working hours. The immediate purpose of those observations would be to count instances of proximate control, sequential control, and referential control in order to realize *temporally comparable* data for computing the first ratio in each cell of a table like Table 6-1. However, the observations should extend to recording instances of allegative, vicarious, modulative, and prelusive social control.[19] If the observations are so extended, then generalizations in Table 6-1 can be tested by using two independent sets of data, those obtained through interviews and those obtained by behavioral observations.

The prescribed research would confront one problem for which there is no satisfactory solution. "Normative consensus" is a quantitative variable, but there is no accepted procedure for its numerical expression. One can think of posing a series of normative questions to members of a social unit and perhaps imagine a defensible formula for expressing the amount of agreement in their answers. However, since seemingly infinite types of human behavior are subject to evaluation, it is inconceivable that the normative questions could be such as to recognize all types of behavior; and the idea of a representative sample of types does not make a great deal of sense.

The alternative to an attempt at the numerical expression of the normative consensus is to assume a close inverse relation between normative consensus and status differentiation.[20] The assumption, in other words, is that as

[19]Such observations are all the more necessary because modulative and prelusive social control are especially likely to go undetected by an examination of accounts of disputes or "accusations of wrongs," for people commonly engage in those types of social control independently of any particular dispute. That is particularly true of the formulation of rules that stipulate negative sanctions to promote general deterrence. Accordingly, each such rule in existence at any time during the year in question would be counted as an instance of vicarious social control. The existence of such rules is not likely to be detected by unobtrusive observations; hence, the interviews of owners or managers would necessarily be extended to subjects beyond particular disputes. Surveillant prelusive control may be such a controversial subject that it cannot be dealt with in interviews; the alternative is to ask owners or managers about the frequency of their requests for letters of recommendation of applicants for employment (which are instances of preemptive prelusive control). Recognizing that some stores are likely to hire more employees than others over some period (e.g. a year), the frequency count of that kind of prelusive social control for any particular store could be: $(P)(Ln)$, where P is the proportion of applicants for which letters of recommendation were requested and Ln is the number of new employees over the period in the store with the greatest number of new employees.

[20]Doubts about the assumption are surely justified. As a case in point, general observations (Allen, 1965; Bullock, 1962) suggest a marked decline of normative consensus in Germany over the years 1914–1932, but it is extremely doubtful that status differentiation increased propor-

individuals come to occupy different statuses they come to disagree in evaluations of conduct.

There is a procedure for expressing the amount of status differentiation (SD) in a social unit, one suggested by the following formula:

$$SD = (N/\Sigma X)\left(1 - \left[\left(\Sigma\left|X-\bar{X}\right|\right)/2\Sigma X\right]\right),$$

where X is the number of individuals in a particular status configuration (e.g. male, 20−24, carpenter, Anglo-Caucasian, married, father, Methodist), N is the number of status configurations occupied by at least one of the social unit's members, and $\bar{X} = \Sigma X/N$. Apart from its postulated inverse relation with normative consensus, status differentiation is a component of socio-cultural differentiation, and the formula is such that there is no necessary relation between the amount of status differentiation and the size of the social unit (number of members).

The Question of Significance

The immediate importance of the proposed line of research lies not in the possibility that the evidence would support the generalizations in Table 6-1. That is the case because the present conceptualization of social control does not stand or fall on those generalizations. However, the research would indicate whether or not the conceptualization can be applied. It is not claimed that in using the conceptualization investigators will confront no difficulties in distinguishing social control behavior and in recognizing types of it, nor is it claimed that investigators will never disagree. Indeed, it may well be that the conceptualization must be modified to realize an acceptable level of empirical applicability, and there is also the awful possibility that the problems in application are so great that the conceptualization is beyond repair. All such considerations cannot be judged a priori; hence, at least initially, ascertaining the empirical applicability of the conceptualization is more important than tests of particular generalizations. That is the case despite the fact that sociologists rarely give more than lip service to the importance of empirical applicability. In sociology the acceptance or rejection of a conceptualization depends not on its empirical applicability but, rather, on whether sociologists regard it as interesting and important. Perhaps that is as it should be. Nonetheless, however interesting and important a conceptualization may appear, it will prove to have no real utility in the long run if its empirical applicability is negligible.

(footnote continued)

tionately during that period. The only way to cope with such possible "historical exceptions" is to increase the number of social units that are examined in tests of the generalizations in Table 6-1.

Even if comparisons of retail stores should yield support for the generalizations in Table 6-1, the importance of the conceptualization would not be obvious, the immediate reason being that sociologists are likely to be bored by a comparison of retail stores. However, that evidence would suggest the possibility that the relations postulated in Table 6-1 also hold for social units that sociologists regard as far more interesting and important, countries or societies in particular. The two principal independent variables (size and socio-cultural differentiation) take on added significance, with recognition of a global trend toward large and highly differentiated social units.[21] If that trend continues and if the generalizations in Table 6-1 are valid, then human beings will become subject to intensities of social control that are largely alien to most contemporary social units.

The current state of sociological theory (including conventional conceptualizations) runs contrary to the foregoing "conditional prophecy," and the state of theory is not now conducive to an appreciation of the importance of the prophecy. That is the case because sociological theory attaches no real significance to social control.[22] With few exceptions throughout the history of the field, theorists have accepted what Lemert has correctly characterized (1972) as the assumption of "automaticity" in social control. Many early theorists, such as Durkheim, ostensibly assumed normative consensus and viewed conformity as stemming from consensus alone. Modern theorists place more emphasis on mechanisms by which shared evaluations of conduct are internalized, but they are content (as in the case of Parsons) to identify socialization as the primary mechanism. Socialization is partially conscious and deliberate (it may even entail some of the types of social control described here), but the term actually denotes "the process by which individuals acquire the knowledge, skills and dispositions that enable them to participate as more or less effective members of groups and of the society.''[23] As such, much of socialization (e.g. emulation) is not conscious and deliberate; it is crescive (i.e. unwitting, unplanned), and that feature of socialization is emphasized in sociological theory. Indeed, rather than emphasize the role of social control in socialization, Parsons (1951) suggests that the social control occurs when

---

[21]Those variables are also important in reconsidering the paucity of instances of social control revealed in well-known and in-depth analyses of social units, notably: Howell's *Hard Living on Clay Street* (1973), Liebow's *Tally's Corner* (1967), Llewellyn and Hoebel's *The Cheyenne Way* (1941), Pospisil's *Kapauku Papuans and Their Law* (1958), and Whyte's *Street Corner Society* (1955). While the paucity of instances may only reflect insufficiently detailed observations by the investigators and/or a possible reluctance on their part to draw inferences about intention, it is significant that the social units in question were relatively small and undifferentiated (socially and culturally).

[22]What passes for "social control theory" in sociology is little more than a debate over the conceptualization of social control [see Martindale's exposition (1978) of "the theory of social control"]. For reasons previously indicated, even the identification of particular theories as pertaining to social control is disputable; and none of them are well-known, let alone accepted (especially the theories about punitiveness).

[23]Brim, quoted by Cook-Gumperz (1973:5).

socialization fails, meaning that it checks deviance due to ineffective socialization.

Since functionalists (like Parsons and Durkheim) emphasize normative consensus but Marxists emphasize conflict, it may appear that the latter are much more appreciative of social control, especially if conceptualized (as here) so as to attribute an intentional quality to it. Yet the aversion of Marxists to reductionism or "psychologizing" is hardly less than that of the functionalists [see Popper's commentary (1950)]; hence, they too have succumbed to the "automaticity" assumption. True, we are informed by Marxists that capitalists control legislators, but little is said about how that control is realized, and the indifference of Marxists to documenting it is monumental. Marxists are prone to describe revolutions as caused by a contradiction between the means of production and economic relations without much comment about the *strategies* of would-be revolutionaries. One must surely wonder why some attempted revolutions fail and why Marxists do not emphasize the possibility that success or failure depends in part on the strategies (including social control) of those who promote and those who oppose the revolution (Russell, 1974).

In light of the foregoing criticisms, Malinowski's castigation of "classical anthropology" (1959:30) extends to contemporary sociology: "Take the real savage, keen on evading his duties, swaggering and boastful when he has fulfilled them, and compare him with the anthropologist's dummy who slavishly follows custom and automatically obeys every regulation. There is not the remotest resemblance between the teachings of anthropology on this subject and the reality of native life." True, sociologists rarely speak of "automatic obedience" but, for that matter, they rarely speak of human behavior. To illustrate, as pointed out by Blumer (1969), sociologists commonly refer to *social roles* as interacting, not individuals. Insofar as their observations bear on human behavior at all, behavior is described as determined by "social structure," as though the latter is somehow distinct from the former. Hence, they speak endlessly of institutional and organizational arrangements, such as social class, familialism, castes, capitalism, marriage, and bureaucracy. The point is not that such terms denote fictions; it is readily admitted that they are essential components of the sociological vocabulary. Nevertheless, insofar as sociologists recognize the notion of social control at all, they are content to depict it as somehow automatically *flowing from* organization and institutions. Not one major sociological theory confronts this question: What kinds of social control are necessary to maintain a given type of institution or organization?[24]

[24]If sociologists are wary of such theories in the fear that they would be a step down the road to reductionism, they should contemplate two questions. First, what features of social control appear necessary for, say, slavery, fascism, capitalism, and universities? Second, why must an answer to the first question be considered "psychological"? The fact that the present conceptualization of social control could be used both in the pursuit of the first question and in the

It falls to individuals who are not prominent sociologists to pose such questions. For example, Hinton (1966:46) described the "social structure" of a Chinese village (Long Bow, prior to the Communist revolution) in terms that sociologists would regard as conventional. However, he went beyond convention in posing these questions: "With so many of Long Bow's peasants on the verge of ruin, how did a handful of landlord and rich peasant families maintain their system of exploitation? How did they enforce the payment of rent and interest through years of famine and war? How did they protect their hoarded wealth from looting and seizure by their tenants and hired laborers who, after all, needed only to join together to bring the whole system down?" Conventional or not, Hinton's observations supply an answer—the system was perpetuated by deterrent vicarious social control (very harsh punishments) and modulative control (the appointment of sychophants as officials).

Let us suppose that sociologists have been correct in tacitly assuming that social control flows from "social structure" and that the former is not necessary to maintain the latter. Even so, it would not follow that the assumption will remain defensible in the future, especially if the trend toward greater socio-cultural differentiation and less normative consensus continues. The argument was summarized by Lester F. Ward (1903): The evolution of social organization is from genesis to telesis. Translated into the present terminology, change is in the direction of greater social control. Sociologists never devoted much attention to Ward's evolutionary principle, but it could be helpful to reconsider it.

The possibility of an evolutionary trend in social control transcends the interests of sociologists (i.e. it is not purely "academic"), especially when one contemplates the expansion of modulative and prelusive social control. Perhaps those two types are not inherently evil, and perhaps they will not be perceived as evil once they become prevalent. Nonetheless, the extensive use of both types of social control by the Nazis could be telling in itself.

The major assumption underlying the generalizations in Table 6-1 has particular implications for penal policy. Restating that assumption briefly: The most effective type of social control tends to be used the most. The notion of effectiveness is vague to the point of defying a precise definition (let alone measurement); even so, there are ample grounds for questioning the effectiveness of a deterrent penal policy, and yet policy makers in the United States and numerous other highly urbanized countries cling tenaciously to the deterrence doctrine in their attempts to prevent criminality. Accordingly, it may appear that there is at least one glaring exception to the "effectiveness—prevalence" assumption, but the effectiveness of one type of social

(footnote continued)
study of "impression management" (Goffman, 1959, 1961b) and other facets of the social psychology of interaction (Weinstein and Deutschberger, 1963; Wood et al., 1967) is hardly a contradiction.

control is to be assessed relative to that of alternative types. Can the reader imagine a criminal justice system based exclusively on referential or allegative social control? Modulative and prelusive control are alternatives; but it is by no means obvious how a criminal justice system could be based on either of those two, especially without abandoning all manner of legality principles (e.g. "due process").

That is not to say that criminal justice can never be other than essentially deterrent vicarious social control. To the contrary, the present conceptualization of social control (including distinctions as to types) is relevant for those who aspire to go beyond the sociology of the "is" to the sociology of the "possible." Criminal justice in the United States and other highly urbanized countries cries out for innovations, for no one appears satisfied with current practices and policies. Innovations in criminal justice are inherently dangerous, and perhaps they are the most dangerous when predicated on the assumption that criminal justice can be apolitical and benign. Indeed, any system of social control is dangerous, but therein lies the real significance of the subject.

References

Adamek, Raymond J. and Jerry M. Lewis (1973) Social control, violence, and radicalization: The Kent State case, *Social Forces* 51:342–347.

Adams, Richard N. (1975) *Energy and Structure: A Theory of Social Power* (Austin, TX: University of Texas Press).

Akers, Ronald L. (1977) *Deviant Behavior,* 2nd ed. (Belmont, CA: Wadsworth).

—— and Richard Hawkins, eds. (1975) *Law and Control in Society* (Englewood Cliffs, NJ: Prentice-Hall).

—— and Edward Sagarin, eds. (1974) *Crime Prevention and Social Control* (New York: Praeger).

Allen, William S. (1965) *The Nazi Seizure of Power: The Experience of a Single German Town, 1930–1935* (Chicago: Quadrangle Books).

Ambrose, Stephen E. (1975) *Crazy Horse and Custer* (Garden City, NY: Doubleday).

Anderson, Alan R. and Omar K. Moore (1957) The formal analysis of normative concepts, *American Sociological Review* 22:9–17.

Aronson, Elliot (1976) *The Social Animal,* 2nd ed. (San Francisco: Freeman).

Ball, Harry V. et al. (1962) Law and social change: Sumner reconsidered, *American Journal of Sociology* 67:532–540.

Bandura, Albert (1969) *Principles of Behavior Modification* (New York: Holt, Rinehart and Winston).

Banton, Michael P. (1964) *The Policeman in the Community* (New York: Basic Books).

Barton, R. F. (1919) *Ifugao Law,* Publications in Archaeology and Ethnology, vol. 15, no. 1 (Berkeley, CA: University of California).

Bates, Frederick L. and Clyde C. Harvey (1975) *The Structure of Social Systems* (New York: Wiley).

Baumgartner, M. P. (1978) Law and social status in colonial New Haven, *Research in Law and Sociology* 1:153−174.

Bean, Philip (1974) *The Social Control of Drugs* (New York: Wiley).

Becker, Howard S. (1955) Marihuana use and social control, *Social Problems* 3:35−44.

───── (1963) *Outsiders* (New York: Free Press).

Bedau, Hugo A. (1978) Retribution and the theory of punishment, *Journal of Philosophy* 75:601−620.

Bell, Robert R. (1971) *Social Deviance* (Homewood, IL: Dorsey).

Bensman, Joseph and Israel Gerver (1963) Crime and punishment in the factory, *American Sociological Review* 28:588−598.

Bernard, L. L. (1939) *Social Control in Its Sociological Aspects* (New York: Macmillan).

Berndt, Ronald M. (1962) *Excess and Restraint* (Chicago: University of Chicago Press).

Beyer, Janice M. and Harrison M. Trice (1979) A reexamination of the relations between size and various components of organizational complexity, *Administrative Science Quarterly* 24:48−64.

Bianchi, Herman et al., eds. (1975) *Deviance and Control in Europe* (New York: Wiley).

Bidney, David (1953) *Theoretical Anthropology* (New York: Columbia University Press).

Bierstedt, Robert (1963) *The Social Order,* 2nd ed. (New York: McGraw-Hill).

Birenbaum, Arnold and Edward Sagarin (1976) *Norms and Human Behavior* (New York: Praeger).

Bittner, Egon (1970) *The Functions of the Police in Modern Society* (Rockville, MD: National Institute of Mental Health).

Black, Donald (1976) *The Behavior of Law* (New York: Academic Press).

Blake, Judith and Kingsley Davis (1964) Norms, values, and sanctions, pp. 456−484 in Robert E. L. Faris (ed.), *Handbook of Modern Sociology* (Chicago: Rand McNally).

Blauner, Robert (1972) *Racial Oppression in America* (New York: Harper and Row).

Blumer, Herbert (1969) *Symbolic Interactionism* (Englewood Cliffs, NJ: Prentice-Hall).

Blumstein, Alfred et al., eds. (1978) *Deterrence and Incapacitation* (Washington, DC: National Academy of Science).

Bodde, Derek and Clarence Morris (1967) *Law in Imperial China: Exemplified by 190 Ch'ing Dynasty Cases* (Cambridge, MA: Harvard Univeristy Press).

Bodenheimer, Edgar (1974) *Jurisprudence,* rev. ed. (Cambridge, MA: Harvard University Press).

Booth, Alan et al. (1977) Correlates of city crime rates: Victimization surveys versus official statistics, *Social Problems* 25:187−197.

Bordua, David J. (1967) Recent trends: Deviant behavior and social control, *Annals of the American Academy of Political and Social Science* 369:149−163.

Bredemeier, Harry C. and Richard M. Stephenson (1962) *The Analysis of Social Systems* (New York: Holt, Rinehart and Winston).

Breed, Warren (1955) Social control in the newsroom: A functional analysis, *Social Forces* 33:326–335.

Broadhead, Robert S. and Ray C. Rist (1976) Gatekeepers and the social control of social research, *Social Problems* 23:325–336.

Brown, Paula (1952) Changes in Ojibwa social control, *American Anthropologist* 54:57–70.

Brown, W. O. (1940) White dominance in South Africa: A study in social control, *Social Forces* 18:406–410.

Bullock, Alan (1962) *Hitler: A Study in Tyranny,* rev. ed. (New York: Harper and Row).

Campbell, Byron A. and Russell M. Church, eds. (1969) *Punishment and Aversive Behavior* (New York: Appleton-Century-Crofts).

Caute, David (1978) *The Great Fear: The Anti-Communist Purge Under Truman and Eisenhower* (New York: Simon and Schuster).

Chambliss, William J. and Milton Mankoff, eds. (1976) *Whose Law? What Order?* (New York: Wiley).

Clark, Alexander L. and Jack P. Gibbs (1965) Social control: A reformulation, *Social Problems* 12:398–415.

Clark, John M. (1939) *Social Control of Business,* 2nd ed. (New York: McGraw-Hill).

Clegg, Stewart (1975) *Power, Rule, and Domination* (London: Routledge and Kegan Paul).

Clinard, Marshall B. and Robert F. Meier (1979) *Sociology of Deviant Behavior,* 5th ed. (New York: Holt, Rinehart and Winston).

Cohen, Albert K. (1966) *Deviance and Control* (Englewood Cliffs, NJ: Prentice-Hall).

Coleman, James W. (1969) *The Molly Maguire Riots* (New York: Arno).

Conger, Rand D. (1976) Social control and social learning models of delinquent behavior: A synthesis, *Criminology* 14:17–40.

Conrad, John P. (1965) *Crime and Its Correction* (Berkeley, CA: University of California Press).

Cook-Gumperz, Jenny (1973) *Social Control and Socialization: A Study of Class Differences in the Language of Maternal Control* (London: Routledge and Kegan Paul).

Cullen, Francis T. and John B. Cullen (1978) *Toward a Paradigm of Labeling Theory,* New Series, no. 58 (Lincoln, NE: University of Nebraska Studies).

Currie, Elliott P. (1968) Crimes without criminals: Witchcraft and its control in renaissance Europe, *Law and Society Review* 3:7–32.

Davies, Nigel (1974) *The Aztecs* (New York: G.P. Putnam's Sons).

Davis, Kingsley (1949) *Human Society* (New York: Macmillan).

Davis, Nanette J. (1975) *Social Constructions of Deviance* (Dubuque, IA: Wm. C. Brown).

DeFleur, Melvin L. et al. (1977) *Sociology: Human Society,* 2nd ed. (Glenview, IL: Scott, Foresman).

Denisoff, R. Serge (1974) *The Sociology of Dissent* (New York: Harcourt, Brace, Jovanovich).

——— and Charles H. McCaghy (1973) *Deviance, Conflict, and Criminality* (Chicago: Rand McNally).

Denzin, Norman K. (1970) Rules of conduct and the study of deviant behavior: Some notes on the social relationship, pp. 120–159 in Jack D. Douglas (ed.), *Deviance and Respectability* (New York: Basic Books).

Deutscher, Irwin, ed. (1973) *What We Say/What We Do* (Glenview, IL: Scott, Foresman).

Dillon, Merton L. (1974) *The Abolitionists* (DeKalb, IL: Northern Illinois University Press).

Dohrenwend, Bruce P. (1959) Egoism, altruism, anomie, and fatalism: A conceptual analysis of Durkheim's types, *American Sociological Review* 24:466–473.

Domhoff, G. William (1978) *The Powers That Be: Processes of Ruling Class Domination in America* (New York: Random House).

Douglas, Jack D. (1967) *The Social Meanings of Suicide* (Princeton, NJ: Princeton University Press).

Dowd, Jerome (1936) *Control in Human Societies* (New York: D. Appleton-Century).

Durkheim, Emile (1949) *The Division of Labor in Society* (New York: Free Press).

——— (1951) *Suicide* (New York: Free Press).

Duster, Troy (1970) *The Legislation of Morality: Law, Drugs, and Moral Judgment* (New York: Free Press).

Edgerton, Robert B. (1976) *Deviance: A Cross-Cultural Perspective* (Menlo Park, CA: Cummings).

Ehrlich, Eugen (1936) *Fundamental Principles of the Sociology of Law* (Cambridge, MA: Harvard University Press).

Elliott, Delbert S. et al. (1979) An integrated theoretical perspective on delinquent behavior, *Journal of Research in Crime and Delinquency* 16:3–27.

Ellis, Desmond P. (1971) The Hobbesian problem of order: A critical appraisal of the normative solution, *American Sociological Review* 36:692–703.

Entwisle, Doris R. and John Walton (1961) Observations on the span of control, *Administrative Science Quarterly* 5:522–533.

Erikson, Kai T. (1962) Notes on the sociology of deviance, *Social Problems* 9:307–314.

——— (1966) *Wayward Puritans* (New York: Wiley).

Etzioni, Amitai (1968) Social control: organizational aspects, pp. 396–402 in David L. Sills (ed.), *International Encyclopedia of the Social Sciences,* vol. 14 (New York: Macmillan).

Feldman, Saul D., ed. (1978) *Deciphering Deviance* (Boston: Little, Brown).

Finn, James, ed. (1971) *Conscience and Command: Justice and Discipline in the Military* (New York: Random House).

Finney, Ross L. (1926) Unemployment: An essay in social control, *Social Forces* 5:146–148.

Frank, Jerome D. (1961) *Persuasion and Healing: A Comparative Study of Psychotherapy* (Baltimore: Johns Hopkins Press).

Friedland, William H. (1973) Book review in *Contemporary Sociology* 2:513–514.

Fuller, Lon L. (1969) *The Morality of Law,* rev. ed. (New Haven, CT: Yale University Press).

Gallo, Max (1972) *The Night of Long Knives* (New York: Harper and Row).

Gamson, William A. (1968) *Power and Discontent* (Homewood, IL: Dorsey).

Genovese, Eugene D. (1974) *Roll Jordan Roll: The World the Slaves Made* (New York: Pantheon).

Gersuny, Carl (1973) *Punishment and Redress in a Modern Factory* (Lexington, MA: Lexington Books).

Gibbons, Don C. and Joseph F. Jones (1975) *The Study of Deviance* (Englewood Cliffs, NJ: Prentice-Hall).

Gibbs, Jack P. (1965) Norms: The problem of definition and classification, *American Journal of Sociology* 70:586−594.

────── (1972) Issues in defining deviant behavior, pp. 39−68 in Robert A. Scott and Jack D. Douglas (eds.), *Theoretical Perspectives on Deviance* (New York: Basic Books).

────── (1975) *Crime, Punishment, and Deterrence* (New York: Elsevier).

────── (1977) Social control, deterrence, and perspectives on social order, *Social Forces* 56:408−423.

────── (1978) The death penalty, retribution and penal policy, *Journal of Criminal Law and Criminology* 69:291−299.

────── and Maynard L. Erickson (1975) Major developments in the sociological study of deviance, *Annual Review of Sociology* 1:21−42.

Goffman, Erving (1959) *The Presentation of Self in Everyday Life* (Garden City, NY: Doubleday).

────── (1961a) *Asylums* (Garden City, NY: Doubleday).

────── (1961b) *Encounters* (Indianapolis, IN: Bobbs-Merrill).

────── (1963) *Stigma* (Englewood Cliffs, NJ: Prentice-Hall).

Golden, Joseph (1958) Social control of Negro−white intermarriage, *Social Forces* 36:267−269.

Goode, Erich (1975) On behalf of labeling theory, *Social Problems* 22:570−583.

Goode, William J. (1972) Presidential address: The place of force of human society, *American Sociological Review* 37:507−519.

Gouldner, Alvin W. (1965) *Enter Plato* (New York: Basic Books).

────── (1968) The sociologist as partisan, *American Sociologist* 3:103−116.

Gove, Walter R., ed. (1975) *The Labelling of Deviance* (New York: Wiley).

Grey, Anthony (1970) *Hostage in Peking* (London: Michael Joseph).

Grunberger, Richard (1971) *The 12-Year Reich* (New York: Holt, Rinehart and Winston).

Grupp, Stanley E., ed. (1971) *Theories of Punishment* (Bloomington, IN: Indiana University Press).

Gulliver, P. H. (1963) *Social Control in an African Society* (Boston: Boston University Press).

Habbe, Stephen (1969) *Company Controls for Drinking Problems*, Personnel Policy Study no. 218 (New York: National Industrial Conference Board).

Hagan, John et al. (1977) Conflict and consensus in the designation of deviance, *Social forces* 56:320−340

Hall, Gwendolyn M. (1971) *Social Control in Slave and Plantation Societies* (Baltimore: Johns Hopkins Press).

Hallett, Jean-Pierre (1968) *Congo Kitabu* (New York: Random House).

Harring, Sidney L. (1977) Class conflict and the suppression of tramps in Buffalo, 1892−1894, *Law and Society Review* 11:873−911.

Hart, H.L.A. (1961) *The Concept of Law* (Oxford, England: Clarendon Press).

Hawkes, Roland K. (1975) Norms, deviance, and social control, *American Journal of Sociology* 80:886−908.

Hay, Douglas et al. (1975) *Albion's Fatal Tree: Crime and Society in Eighteenth-Century England* (New York: Pantheon Books).

Hayes, Wayland J. (1936) The Southern crisis and social control, *Social Forces* 15:21–29.

Heaton, John W. (1939) *Mob Violence in the Late Roman Republic 133 –49 B.C.,* vol. 23, no. 4, Illinois Studies in the Social Sciences (Urbana, IL: University of Illinois Press).

Heer, Clarence (1937) Taxation as an instrument of social control, *American Journal of Sociology* 42:484–492.

Hinton, William (1966) *Fanshen: A Documentary of Revolution in a Chinese Village* (New York: Random House).

Hirschi, Travis (1969) *Causes of Delinquency* (Berkeley, CA: University of California Press).

Hirst, Paul A. (1972) Marx and Engels on law, crime, and morality, *Economy and Society* 1:28–56.

Hitler, Adolf (1940) *Mein Kampf* (New York: Reynal and Hitchcock).

Hobbes, Thomas (1953) *Leviathan* (Oxford, England: Claredon Press).

Hoebel, E. Adamson (1954) *The Law of Primitive Man* (Cambridge, MA: Harvard University Press).

Hollingshead, August B. (1941) The concept of social control, *American Sociological Review* 6:217–224.

Homans, George C. (1961) *Social Behavior* (New York: Harcourt, Brace and World).

——— (1974) *Social Behavior,* rev. ed. (New York: Harcourt Brace Jovanovich).

Howard, Alan and Irwin Howard (1964) Pre-marital sex and social control among the Rotumans, *American Anthropologist* 66:266–283.

Howell, Joseph T. (1973) *Hard Living on Clay Street* (Garden City, NY: Doubleday).

Hughes, J.R.T. (1976) *Social Control in the Colonial Economy* (Charlottesville, VA: University Press of Virginia).

Humphreys, Laud (1972) *Out of the Closets: The Sociology of Homosexual Liberation* (Englewood Cliffs, NJ: Prentice-Hall).

Huxley, Aldous (1946) *Brave New World* (New York: Harper and Row).

Inciardi, James A., ed. (1979) Special issue on radical criminology, *Criminology* 16:no. 4.

Janowitz, Morris (1968) *Social Control of Escalated Riots* (Chicago: University of Chicago Center for Policy Study).

——— (1975) Sociological theory and social control, *American Journal of Sociology* 81:82–108.

——— (1976) *Social Control of the Welfare State* (New York: Elsevier).

Johnson, Harry M. (1960) *Sociology* (New York: Harcourt, Brace and World).

Jones, Harry W. (1969) *The Efficacy of Law* (Evanston, IL: Northwestern University Press).

Julian, Joseph (1968) Organizational involvement and social control, *Social Forces* 47:12–16.

Kamen, Henry (1967) *The Rise of Toleration* (New York: McGraw-Hill).

Kanfer, Stefan (1973) *A Journal of the Plague Years* (New York: Atheneum).

Kantorowicz, Hermann (1958) *The Definition of Law* (Cambridge, England: University Press).

Kaplan, Howard B. (1975) *Self-Attitudes and Deviant Behavior* (Pacific Palisades, CA: Goodyear).

Kelsen, Hans (1967) *Pure Theory of Law* (Berkeley, CA: University of California Press).

Kirchheimer, Otto (1961) *Political Justice: The Use of Legal Procedure for Political Ends* (Princeton, NJ: Princeton University Press).

Kisch, Guido (1970) *The Jews in Medieval Germany,* 2nd ed. (New York: Ktav Publishing House).

Kitsuse, John I. (1962) Societal reaction to deviant behavior, *Social Problems* 9:247–256.

——— (1975) The "new conception of deviance" and its critics, pp. 273–284 in Walter R. Gove (ed.), *The Labelling of Deviance* (New York: Wiley).

Kittrie, Nicholas N. (1971) *The Right to be Different: Deviance and Enforced Therapy* (Baltimore: Johns Hopkins University Press).

Klapp, Orrin E. (1954) Heroes, villains and fools, as agents of social control, *American Sociological Review* 19:56–62.

——— (1973) *Models of Social Order* (Palo Alto, CA: National Press).

Kluckhohn, Clyde and Dorthea Leighton (1951) *The Navaho* (Cambridge, MA: Harvard University Press).

Kogon, Eugen (no date), *The Theory and Practice of Hell: The German Concentration Camps and the System Behind Them* (New York: Farrar Straus).

Krohn, Marvin D. and Ronald L. Akers (1977) An alternative view of the labelling versus psychiatric perspectives on societal reaction to mental illness, *Social Forces* 56:341–361.

Krüger, Marlis and Frieda Silvert (1975) *Dissent Denied: The Technocratic Response to Protest* (New York: Elsevier).

Lachenmeyer, Charles W. (1971) *The Language of Sociology* (New York: Columbia University Press).

Landis, Paul H. (1956) *Social Control,* rev. ed. (Philadelphia: Lippincott).

LaPiere, Richard T. (1954) *A Theory of Social Control* (New York: McGraw-Hill).

Laquer, Walter (1977) *Terrorism* (Boston: Little, Brown).

Larson, Calvin J. (1977) *Major Themes in Sociological Theory,* 2nd ed. (New York: David McKay).

Lea, Henry C. (1963) *The Inquisition of the Middle Ages: Its Organization and Operation* (London: Eyre and Spottiswoode).

Lee, Frank F. (1954) Social control in the race relations pattern of a small New England town, *Social Forces* 33:36–40.

Leites, Nathan and Charles Wolf, Jr. (1970) *Rebellion and Authority: An Analytic Essay on Insurgent Conflicts* (Chicago: Markham).

Lemert, Edwin M. (1945) The grand jury as an agency of social control, *American Sociological Review* 10:751–758.

——— (1972) *Human Deviance, Social Problems, and Social Control,* 2nd ed. (Englewood Cliffs, NJ: Prentice-Hall).

Lens, Sidney (1969) *Radicalism in America* (New York: Crowell).

LeVine, Robert A. (1959) Gusii sex offenses: A study in social control, *American Anthropologist* 61:965–990.

Lieban, Richard W. (1962) The dangerous Ingkantos: Illness and social control in a Philippine community, *American Anthropologist* 64:306–312.

Liebow, Elliot (1967) *Tally's Corner* (Boston: Little, Brown).

Lipset, Seymour M. (1976) *Rebellion in the University* (Chicago: University of Chicago Press).

Lipton, Douglas. et al. (1975) *The Effectiveness of Correctional Treatment: A Survey of Treatment Evaluation Studies* (New York: Praeger).

Litwak, Eugene (1956) Three ways in which law acts as a means of social control, *Social Forces* 34:217–223.

Llewellyn, K. N. (1951) *The Bramble Bush* (New York: Oceana Publications).

———— and E. Adamson Hoebel (1941) *The Cheyenne Way* (Norman, OK: University of Oklahoma Press).

Lofland, John (1969) *Deviance and Identity* (Englewood Cliffs, NJ: Prentice-Hall).

London, Perry (1964) *The Modes and Morals of Psychotherapy* (New York: Holt, Rinehart and Winston).

———— (1969) *Behavior Control* (New York: Harper and Row).

Lowenthal, Leo and Norbert Guterman (1970) *Prophets of Deceit,* 2nd ed. (Palo Alto, CA: Pacific Books).

Lumley, Frederick E. (1925) *Means of Social Control* (New York: Century).

Macaulay, Stewart (1977) Elegant models, empirical pictures, and the complexities of contract, *Law and Society Review* 11:507–528.

Machiavelli, Niccolò (1952) *The Prince* (New York: Mentor, New American Library of World Literature).

Malinowski, Bronislaw (1959) *Crime and Custom in Savage Society* (Paterson, NJ: Littlefield Adams).

Mandell, Betty R., ed. (1975) *Welfare in America: Controlling the 'Dangerous Classes'* (Englewood Cliffs, NJ: Prentice-Hall).

Marshall, James (1968) *Intention—In Law and Society* (New York: Funk and Wagnalls).

Marshall, Kim (1972) *Law and Order in Grade 6-E* (Boston: Little, Brown).

Martindale, Don (1978) The theory of social control, pp. 46–58 in Joseph S. Roucek (ed.), *Social Control for the 1980's* (Westport, CT: Greenwood Press).

Marx, Gary T. (1974) Thoughts on a neglected category of social movement participants: The agent provocateur and the informant, *American Journal of Sociology* 80:402–442.

Marx, Karl (1909) *Capital,* 3 vols. (Chicago: Charles H. Kerr).

Matza, David (1969) *Becoming Deviant* (Englewood Cliffs, NJ: Prentice-Hall).

May, Geoffrey (1931) *Social Control of Sex Expression* (New York: W. Morrow).

Mercurio, Joseph A. (1972) *Caning: Educational Rite and Tradition* (Syracuse, NY: Syracuse University, Division of Special Education and Rehabilitation).

Merrill, Francis E. (1938) The stock exchange and social control, *American Journal of Sociology* 43:560–574.

Merton, Robert K. (1957) *Social Theory and Social Structure,* rev. ed. (New York: Free Press).

———— (1966) Social problems and sociological theory, pp. 775–823 in Robert K. Merton and Robert Nisbet (eds.) *Contemporary Social Problems,* 2nd ed. (New York: Harcourt, Brace and World).

———— (1971) Social problems and sociological theory, pp. 793–845 in Robert K.

Merton and Robert Nisbet (eds.), *Contemporary Social Problems,* 3rd ed. (New York: Harcourt Brace Jovanovich).

Michels, Robert (1915) *Political Parties* (New York: Hearst's International Library).

Mills, C. Wright (1959) *The Power Elite* (New York: Oxford University Press).

Mitford, Jessica (1973) *Kind and Usual Punishment* (New York: Knopf).

Modlin, George M. and Archibald M. McIsaac (1938) *Social Control of Industry* (Boston: Little, Brown).

Monahan, John (1977) Empirical analyses of civil commitment: Critique and context, *Law and Society Review* 11:619−628.

Moore, Barrington, Jr. (1966) *Social Origins of Dictatorship and Democracy* (Boston: Beacon Press).

Moore, Sally F. (1958) *Power and Property in Inca Peru* (New York: Columbia University Press).

Morris, Norval (1966) Impediments to penal reform, *University of Chicago Law Review* 33:627−656.

Morris, Richard T. (1956) A typology of norms, *American Sociological Review* 21:610−613.

Mosca, Gaetano (1939) *The Ruling Class* (New York: McGraw-Hill).

Nadel, S. F. (1953) Social control and self-regulation, *Social Forces* 31:265−273.

Nagel, Jack H. (1975) *The Descriptive Analysis of Power* (New Haven, CT: Yale University Press).

Newcomb, Theodore M. (1950) *Social Psychology* (New York: Dryden).

Orwell, George (1949) *Nineteen Eighty-Four* (New York: Harcourt, Brace and World).

Packer, Herbert L. (1968) *The Limits of the Criminal Sanction* (Stanford, CA: Stanford University Press).

Parenti, Michael (1978) *Power and the Powerless* (New York: St. Martin's Press).

Pareto, Vilfredo (1963) *The Mind and Society,* 2 vols. (New York: Dover).

Parsons, Talcott (1951) *The Social System* (New York: Free Press).

——— (1962) The law and social control, pp. 56−72 in William M. Evan (ed.), *Law and Sociology:* (New York: Free Press).

Pennock, J. Roland and John W. Chapman, eds. (1972) *Coercion* (Chicago: Aldine).

Phelps, Clyde W. (1951) The social control of consumer credit costs: A case study, *Social Forces* 29:433−442.

Pitts, Jesse R. (1968) Social control: The concept, pp. 381−396 in David L. Sills (ed.), *International Encyclopedia of the Social Sciences,* vol. 14 (New York: Macmillan).

Piven, Frances F. and Richard A. Cloward (1971) *Regulating the Poor: The Functions of Public Welfare* (New York: Random House).

Platt, Anthony M. (1969) *The Child Savers* (Chicago: University of Chicago Press).

Pollinger, Kenneth J. and Annette C. Pollinger (1972) *Community Action and the Poor: Influence vs. Social Control in a New York City Community* (New York: Praeger).

Pope, Liston (1942) *Millhands and Preachers* (New Haven, CT: Yale University Press).

Popper, Karl R. (1950) *The Open Society and Its Enemies* (Princeton, NJ: Princeton University Press).

Pospisil, Leopold (1958) *Kapauku Papuans and Their Law,* no. 54 (New Haven, CT: Yale University Publications in Anthropology).

Pound, Roscoe (1968) *Social Control Through Law* (Hamden, CT: Archon Books).

Quinney, Richard (1970) *The Social Reality of Crime* (Boston: Little, Brown).

——— (1974) *Critique of Legal Order: Crime Control in Capitalist Society* (Boston: Little, Brown).

Radine, Lawrence B. (1977) *The Taming of the Troops: Social Control in the United States Army* (Westport, CT: Greenwood Press).

Radzinowicz, Leon (1948) *A History of English Criminal Law and Its Administration from 1750,* vol. I (London: Stevens and Sons).

Ranulf, Svend (1938) *Moral Indignation and Middle Class Psychology* (Copenhagen: Levin and Munksgaard).

Raz, Joseph (1970) *The Concept of a Legal System* (Oxford, England: Clarendon Press).

Reay, Marie (1953) Social control amongst the Orokaiva, *Oceania* 24:110–118.

Reid, Sue T. (1979) *Crime and Criminology,* 2nd ed. (New York: Holt, Rinehart and Winston).

Riesman, David et al. (1953) *The Lonely Crowd* (Garden City, NY: Doubleday).

Robertson, Roland and Laurie Taylor (1973) *Deviance, Crime and Socio-Legal Control* (London: Martin Robertson).

Rock, Paul (1973) *Making People Pay* (London: Routledge and Kegan Paul).

——— and Mary McIntosh, eds. (1974) *Deviance and Social Control* (New York: Barnes and Noble).

Rommetveit, Ragnar (1955) *Social Norms and Roles* (Minneapolis: University of Minnesota Press).

Ross, E. A. (1901) *Social Control* (New York: Macmillan).

Roucek, Joseph S. (1978) The concept of social control in American sociology, pp. 3–19 in Joseph S. Roucek (ed.) *Social Control for the 1980's* (Westport, CT: Greenwood Press).

Rowan, Carl (1978) Column in *Tennessean* 21 1978 August, p. 7 (Nashville).

Rubington, Earl and Martin S. Weinberg (1973) *Deviance: The Interactionist Perspective,* 2nd ed. (New York: Macmillan).

Rusche, Georg and Otto Kirchheimer (1939) *Punishment and Social Structure* (New York: Columbia University Press).

Rushing, William A. and Jack Esco (1977) Status resources and behavioral deviance as contingencies of societal reaction, *Social Forces* 56:132–147.

Rushing, William A. and Suzanne T. Ortega (1979) Socioeconomic status and mental disorder: New evidence and a sociomedical formulation, *American Journal of Sociology* 84:1175–1200.

Russell, D. E. H. (1974) *Rebellion, Revolution, and Armed Force* (New York: Academic Press).

Sanders, William B. (1976) *Juvenile Delinquency* (New York: Praeger).

Scheff, Thomas J. (1966) *Being Mentally Ill: A Sociological Theory* (Chicago: Aldine).

——— (1967) Toward a sociological model of consensus, *American Sociological Review* 32:32–46.

Schellenberg, James A. (1970) *An Introduction to Social Psychology* (New York: Random House).

Schreiber, Jan (1978) *The Ultimate Weapon: Terrorists and World Order* (New York: William Morrow).

Schur, Edwin M. (1965) *Crimes without Victims* (Englewood Cliffs, NJ: Prentice-Hall).

───── (1971) *Labeling Deviant Behavior* (New York: Harper and Row).

Scott, John F. (1971) *Internalization of Norms* (Englewood Cliffs, NJ: Prentice-Hall).

Scott, John P. and Sarah F. Scott (1971) *Social Control and Social Change* (Chicago: University of Chicago Press).

Scott, Robert A. (1972) A proposed framework for analyzing deviance as a property of social order, pp. 9–35 in Robert A. Scott and Jack D. Douglas (eds.), *Theoretical Perspectives on Deviance* (New York: Basic Books).

Selznick, Philip (1961) Sociology and natural law, *Natural Law Forum* 6:84–108.

Shapiro, Michael H. (1972) The uses of behavior control technologies: A response, *Issues in Criminology* 7:55–93.

───── (1973) Legislating the control of behavior control: Autonomy and the coercive use of organic therapies, *Southern California Law Review* 47:237–356.

Sherif, Muzafer (1936) *The Psychology of Social Norms* (New York: Harper).

Short, James F., Jr. (1979) On the etiology of delinquent behavior, *Journal of Research in Crime and Delinquency* 16:28–33.

Shorter, Edward and Charles Tilly (1974) *Strikes in France, 1830–1968* (London: Cambridge University Press).

Simmel, Georg (1950) *The Sociology of Georg Simmel,* edited and translated by Kurt H. Wolff (New York: Free Press).

Simmons, J. L. (1965) Public stereotypes of deviants, *Social Problems* 13:223–232.

Sites, Paul (1973) *Control: The Basis of Social Order* (New York: Dunellen).

Skinner, B. F. (1971) *Beyond Freedom and Dignity* (New York: Knopf).

Skolnick, Jerome H. (1966) *Justice Without Trial* (New York: Wiley).

───── (1968) *The Police and the Urban Ghetto* (Chicago: American Bar Foundation).

───── (1969) *The Politics of Protest* (New York: Simon and Schuster).

Sorel, Georges (1915) *Reflections on Violence* (London: George Allen and Unwin).

Sorokin, Pitirim A. (1937) *Social and Cultural Dynamics,* vol. 2 (New York: American Book Co.).

Spector, Malcolm (1976) Labelling theory in *Social Problems:* A young journal launches a new theory, *Social Problems* 24:69–75.

Spiller, Robert E., ed. (1960) *Social Control in a Free Society* (Philadelphia: University of Pennsylvania Press).

Spitzer, Steven (1975a) Punishment and social organization: A study of Durkheim's theory of penal evolution, *Law and Society Review* 9:613–637.

───── (1975b) Toward a Marxian theory of deviance, *Social Problems* 22:638–651.

───── and Andrew T. Scull (1977) Privatization and capitalist development: The case of the private police, *Social Problems* 25:18–29.

Stampp, Kenneth M. (1967) *The Peculiar Institution: Slavery in the Ante-Bellum South* (New York: Knopf).

Steadman, Henry J. (1972) The psychiatrist as a conservative agent of social control, *Social Problems* 20:263–271.

Steffensmeier, Darrell J. and Robert M. Terry, eds. (1975) *Examining Deviance Experimentally* (Port Washington, NY: Alfred).

Stewart, Phyllis L. and Muriel G. Cantor, eds. (1974) *Varieties of Work Experience: The Social Control of Occupational Groups and Roles* (New York: Wiley).

Stinchcombe, Arthur L. (1968) *Constructing Social Theories* (New York: Harcourt, Brace and World).

Stoll, Clarice S. (1968) Images of man and social control, *Social Forces* 47:119—127.

Stone, Julius (1961) *The Province and Function of Law* (Sydney: Maitland).

Sutherland, Edwin H. and Donald R. Cressey (1974) *Criminology,* 9th ed. (Philadelphia: Lippincott).

Sykes, Gresham M. (1958) *The Society of Captives* (Princeton, NJ: Princeton University Press).

———— (1974) The rise of critical criminology, *Journal of Criminal Law and Criminology* 65:206—213.

Szasz, Thomas S. (1965) *Psychiatric Justice* (New York: Macmillan).

Taylor, Ian et al. (1973) *The New Criminology* (London: Routledge and Kegan Paul).

Thibaut, John W. and Harold H. Kelley (1959) *The Social Psychology of Groups* (New York: Wiley).

Thio, Alex (1978) *Deviant Behavior* (Boston: Houghton Mifflin).

Thomas, Lately (1973) *When Even Angels Wept* (New York: William Morrow).

Tilly, Charles et al. (1975) *The Rebellious Century, 1830—1930* (Cambridge, MA: Harvard University Press).

Tittle, Charles R. et al. (1978) The myth of social class and criminality, *American Sociological Review* 43:643—656.

Traub, Stuart H. and Craig B. Little, eds. (1975) *Theories of Deviance* (Itasca, IL: Peacock).

Turk, Austin T. (1969) *Criminality and Legal Order* (Chicago: Rand McNally).

Vallier, Ivan (1970) *Catholicism, Social Control, and Modernization in Latin America* (Englewood Cliffs, NJ: Prentice-Hall).

von Wright, George H. (1963) *Norm and Action* (New York: Humanities Press).

Waite, Robert G. L. (1977) *The Psychopathic God: Adolf Hitler* (New York: Basic Books).

Wakeman, Frederic, Jr. and Carolyn Grant, eds. (1975) *Conflict and Control in Late Imperial China* (Berkeley, CA: University of California Press).

Ward, Lester F. (1903) *Pure Sociology* (New York: Macmillan).

Watkins, C. Kenneth (1975) *Social Control* (New York: Longmans).

Weber, Max (1930) *The Protestant Ethic and the Spirit of Capitalism* (London: G. Allen).

———— (1954) *Max Weber on Law in Economy and Society,* edited by Max Rheinstein (Cambridge, MA: Harvard University Press).

———— (1968) *Economy and Society,* 3 vols. (New York: Bedminster Press).

Weinberg, S. Kirson (1974) *Deviant Behavior and Social Control* (Dubuque, IA: Wm. C. Brown).

Weinstein, Eugene A. and Paul Deutschberger (1963) Some dimensions of altercasting, *Sociometry* 26:454—466.

Wheeler, Stanton, ed. (1969) *On Record: Files and Dossiers in American Life* (New York: Russell Sage).

Whyte, William F. (1955) *Street Corner Society,* 2nd ed. (Chicago: University of Chicago Press).

Wighton, Charles (1962) *Heydrich: Hitler's Most Evil Henchman* (Philadelphia: Chilton).

Wilkinson, Paul (1977) *Terrorism and the Liberal State* (New York: Wiley).

Williams, Robin M., Jr. (1968) The concept of norms, pp. 204–208 in David L. Sills (ed.), *International Encyclopedia of the Social Sciences,* vol. 11 (New York: Macmillan).

Wilson, Amy A. (1977) Deviance and social control in Chinese society: An introductory essay, pp. 1–13 in Amy A. Wilson et al. (eds.) *Deviance and Social Control in Chinese Society* (New York: Praeger).

———— et al., (1977) *Deviance and Social Control in Chinese Society* (New York: Praeger).

Wilson, John (1977) Social protest and social control, *Social Problems* 24:469–481.

Wise, David (1976) *The American Police State: The Government Against the People* (New York: Random House).

Wolfe, Alan (1978) *The Seamy Side of Democracy: Repression in America,* 2nd ed. (New York: Longman).

Wood, Arthur L. (1974) *Deviant Behavior and Control Strategies* (Lexington, MA: D. C. Heath).

Wood, James R. et al. (1967) Children's interpersonal tactics, *Sociological Inquiry* 37:129–138.

Wrong, Dennis H. (1961) The oversocialized conception of man in modern sociology, *American Sociological Review* 26:183–193.

Zald, Mayer N. (1978) On the social control of industries, *Social Forces* 57:79–102.

Ziegenhagen, Eduard A. (1977) *Victims, Crime, and Social Control* (New York: Praeger).

Name Index

Subject Index

Date Due

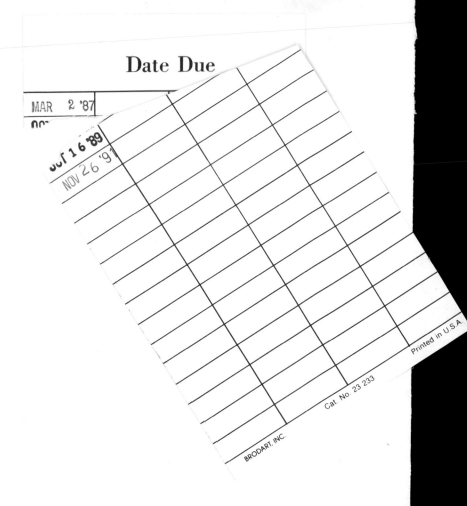

MAR 2 '87

OC

JUL 16 '89

NOV 26 '91